Resisting Corporate Corruption

Resisting Corporate Corruption

Lessons in Practical Ethics from the Enron Wreckage

Stephen V. Arbogast

Executive Professor of Finance at the
Bauer College of Business, Houston, Texas, USA

M&M Scrivener Press

Published by   M & M Scrivener Press
3 Winter Street, Salem, MA 01970

http://www.mmscrivenerpress.com

Copyright © 2008 M & M Scrivener Press

Conflicts and Trends™in Business Ethics
Series Editor, Nicholas Capaldi

Cover design by Hannus Design

Library of Congress Cataloging-In-Publication Data
Arbogast, Stephen V., 1948-
  Resisting corporate corruption : lessons in practical ethics from the
  Enron wreckage / Steven V. Arbogast.
      p. cm.
  Includes bibliographical references and index.
  ISBN 978-0-9764041-4-9 (alk. paper)
  1. Business ethics. 2. Industrial management--Moral and ethical aspects.
  3. Enron Corp.--Corrupt practices--Case studies. I. Title.

HF5387.A695 2008
174'.4--dc22

                        2007040681

ISBN: 978-0-9764041-4-9   (hardcover : alk. paper)

Printed in the United States on acid-free paper.

Contents

Acknowledgments

THIS WORK WOULD NOT HAVE BEEN POSSIBLE without the encouragement of Professor Nicholas Capaldi of Loyola University, New Orleans, and Martin Scrivener, the publisher. These individuals published an earlier paper of mine on the American Catholic Bishops' Pastoral Letter on the Economy. When it came to their attention that I had also authored several Enron ethics case studies, they were quick to encouraged expansion into a book. Throughout this process, they have consistently provided helpful feedback and a ready ear to sort out the inevitable dilemmas.

Jordan Mintz, Vince Kaminski, and Sherron Watkins have been instrumental in the realization of this project. Contacted separately, each responded generously with time and interest. Despite being caught up in their own career changes and in Mintz's case, an ongoing SEC investigation, they took the matter of training the next generation of business students in ethics most seriously. In talking to them over the course of interviews that stretched out over two years in some cases, it became clear that the scars of Enron are still fresh. All continue to reflect on what went wrong and how it could have been avoided. Reading these cases could have been a perfect chance to say "it wasn't that way". Instead, their reaction was uniformly that the cases were representative of what happened; they also were helpful in correcting details, such as the workings of the 'Total Return Swap'. Conversations with all three helped clarify the overriding ethics matters and the realistic options for addressing them.

Dean Arthur Varga and Professor Praveen Kumar, Chairman of the Finance Department of the Bauer College of Business, University of Houston (UH), were consistently encouraging throughout this project. Both were insistent that business schools must do a better job teaching ethics to their students. Dean Varga has made this part of the curriculum at the Bauer College; Dr. Kumar approved a new course based on these Enron cases.

Professors Jacqueline Weaver and Leslie Griffin at the UH Law Center read multiple cases and provided extensive comments. Both also helped sensitize me to the ongoing legal struggle between the bar associations and the SEC over an attorney's responsibility to "turn in" clients to regulators when fraud is suspected. This issue continues to affect several former in-house Enron counsels, including Jordan Mintz.

Frank Risch and Brian Maher, former treasurer and assistant treasurer of ExxonMobil Corporation, respectively, read several cases and/or Teaching Notes and provided helpful comments. Both have considerable experience with the ExxonMobil system of financial control, which perspective helped ground this work. Brian, also a former finance director of Esso Italiana, Spa., was particularly helpful in discussing the background of Exxon's Cazzaniga affair and the subsequent consent decree entered into with the SEC.

Walter C. Arzonetti, a former Exxon assistant treasurer, helped ensure that I had an Exxon career within which I could learn to value sound financial control. James D. Gibbons, Stephen L. B. Penrose, the late Carol C. Tatkon, and the late Edgar A. Robinson all helped provide me with opportunities in my Exxon career and wise counsel that contributed to my financial education.

Father Donald Nesti C.S.Sp., director of the Center for Faith and Culture at the University of St. Thomas School of Theology (UST), also read several cases. Father Nesti brought to these works a completely different sensibility and a quickness to see ethics issues that might remain hazy to other eyes. His comments served as a strong reminder that the notion of right and wrong enters into these questions more than many business executives care to admit. Chris Carmouche, an attorney and colleague in seminary classes, was instrumental in the development of these cases when he crafted a continuing legal education' (CLE) session for the St. Thomas Moore Society (Catholic lawyers) using two of the case studies.

My brother, Dr. Gordon W. Arbogast, Associate Dean of the Business School at Jacksonville University, used a case about Jordan Mintz in one of his Executive MBA classes. This event, coming to Jordan Mintz's attention, helped start the process that ended in this work. Gordon, West Point class of 1963, brings a sorely needed ethical sensibility to his business classrooms.

This work gives me an opportunity to thank Walter F. LaFeber, Professor Emeritus of Diplomatic History at Cornell University. Professor LaFeber set the standard for effective teaching when I had him in 1967-'68. Over the subsequent thirty-nine years, we have almost never agreed on the specifics (or generalizations) of U.S. foreign policy and been better off for the lively discussions. Throughout this, Professor LaFeber's concern to instill a higher ethical component into public policy served as a reminder that such matters are ignored at our peril. Since we likely will never agree on foreign policy, this work constitutes a small measure of payback in an area where perhaps we can agree on what went wrong and what needs to be done better.

Finally, I would like to thank my wife, Debbie, whose love, support, and patience have enabled me to attempt and complete this first book. She has been there for me at each turn and at the end of each day, for which I am grateful beyond words.

Preface

WHY PREPARE A BOOK OF ETHICS CASE STUDIES? Why focus that book on Enron, a company that can easily be regarded as the antithesis of an ethical corporation?

This book was written in the belief that individuals need to be trained to handle the ethics dilemmas of corporate life. Their ethical formation as private individuals is not enough. Most corporate ethics situations are too complex and challenging to be faced without careful preparation.

This book was also written in the belief that much of the existing literature on corporate ethics underestimates the practical dilemmas of corporate life. Successfully managing a major ethics challenge often requires employees to cope with not one or two but four dimensions of the problem. Without training in recognizing this complexity and practice in devising solutions, the individual likely will not be up to the task.

As for Enron, it has provided us with not only the most public but also the most complete and devastating example of consequences that can flow from disregarding ethics in the conduct of business. Enron's history is replete with cases in which individuals either ignored the ethics decision in front of them or chose to act in conscious disregard of Enron's own policies or the law. The Enron story is thus the ultimate cautionary tale. Told chronologically, this story is a tangled one. Several good corporate histories have tried to capture it, cutting back and forth among diverse businesses, locales, and oversized personalities. This book approaches Enron's history from a different angle: key ethics thresholds. Readers will have the chance to see how Enron proceeded, step by step, to cross invisible lines that left it both corrupted and blind to its own inner decay.

Perhaps more surprising, Enron also provides cases in which individuals chose to see the ethics issue and to resist unethical practices. In several of these cases, the 'resisters' were at least partially successful. Resisters here refer to individuals who openly opposed activities or transactions subsequently deemed ethically questionable or illegal. As the cases make clear, these resisters had success because they were able to decode the complexities of their situations and to devise plans for working on multiple fronts.

Using Enron as a focal point thus affords the opportunity to examine business ethics under severe conditions. One can see how early decisions allowed the ethics environment to deteriorate, and one can also examine how effective resistance, which was certainly possible in the early going, was still a possibility even as the final crisis approached.

The Enron file thus provides valuable history on how individuals and companies move, decision by decision, down a road to corruption and on what it takes to oppose this descent successfully. This book seeks to harvest Enron's history lessons and make them available in a format useful for training tomorrow's executives.

How This Book Came to Be Written

Jordan Mintz's story provided the inspiration for this book. It was May 2004 and I was in the last months of my career with ExxonMobil. Knowing that I was planning to teach and was interested in corporate ethics, Bear Sterns investment banker, Telly Zachariades, sent me his copy of *The Smartest Guys in the Room.* I found it engrossing. Then I started shaking my head at the progressively brazen flouting of accounting principles, sound practices, and the law. Then I came across Jordan Mintz.

Mintz was a tax attorney who joined Andy Fastow's Global Finance as general counsel in 2000. Mintz quickly encountered and was appalled by Fastow's self-dealing LJM partnerships. What caught my attention, however, was the resourceful way in which Mintz went about tackling Fastow's little empire. Mintz picked a target with exquisite care: the amount of Fastow's LJM compensation. This target had two advantages. First, it involved a matter on which Fastow had been less than truthful to his superiors and the Enron board. Thus, Fastow's reputation was vulnerable; revealing Fastow's true compensation would discredit him within Enron. Second, the target provided attorney Mintz with a legal path to force disclosure. Mintz could argue from the law that Fastow needed to disclose his compensation in Enron's SEC filings. Mintz would back up this argument with an opinion from outside counsel, which as Global Finance's general counsel, he could obtain without asking permission from anyone else. Armed with this ammunition, Mintz continued to press Fastow, Rick Causey, and others to disclose Fastow's compensation. Mintz also sent materials to Jeff Skilling, advising that he had failed to sign off on Enron's deals with LJM and needed to do so. These cumulative efforts worked. Shortly thereafter, Skilling forced Fastow to choose between working for Enron or LJM. Fastow's prestige within Enron was never the same. As more facts about Enron's related party transactions appeared in the press, Fastow turned into a liability. In October 2001, he was fired.

This tale of Fastow's demise was satisfying, but what really caught my attention was the complexity of Mintz's situation. This is how ethical situations present themselves in corporate life. They come dressed up in circumstances that blur the clarity of the moral issues and are loaded with personal risks that intimidate people inclined to do the right thing. I resolved to capture this reality in a case study: New Counsel for Andy Fastow. It was the first of the cases that would make up this book.

This case was used in a course at a Florida university; somehow Jordan Mintz heard about it. We met and began to discuss the realities of trying to act ethically inside a corrupted corporation. At about the same time, Kurt Eichenwald published *Conspiracy of Fools*. This work provided even more details on Enron's dubious deeds, as well as the efforts of Mintz and others to combat such practices. In particular, I was impressed by the accounts involving Vince Kaminski and Sherron Watkins. Their case histories reinforced the lessons of Mintz's story. Yes, it takes personal courage to confront a difficult corporate ethics dilemma. But it takes a lot more – it takes practical skills of particular types to have a chance to succeed.

I wrote two more cases, 'Adjusting the Forward Curve in the Back Room' and 'Investigating Accounting Improprieties at Jayen Corporation' to document the point further. These cases were used in a continuing legal education program for a group of Houston attorneys. Their response suggested that they had not previously encountered ethics training materials of this type.

I then resolved to prepare a set of cases to cover the complete trajectory of Enron's ascent and implosion. At a minimum this case set would show two things. First, it would illustrate how a corporation can go bad by stages. This would serve the purpose of emphasizing certain thresholds that must be held if a company is to avoid ethics decomposition. Second, the case set would show not only the complexity of each individual ethics situation but, also, how these grew ever more difficult as Enron grew more corrupt.

Finally, I decided to focus most of the cases not on the most prominent figures of the Enron drama, but on individuals one or two levels down. Ken Lay, Jeff Skilling, and Andy Fastow appear in these cases. However, with the exception of Lay, they are not the focal points. Rather, the cases present the dilemmas of such people as Jordan Mintz in the hope that their situations will more closely resemble the problems that today's students might eventually have to face.

For Whom This Book Is Written

The primary audience for this book is students preparing for a career in business. Hopefully, most will never face the acute ethics dilemmas Enron provided. Most, however, will likely face one or more tough ethics problems if they stay in corporate life. This book is intended to help them identify the complexities of their situation and to practice devising solutions. It should be similarly helpful to law students training for careers advising or regulating the private sector.

This book is also intended for professionals specializing in audit or financial controls advisory work. The book's set of cases serves as a cautionary tale for what can happen when financial control is deemphasized. Controls organizations may find it helpful to use the whole book when training their less-experienced professionals; individual cases may also be useful in controls training for line organizations.

Seminary students studying for careers involving pastoral work with corporate workers can benefit from learning about the complexities of business ethics. Pastors are often a source of advice and support to individuals dealing with personal ethics issues. The material in this book can be of assistance in extending this pastoral reach to parishioners' professional dilemmas.

Finally, this book is offered to all those appalled by what happened at Enron and still asking how things ever could have gone so wrong. Following the arc of these cases should reveal the destructive synergy between Enron's early weakening of its controls environment and its later deceptive responses to business failures. Collectively, the cases show that things went so wrong because Enron decided early on that financial control was not a priority.

How to Use This Book

Although individual cases can be used within various types of training courses, the primary purpose of this book is to provide material for a full-semester graduate school course. The basic structure seeks to provide students with repeat practice in devising solutions to business ethics issues. Enron's story provides a moving target for these efforts, with the issues changing and increasing in difficulty as the cases unfold.

By the end of working these seventeen cases, students and other readers should have internalized a framework for spotting and working ethics issues. This framework should then serve as an internal guide for real situations that students may encounter during their careers. Knowing that even seemingly intractable ethics situations can yield to rational thinking and tactical planning should fortify students' and readers' personal resolve to respond ethically if and when tested.

Much of the focus of these cases involves tactical planning within the corporate setting. That may seem a strange preoccupation for cases studying ethics. It is not when the ethical issues arise in a business setting. Anyone who has worked a business ethics issue knows that figuring out the right and wrong of it is only the first and maybe not the most difficult step. The more challenging part often involves a form of bureaucratic politics and maneuver. Such maneuvers are not unlike those involved in championing a new idea or an unpopular cause within a company. Sometimes, it involves getting to the right people with the right message and the right evidence to back it up. Sometimes, it involves waiting for the right moment to press hard, taking advantage of events that may have vindicated a prior warning. Sometimes, it involves managing a meeting with a very senior person or dealing with the investigation he or she may have set in motion. A lot of this type of content is incorporated into the cases in this book. Winning the corporate ethics decision involves winning within the organization. Without the skills to do this, employees' ethical stances become gestures of protest: poignant but ineffectual. In order to be able to act ethically in challenging situations, business students need to practice being tactically skillful within the corporate organization. As is emphasized throughout this book, this kind of tactical planning forms part of how students should approach every case.

For a semester course, students should begin by reading Essay 1, which provides an overview of the recommended approach for working ethics cases. This essay also introduces some key concepts, such as the stages of Enron's ethical decomposition, the four dimensions that arise within most ethics issues, and the definition of tactical planning in ethics cases.

Next, read Case Study 1, on Enron Oil Trading. This case introduces the complexities alluded to in Essay 1 and illustrates how difficult it is to craft tactical plans that adequately address all four dimensions. Instructors play a key role here; they must show how the concepts and approach laid out in the initial essay connect to possible case solutions. Students and readers will then be ready for Essay 2, which explores the importance of tactical planning when handling ethics issues. This essay also discusses which tactical paths may be most effective, depending on the stage of a firm's ethical decomposition.

This tactical guidance can then be applied to Case Studies 2 and 3. Enron was still in an early stage of ethical decay at this point. Students should be able to see that there were both more options available for successful resistance and a disturbing pattern of near-term financial considerations trumping sound practice. Students will get a chance to work on the question of whether this situation could have been arrested early on.

Essay 3 follows. This essay elaborates on the nature and importance of financial control. Its most important theme, however, is the economic rationale for maintaining sound controls. Although the battle to maintain the integrity of Enron's controls was lost fairly early, the rationale for financial control remained relevant throughout. This rationale provides arguments that resisters could have used each time they tried to halt Enron's slide. Grasping these economic arguments is important to effective resistance and to crafting solutions for all the cases that follow.

Students then have a choice. They can jump to the back of the book and read Essay 4. This essay reflects on the overall lessons of these Enron cases. These lessons learned may provide further clues as to how to approach individual cases. Alternatively, students can attack the cases in order, draw their own conclusions, and see how they compare with Essay 4's summary. This latter approach is recommended for both its value in forcing students to think more for themselves and its potential to turn up different or additional lessons learned.

Do the cases in the order provided in the book. This sequence mirrors Enron's history and provides students with some sense of what it was like to be a long-service Enron employee. Experiencing even a small sense of what it was like to work for a company that grew increasingly more corrupt will itself create a valuable instinct for resisting similar tendencies elsewhere.

Finally, students are encouraged to put themselves in the shoes of the individual who in each case faces the ethics dilemma. All cases are set up to present an individual who had the task of confronting one of Enron's ethics challenges. Students will want to role play this individual. Each case also provides background about that person's personal and/or career situation. Acting as if you share the temptations or threats this person faced will best replicate the conditions students might need to overcome sometime in your career.

Financial Content

Most cases contain a generous dose of financial content. This can vary from a description of the workings of 'mark-to-market' accounting to the byzantine structuring of the Chewco transaction. Although an effort has been made to present this material in a fashion accessible to non-technical case readers, inclusion of this content is deemed important to a proper consideration of real-world ethics issues. Those who push the ethics envelop frequently use technical complexities to hide their tracks. As discussed in the essays, the keys to successfully opposing such efforts also are often found down in the details.

Accordingly, students are encouraged to digest the technical content as they read the cases. It will enhance appreciation of both the skillfulness with which corrupting agents wrap their schemes in defensible fabric and the huge risks and loose ends they often leave hiding in the fine print.

How Historical Are the Cases: Origins and Disclaimers

These cases are historically-based but are not history. This means that the facts given in each case are grounded in the accounts of the episode provided in one or more of the published accounts on Enron. Most of the cases draw heavily on the books *The Smartest Guys in the Room, Conspiracy of Fools, and Power Failure*. Cases later in Enron's history also reflect findings from the *Powers Committee's Report of the Special Investigation Committee*, commissioned by Enron's board late in 2001. Several of the cases have been read and commented on by Enron resisters Jordan Mintz, Vince Kaminski, and Sherron Watkins. A complete list of sources appears at the end of the book.

In order to provide cases that position students at key decision moments, it was necessary to create some material that is not historical. For example, there is no record of Ken Lay's private thoughts on the evening after Jeff Skilling resigned. If students are going to practice standing in Ken Lay's shoes, they need to imagine what was going through Lay's mind at the time.

The historical record provides some basis for doing so. However, what's portrayed in the case as Lay's private thoughts is only that - 'historically based speculation' and should be considered as such.

Formatting has been used to highlight this creation process. Created internal thoughts or dialogues appear in different typeface and are not placed within quotation marks. These include the passages under each case title, which are there to set a tone for the case. Material that does appear within quotation marks can be regarded as historical. Each case concludes with an Author's Note that cites the sources used to set up the facts for the case. As the notes make clear, the cases are firmly based on the historical facts as documented by the major published Enron accounts. These notes also identify which material has been created or imagined as part of the case-writing process. Attachments that have been created for the same purpose are labeled Historical Recreation (HRC). All readers interested in Enron's story are advised to read these Author's Notes carefully before concluding that anything in these cases provides new information. In fact, the basic mode of this book is one of recapturing stories from published accounts and reshaping them to enable students to revisit key moments when ethics matters were at stake.

For the most part, real names are used in the cases. The Enron story is now very public. An extensive record exists for almost all the incidents covered in the cases. One exception is the incident on which Case 7 – 'Adjusting the Forward Curve in the Back Room' - is based; this incident gets only fleeting attention in published accounts. The case facts presented here come from the recollections of one Enron figure, as is noted in the case's Author's Note. Because of this less plentiful-source basis, the names in this case have been fictionalized.

A more significant exception is case study 17 – 'Investigating Accounting Improprieties at Jayen Corporation'. This case and all the names have been thoroughly fictionalized. The case relates to an Enron investigation that occurred following Sherron Watkins' submission of her anonymous letter. However, the case focuses on a law firm rather than on Enron. There is little historical record concerning the deliberations of this law firm. In recognition of this circumstance and of the fact that the case portrays deliberations that may not remotely resemble what actually happened, it was decided to disguise the case fully and to state explicitly that it is not intended to represent the events or conduct of any law firm or of the members of any firm.

Solutions Manual

Case studies by definition are amenable to multiple solutions. However, in an effort to provide material that instructors can use to jump-start students' thinking, solutions have been developed for each case. These discussions are organized as Solution Notes and are available in CD form from the publisher.

Essay 1

Overview of the Case Studies and How to Approach Them

THIS ESSAY IS INTENDED TO HELP STUDENTS analyze each Enron case by identifying the ethics issue, the surrounding business and personal complications, and the opportunities for achieving a successful ethical and business outcomes. To be able to do this, students need to look for issues on multiple levels. Serious ethics problems typically present a complex, intertwined set of issues. Focusing on only one or two dimensions can result in being blindsided on another level. This essay provides a structured approach to mapping the issues that are shaping each case's ethics problem.

It next provides guidance to students on crafting the tactical plans necessary to pursue an issue to a successful ethical and business outcome. Although tactical planning must respond to the particulars of each case, some general points can be made; this book's cases present a variety of tactical situations within which students will have to decide whether to work issues within a firm or by contacting outside agents. This essay enumerates several of these situations and makes some general observations on how to work successfully within these different circumstances.

An Overview of the Approach

Business ethics issues vary widely in degree of difficulty. Much of this variation is a function of a company's stage of ethical decomposition. The more decayed a company's financial control environment, the fewer options an employee will have to pursue an ethical outcome; as decay advances, personal risks also become starker and more severe.

This reality requires that employees facing an ethics issue first assess the stage of their firm's controls environment. To the extent that controls remain satisfactory, employees can work ethics issues within established channels. Where controls have been systematically compromised or neglected by management, employees may need to develop tactical plans that are essentially political in nature. These plans may focus on reaching and influencing key

1

S.V. Arbogast, *Resisting Corporate Corruption* (pp. 1–8)

decision makers with authority to shape the firm's conduct. If the decomposition is advanced, adequate outcomes may be achieved only by turning to oversight agents outside the firm.

Thus, the approach begins by assessing the firm's stage of controls integrity to determine whether the ethics issue can be worked (1) in or outside of the firm's management structure and (2) in a normal as opposed to a political fashion.

From there, students need to define the ethics issue(s) at stake. This definition should be laid out in a manner divorced from complicating business and personal interests. A clear statement of the ethics issue is needed to arrive at a definition of an acceptable ethical outcome. Students should next set a minimum acceptable ethical outcome as a boundary condition for their case solution. For example, let's consider the situation of Jordan Mintz, the tax attorney who went to work for Andy Fastow early in 2001 (see Case Study 12 'New Counsel for Andy Fastow'). Mintz examined Fastow's LJM related-party vehicles and found them replete with conflicts of interest and internal approval issues. Facing an array of ethics issues, Mintz set his boundary condition for an acceptable outcome: (1) Fastow's compensation needed to be disclosed, or (2) Fastow needed to resign from LJM. (Mintz helped achieve the latter.) With an ethical boundary condition thus defined, Mintz was then able to shape tactical plans around achieving that minimum outcome. Students are encouraged to follow this general approach as they consider each of the cases.

This overall approach has referred to several concepts that need further elaboration: (1) a firm's financial control environment, (2) stages of decomposition of controls, and (3) the complexity of business ethics problems. This essay provides a brief explanation of each point. Essay 2 goes into more depth, especially about the tactical planning needed to secure ethical outcomes. Essay 3 elaborates on the economic importance of good financial control and how knowledge of these rationales can be helpful when developing one's tactical plans.

The Company Financial Control Environment

A company's financial-control environment is an important concept for using this recommended approach. Financial control pertains to a firm's need to ensure that company assets remain in company possession and are used for purposes beneficial to the firm's ownership, that the firm's accounting records accurately reflect the firm's activities, and that the firm's operations are in compliance with applicable laws and regulations. The vast majority of business ethics issues involve one or more of these activities. Business ethics and financial control are thus deeply intertwined. As was noted earlier and is reinforced by the cases, an individual's ability to act ethically is gravely hampered when a firm's financial controls are weak.

Controls environment refers to the firm's: (1) formal structure of governance, (2) financial control structure, and (3) the integrity of these structures. These structural features include corporate policies, standards of business conduct, delegations of authority and capital budgeting procedures. The controls environment also includes the effectiveness and frequency of audits, the attention paid to audit findings, the extent to which line managers are required to take responsibility for controls, the investigation and adjudication of irregularity cases, and whether the firm exempts powerful figures from rules applied to other employees.

Senior management has the major responsibility for ensuring the integrity of the controls environment. In a myriad of ways, senior management determines the effectiveness of any controls system. Through the importance and attention they devote to financial control, senior managers determine its priority within the various competing objectives firm managers must pursue. Through their personal conduct, they signal whether controls are substantive and fair or largely optics. Much more will be said on this in Essay 2.

Control systems are set up anticipating that business ethics problems will occur. Virtually all firms have experienced employees trying to steal money, abuse expense accounts, or get ahead by means that violate the law. Control systems are structures intended to limit such behavior; controls reinforce the ethical behavior of individuals by providing clear standards, the means of discovering violations, and procedures for punishing offenders. Good control structures ensure that ethical behavior is the expected norm. Weak controls allow the dangerous sense to spread that individuals can get ahead in disregard of internal rules and/or the law.

Normal business is always putting pressure on controls systems. Normal business is always threatening someone with failure or holding out the promise of success if only some inconvenient obstacle can be overcome. Control systems "get in the way" of what people sometimes think they need to do to succeed or avoid failure; controls are intended for exactly that purpose. Naturally, those who would respond to business pressure by evading controls will devise rationales and tactics to justify such an evasion. The integrity of a firm's control system is demonstrated by when controls are given priority over the pressures of the day; this integrity is preserved when the essence of an ethics issue remains the focal point for consideration despite all tactics of disinformation and deception that perpetrators may use.

The trajectory of Enron's controls history is visible in this set of cases. The cases cover Enron's history from 1986 to 2001. Over this span, the firm traversed an arc that took it from a conventional company to a home for felons. This trajectory had distinct stages. Specific cases illustrate all these phases. Since students will need to vary their case solutions by stage, the differences among them are worth noting. Enron's stages, their differing characteristics, and the cases associated with each are enumerated next.

Stages of Enron's Ethical Decomposition

Enron is only one company. Thus, its history can hardly be used as a paradigm for all corporate ethical decomposition. It is, however, a well-documented example of severe decomposition. As such, it can serve as the best-available case study of severe ethical decay. For those who would ask how did Enron go so far wrong, this book's cases show that Enron got there by crossing thresholds between four distinct stages. These stages were:

- **Stage 1: Normal firm, with standard ethics policies, accounting, and internal control.** The key threshold here was the maintenance of integrity for its internal control system. Enron chose to deemphasize controls early on; it also neutralized and then dismantled its internal audit function, crossing a threshold to the next stage.

The cases covering Enron in Stage 1 are:
1. Enron Oil Trading (A): Untimely Problems from Valhalla
2. Enron Oil Trading (B): The Future of Enron Internal Audit
3. Enron Oil Trading (C): An Opening for Enron Audit?

- **Stage 2: Normal company, with a weak controls environment.** Powerful, self-interested executives are common within corporations. When controls are weak, some executives may act in ways which signal others that careers can be made by bending (or breaking) the rules. To succeed via this route, these executives try to neutralize the firm's ethics 'gatekeepers'. Here, gatekeepers refers to the firm's internal accountants, external auditor, and inside and outside legal counsels. In Enron's case, self-interested executives were able to demonstrate that the gatekeepers could be neutered, thus carrying the corporation into a third stage.

The cases covering Enron in Stage 2 are:
1. Enter Mark-to-Market (A): Exit Accounting Integrity?
2. Enter Mark-to-Market (B): Accounting & the Aggressive Client
3. Enter Mark-to-Market (C): The Disease Spreads to Enron Clean Fuels

- **Stage 3: Impaired company, with a self-promoting culture.** The main characteristic of this stage was widespread recognition that Enron's gatekeepers could be "worked". Worked didn't mean ceasing to pay attention to rules and laws. Rather, it meant that when it mattered enough to someone powerful, the gatekeepers could be induced or pressured to drop their objections; instead of advising which lines should not be crossed or which risks were too great, Enron's gatekeepers were maneuvered into becoming technical support for the rule-benders. "Make it work" for the business/client became the mantra; as such, the gatekeepers provided advice on how to work around applicable rules, regulations or laws. Once this mantra was understood within the company, individual and competitive drives caused more and more executives to pursue deals in which their personal agendas were paramount. In these cases, Enron's interests became secondary, and constraining rules or laws came to be regarded as barriers to be overcome.

Ethical decomposition began to accelerate at this point. Without realizing it, the quality of information available to senior managers decayed; self-interested parties manipulated it in pursuit of other agendas. Business performance then suffered as more energy went into self-promotion or disguising problems. Deal structures got sloppy. What mattered was getting the deal closed, not how it would stand up down the road. In this stage, it became increasingly clear that doing the right (and difficult) thing was not necessarily the best way to get ahead. The stage was thus set for crossing the final threshold; now, an agent of corruption entered Enron's picture, and the corporation entered Stage 4.

The cases covering Enron in Stage 3 are:
1. Adjusting the Forward Curve in the Back Room (A)
2. Adjusting the Forward Curve (B): Managing the Showdown Meeting
3. Enron's SPEs: A Vehicle too Far?

- **Stage 4: Corrupted Company, with secrets to hide.** The distinguishing characteristics of Enron's corrupting agent were these: Whereas others would bend rules while maintaining technical compliance, Andy Fastow was willing to break them on the assumption that he wouldn't get caught. Fastow also endeavored to draw others into his schemes, the better to expand his reach and preserve secrecy. This burdened Enron with regulatory and legal violations, rendering it vulnerable to exposure and its consequences: investor and customer flight, shareholder litigation, regulatory investigation, and criminal penalties. For those Enron employees still inclined to resist unethical practices, Fastow's deals raised doubts about whether Enron's management could be trusted. At this point, the breakdown in Enron's financial control environment was complete.

The cases covering Enron in Stage 4 are:
1. Jeff Skilling and LJM (A): The "Shoot the Moon" Meeting
2. Jeff Skilling and LJM (B): Managing the Meeting's Aftermath
3. New Counsel for Andy Fastow (A)
4. New Counsel for Andy Fastow (B): Attorney Responsibility to Report Fraud
5. Nowhere to Go with "the Probability of Ruin"
6. Lay Back…and Say What?
7. "Whistleblowing" before Imploding in Accounting Scandals
8. Investigating Accounting Improprieties at Jayen Corporation

Students should note how tactical options available in the earlier stages are gone by stage 4. By the last stage, there is no internal control organization to which one can appeal. A resister at this stage no longer feels that the advice of Enron's auditor or its more frequently used outside law firms can be trusted. Consequently, several resisters considered more extraordinary means to resist: direct appeals to the company's chief operating officer, private consultations with and opinions from non-customary outside counsel, anonymous letters to Enron's chairman, and disclosing company information to the media and/or regulatory bodies.

The concentration of cases in stage 4 allows readers to consider the utility of such extraordinary measures when combating an entrenched corporate corruption. These cases also explore the legal issues and personal consequences that affect individuals in such circumstances. By this stage, it should be evident that Enron's ethics cases pose manifold complexities for resisters.

The Complexity of Business Ethics Problems

The complexity of business ethics problems has been mentioned several times. What this means will now be spelt out in more detail.

Most ex-post facto discussions of corporate scandals take a one-or-two dimensional approach to the subject. Once a scandal has burst into the open it is fairly straightforward to identify the business principle, internal policy, law, or regulation that was disregarded. This discussion may be supplemented by identifying the personal temptations or structural weaknesses in corporate governance that caused the ethical breach.

This approach needs to be extended to do justice to the circumstances employees typically face. As the cases illustrate, serious ethics dilemmas typically display four intertwined aspects:

1. **The ethics issue itself.** Those proposing something questionable usually deploy pragmatic, legal or authority arguments to blur the ethical question at issue. Employees need the ability to disengage ethics issues from these complications and to give them clear definition; employees also need to be able to distinguish between minor issues typical of corporate life and serious issues that threaten the firm's ethical environment.

2. **Understanding threats to personal interests and the alternatives to mitigate these.** Ethics issues come with temptations and threats. "Going along" can promote immediate career interests whereas resisting can put reputation, career, and family well-being at risk. Many people in corporate life find themselves unprepared for the emotional tugs and pulls of this sort and find their planning and decision-making faculties impaired as a result.

3. **Understanding how acting ethically can be combined with an acceptable business outcome.** This dimension is often overlooked. Those proposing questionable practices usually try to establish such actions as crucial to a needed business outcome. Indeed, they may assert that it is the only way to achieve that outcome. This can cause those insisting on ethical behavior to be portrayed as unrealistic or uncreative. Ethical executives often find that they can't beat "something with nothing", and end up conceding the issue. Spotting effective business alternatives that can be pursued ethically is essential to successful resistance–as these cases show. Being able to articulate in economic terms the longer term benefits of sound controls is also essential to rebutting expedient business arguments.

4. **Developing a viable tactical plan.** Perhaps the most overlooked dimension, this aspect also requires the most practical training to do well; anyone who has successfully moved a major project through a corporate structure knows that it takes a tactical plan. This plan supplements following the formal review process. The right people have to be brought on board. The right evidence has to be marshaled. Opposition has to be faced down. All these activities are involved in a business ethics situation, where it can be even more difficult to achieve results. Ethics violators may hold high positions within management. Indeed, they may include one's boss. Formal procedures for handling ethics issues may also be broken or corrupted. Potential allies may be intimidated by possible ramifications for them personally.

Given this multidimensional nature of ethics problems, effective solutions require tactical plans that work on all fronts. These solutions have to integrate not only "doing the right thing" but also measures to secure an acceptable business outcome; actions that mitigate the threats to personal interests need to be included, if only to preserve a resister's ability to face down corrupting agents. Assuming that the firm has not decayed beyond Stage 3, tactical plans have to devise means, that is arguments, evidence, external threats, and internal pressure points, to attract allies and win the internal decision. If, however, corruption is well advanced, plans may need to be premised on the fact that an internal resolution is not possible; then, the tactical plan likely involves going outside to agents whose function it is to oversee corporate behavior. If the questionable activities are likely illegal, this need to 'go outside' obviously intensifies.

Developing such plans is extraordinarily demanding, as these cases make clear. Indeed, one can argue that Mintz, Kaminski, and Watkins enjoyed only mixed success after much trial and error. Studying their stories will ideally help the tactical planning of future resisters.

A Final Word Before the Cases

The cases that follow vary greatly in terms of when they happened, the issues at stake, and the immediate and longer-term consequences that followed. In one sense, however, they share a common thread. With one exception, the cases are written from the point of view of a midlevel or lower senior executive. The cases involve some names you may recognize–Sherron Watkins, Jeff McMahon, and Ben Glisan, and others less familiar–David Woytek and Jordan Mintz. The book focuses on these individuals, the better to provide cases with issues that students may have to confront sooner in their careers.

The exception concerns Ken Lay. Three cases involving Lay open the book; another forms the penultimate case. Because of the importance of the CEO in preserving the integrity of a controls environment, students need to step into Lay's shoes. From there, students can consider ethics issues through the prism of the interests and responsibilities of the top executive. Later, when "looking upward" while working a case, they can better anticipate senior manager reactions to their plans.

Enron's ethics casebook now begins, with Ken Lay considering events in an unlikely location: Valhalla, N.Y.

Case Study 1

Enron Oil Trading (A): Untimely Problems from Valhalla (A)

This environment is hardly giving us room to breathe.
The last thing we need is a public scandal.

IT WAS THE END OF THE BUSINESS DAY, February 1, 1987. Ken Lay, CEO of Enron Corporation, sat at his desk, ruminating over his agenda for the following day. Tomorrow's schedule showed a morning meeting with Internal Audit and two top officers from Enron Oil Trading (EOT). Louis Borget, president of EOT and Tom Mastroeni, the treasurer, were coming down from their headquarters in Valhalla, New York. They had been called to Houston to answer charges of opening undisclosed bank accounts to conduct unauthorized transactions.

Lay had already heard a bit about the controversy. He again skimmed an Internal Audit memo (Attachment 1) that summarized the issues. The essence of the matter concerned an account opened by EOT at the Eastern Savings Bank. Borget and Mastroeni were the authorized signatories on the account but had failed to report its existence to Enron's Houston headquarters. Millions of dollars from EOT trades had found their way into this account. More worrisome, some $2 million had then been transferred into Mastroeni's personal account at the same bank. Internal Audit suspected that Borget and Mastroeni had EOT engaging in unauthorized and/or fictitious trading, skimming money for personal gain.

Houston oversight of EOT was the responsibility of John Harding and Steve Sulentic. Lay sought out their views upon receiving Internal Audit's report. Eventually, they got back to Lay with a story that the undisclosed account involved transactions that were legitimate and in Enron's interests. The transactions in question were "twinned trades": equal and offsetting buy/sell transactions used to move profits from one accounting quarter to another; such trades, they observed, were not uncommon in the trading business. Borget and Mastroeni would come to Houston, bring their bank records, and explain everything. Lay had pressed lightly on the point of

9

S.V. Arbogast, *Resisting Corporate Corruption* (pp. 9–21)
© 2008 by M & M Scrivener Press

EOT's not reporting the Eastern Savings account to Houston and had gotten an answer to the effect that perhaps some unfortunate shortcuts had been taken but the underlying motives were ok.

Ken Lay hoped that this would turn out to be true. As he pondered how to run tomorrow's meeting, his mind wandered back over Enron's recent history and current predicaments.

Natural Gas Pipelines in Crisis

Ken Lay had only joined Enron in June 1984. It was not then known as Enron; the company that Lay took over as chairman and CEO was called Houston Natural Gas (HNG). Lay had assumed the helm at a difficult transition time for the natural gas pipeline industry. Long-standing players, such as HNG, were finding that the industry business model was rapidly changing. Prior to the mid-1980s, natural gas producers sold gas to pipeline owners under long-term contracts. In order to induce producers to commit their gas, pipeline owners customarily provided long term deals with floor prices and a commitment to "take or pay" for gas: take a minimum volume of gas at a stipulated price or pay the cash equivalent of having taken the specified gas amount.

Two things happened in the 1980s to destabilize this model. The first concerned the value of newly produced natural gas; prices had fallen to rock-bottom levels, below $2 per million BTUs. The second was a regulatory change. No longer would pipeline operators be able to "lock out" producers who didn't commit to ship through their lines. Instead, gas producers were now able to sell directly to end users and require pipelines to ship their volumes for a simple transport tariff.

These changes rocked the gas pipeline industry. Newly developed gas started finding its way directly to end users at the low spot market price. Major carriers increasingly found themselves burdened with gas purchased earlier at higher prices under take-or-pay contracts. Pipeline company financial conditions deteriorated. Debt ratings were downgraded. The carriers labored to work their way out from under disadvantageous contracts. HNG was no exception.

Ken Lay thought he knew how things would play out. His assessment was that natural gas market deregulation would continue to progress; from this, he concluded that future profitability would become a function of scale–that is, the biggest pipeline companies with the most extensive networks would become low-cost providers and would end up dominating a market of natural gas production sold largely at spot prices and moved via low-cost logistics.

As if on cue, the gas pipeline industry began to consolidate. Again, HNG was no exception. In April 1985, a call came from Omaha-based Inter-North suggesting a merger. Inter-North was approximately three times the size of HNG. However, its senior management was aging, its board was divided and both were uncertain about how to cope with the deregulated market. A corporate raider, Irwin Jacobs, was stalking the company. Inter-North needed a deal.

Immediately prior to the merger talks, HNG stock was trading at $45 a share. In just eleven days, Lay was able to extract both a $70 per HNG share price (a 56 percent "control" premium) and a commitment that he would move up to CEO after a couple of years. The Inter-North/HNG merger closed within the year, and the new entity was christened Enron in 1986.

Unfortunately, the merger did little to alleviate the pipeline company's immediate economic straits. Profitability was miserable. The natural gas glut seemed to produce ever-lower prices. Enron had to face this deteriorating environment with more than $1 billion in take-or-pay contract liabilities. Enron reported a $79 million loss for 1985, its first year of operation. Attachment 2 details Enron's financial performance for 1985-'86. Although Enron reported net profits of $556 million for 1986, the bulk of that reflected recoveries of past income taxes. Enron's financial condition was more accurately reflected by the following: earnings before interest and taxes (EBIT) $230 million; interest expense: $421 million.

Enron was now heavily debt laden, the product of Inter-North's having used debt to fund the premium price for HNG's stock. To some extent, this "leveraging up" of the company had been intentional. Irwin Jacobs' group was being paid $350 million to hand over its Inter-North stake and go away. Inter-North thus reckoned that a heavy debt burden would act as shark repellant for future raiders; however, high debt levels also hamstrung the newly merged entity. Ken Lay found that his firm's bank loans contained covenants requiring quarterly interest expense to be covered 1.2 times by EBIT; failure to do so would mean an event of default. Enron would be especially exposed in such case, as the firm also had more than $1 billion of commercial paper outstanding. These unsecured short-term promissory notes had to be rolled over continuously. A "hiccup" on bank loan covenants could spark a full-fledged financial crisis should it lead commercial paper buyers to flee from Enron's paper.

In January 1987, Moody's Investors Service downgraded the company's long term rating to below investment grade, i.e. to "junk" status.

This perilous financial condition meant that Ken Lay spent much of 1986 focused on maintaining liquidity and avoiding the default triggers in Enron's bank loans. Lay froze senior executive pay and sold some pipeline assets. Enron stayed afloat, but the company was barely scraping by.

In fact, a good portion of the company's razor-thin margin for error was being contributed by a little-known and understood entity, EOT. Inter-North had created the subsidiary back in 1984. Trading oil commodities was a relatively new business at that time. Inter-North chose to enter the business by hiring an established trader, Louis Borget. Inter-North lured him away from Gulf States Oil and Refining, where Borget had set up a similar unit three years earlier. The package to induce Borget to move included bonuses tied to the profits produced by the trading operation.

EOT immediately began to report profits. In 1985, when the merged Inter-North/HNG lost $79 million, EOT made $10 million. In 1986, when Enron couldn't cover interest expense with operating earnings, EOT reported profits of $28 million.

Ken Lay still wasn't sure what to do immediately to fix Enron's financial problems. He believed that long term, deregulation would reward his company. For the near term, Enron seemed bogged down in a bad business environment of low prices, intense competition, and the burdens of high debt. One thing he did know was that EOT's contribution was helping the company cope in the short run while it waited for the longer run to bring improved conditions.

Lay had another, more political problem closer to home. The board of Inter-North had rebelled against his predecessor, Sam Segnar, concluding that he had caved in to HNG's demands during the merger negotiations. Segnar had ended up paying with his corporate head. Lay replaced him but soon faced bitter resistance from former Inter-North directors on a series of secondary but highly symbolic issues: the appointment of public accountants and the relocation of Enron's headquarters to Houston. The issues eventually were resolved, with Lay getting his way on the relocation. Lay had also begun to replace former Inter-North directors with selections more supportive of his leadership. Still, at the outset of 1987, Ken Lay was a CEO under the microscope, facing a board that was divided and in some cases personally bitter toward him.

None of this was lost on Ken Lay as he skimmed over Internal Audit's memo yet another time.

Considering the Options

Lay's mind quickly focused on shaping an outcome for the meeting.

What do I do to resolve this issue? I'd better walk into this meeting with some idea of the answer we want at the end.

What really matters here? What issues take priority over others? I have to give preference to the financial condition of our company. This means that EOT's profit-generating capability needs to be preserved. Moreover, a financial scandal right now could be devastating. Not only might EOT's profit contributions be affected, but also Enron's past financial results might have to be restated. Accounting restatements are yellow flags, signs that something major is amiss inside a company. It wouldn't be long before Enron's equity analysts and lenders get wind of unreported bank accounts, and dubious transactions. They'd assume the worst and wonder what else they didn't know. The result could be a major crisis of confidence in the financial markets, possibly leading to a liquidity crisis for Enron.

Borget and Mastroeni have undoubtedly broken some rules. That's not a total surprise coming from traders and their culture. We have to find some means to limit abuses while leaving EOT's risk-taking culture intact.

What exactly are the allegations of wrong doing here? It seems that Borget and Mastroeni either received or thought they'd received signals from Houston to manage the timing of EOT's reported profits. They responded by doing some of what others in their industry also do—twinned trades that give another party profits in one period to be offset by profits returned in the subsequent period. Such trades are not illegal. They altered quarterly results, but that's not uncommon: Everybody "manages earnings" one way or another. The worst that can be said is that they executed these trades in a fashion that was less than above board. Clearly, they must have assumed that not everyone in Houston was on board with managing earnings. Why else would they have not reported the new bank accounts? And what's this about company money going into Mastroeni's personal account? Whatever the reason, and I'm sure they'll have one, that's got to stop.

What to do about it all? How best to keep the big picture in mind but still send a message that excess won't be tolerated?

With this, Ken Lay picked up a pen and began to outline a set of options. He began by listing categories of possible remedial actions:

- Immediate issue management
- Personnel discipline
- Organizational reform
- Transactional rules
- Process reform
- Organizational oversight

He then expanded each bullet point with possible options to consider:

- Immediate issue management
  - o Define the transgressions associated with EOT bank accounts, trades, and the mingling of corporate money with personal accounts, and the mitigating circumstances.
  - o Ensure that Enron's financial condition is a major factor shaping any resolution of the incident.
  - o Determine the "materiality" of accounting issues and the need for any restatement of public financial reports.
- Personnel discipline: options
  - o Terminate Borget or Mastroeni or both.
  - o Terminate Harding or Sulentic, or both.
  - o Discipline some or all of the above in terms of future compensation, responsibilities, and title.

- Possible organizational reforms
  - o Revise Houston's oversight of EOT, either changing out current management and/or intensifying oversight in terms of stewardship reviews and/or oversight of controls.
  - o Embed new management at EOT:
    - New trading personnel loyal to Houston management, charged to learn EOT's business model.
    - New financial management loyal to Houston charged to ensure that controls are sound and rules are respected.
    - A financial controls advisor assigned to EOT for the indefinite future.
- Transactional rules
  - o Have Internal Audit recommend new/clarified rules for authorizing and reporting bank accounts, trades, and unit financial results.
  - o Have the chief accounting officer and/or Arthur Anderson opine on the acceptability of twinned trades done solely for the purpose of managing earnings; consider whether such trades might have other economic rationales.
- Process reform
  - o Reconsider established EOT trading limits and Enron's process for obtaining exceptions; ensure that limits are proportionate to unit profit objectives
- Organizational oversight
  - o Decide whether EOT merits a full-time Internal Audit presence; determine also the frequency and timing of audits and the role of Arthur Anderson as external auditor.
  - o Review who should be EOT's legal counsel and whether that presence should be in Houston or Valhalla.

Well, I clearly have a range of options available. Possibly I can blend a couple of different actions to not upset the apple cart while still making it clear to EOT that there are boundaries.

It flitted through Lay's mind that the meeting's outcome would go some distance toward setting the tone on financial control for the newly merged company:

There have been whispers in Houston that EOT is not respecting its oil-trading limits. The division's open position is not supposed to exceed eight million barrels; if losses exceed $4 million, the open position is to be liquidated. Some of Enron's Houston-based traders are questioning how EOT could generate the profits it was reporting without breaching these boundaries. After all, trading limits work to contain the magnitude of gains as well as losses. Still, nothing hard has surfaced. Perhaps this is only professional jealousy at work.

Whatever I decide, it will have to be smoothly executed. Enron is in no position to absorb public scandal. This will have to be handled carefully.

It also occurred to Lay that this episode could contain an opportunity. Sometimes, rule breaches are expressions of pressures that need to be resolved; under such pressures, managers sometimes choose the path of least resistance rather than a course more likely to yield fundamental improvement. Was EOT one of these cases? If so, was there a way Lay could use EOT to deliver a message that might reverberate positively throughout the struggling pipeline business?

Lay packed up his notes without making a firm decision on a course of action. He found himself leaning toward correcting the abuses without firing anybody. However, he would reserve judgment on the severity of corrective actions until he heard the full story. Lay also reflected that the oil-trading business was something of a mystery. It was relatively new and not a heritage HNG business; profits seemed be closely tied to the quality of the individuals doing the trading. In 1986, Borget himself had told the Enron Board that oil trading "as done by professionals in the industry today, using the sophisticated tools available, can generate substantial earnings with virtually no fixed investment and relatively low risk"[1]

Lay resolved to listen carefully to what emerged between the lines at tomorrow's meeting–especially to the "vibes" regarding how EOT generated its profits. Would there be anything more to the auditors' allegations than what he had already seen in writing and heard from Harding and Sulentic? If so, Lay might have to adjust his plan of action right there at the meeting.

The Meeting with Internal Audit

The meeting convened with Borget and Mastroeni present, along with Enron general counsel Rich Kinder, as well as Harding and Sulentic. David Woytek and John Beard represented Internal Audit. Lay opened the meeting, calling on EOT president Lou Borget to address Internal Audit's concerns.

Borget and Mastroeni laid out the following facts. EOT had been highly profitable in 1986. As this became known, company managers requested that they find a way to shift some profits into 1987. They were told to do this by "whatever legitimate business practice we could." As a result, EOT resorted to matched, or twinned, trades that would net out over the period 1986-'87. Borget observed that such trades were commonly used by other trading companies. Mastroeni stated that EOT had identified three firms interested in boosting their 1986 profits: Isla Petroleum, Southwest Oil and Commodities, and Petropol Energy. EOT then entered into trades with those three entities, selling oil at prices that delivered profits to them during December 1986; the deal was for EOT to buy back oil and recoup equal gains during the first part of 1987. Mastroeni explained that they opened the Eastern Savings Bank account as a place to hold cash proceeds from the 1986 sales. However, because this account was in Enron's name, Mastroeni stated that he had moved money to his personal account to avoid attracting attention and complicating Enron's year-end statements. Their intention was to return all funds to Enron in 1987.

Sulentic then added that it was all a misunderstanding, that Borget and Mastroeni believed that they were acting in Enron's best interests. He added: "I say we accept that mistakes were made, do what needs to be done to correct them, and move on to a profitable 1987."[2]

Ken Lay then spoke, making it clear that he disapproved of the methods EOT had used to accomplish its goals. He asked whether anyone else at the meeting had anything to add.

David Woytek spoke up, pointing out that the bank statements EOT had brought to the meeting had been altered. Transactions showing funds transfers into and out of the accounts had been removed. Woytek had the statements provided by the Eastern Savings Bank to document the point.

Mastroeni then explained that the deleted transactions referred to a disputed bonus paid to a trader. The individual in question had been fired near the end of 1985. He had retained a lawyer and threatened to sue the company if his anticipated year-end bonus was not paid. After some discussion, a close-out settlement of $250,000 had been agreed on. Woytek asked Mastroeni why, if that were so, there was any need to alter the bank records. Mastroeni replied that the incident had nothing to do with the transactions under discussion at this meeting, so they simply took them out of the bank statements to avoid confusing the issues.

Lay listened to the conversation as it surged back and forth. What he had just heard amounted to new information; Borget and Mastroeni had brought doctored bank records to the meeting.

They had made a decision not "to confuse" the issues, in the process attempting to prevent some transactions from coming under scrutiny.

It was getting close to the moment when Lay would need to end the discussion and focus the meeting on what actions should be taken. Lay had now heard Borget/Mastroeni's stories explaining the opening of the unreported bank account, the origins of the funds transfers into the account and the outflow of money to Mastroeni's account. How much could he take those stories at face value? And how should this new information—that EOT's managers had altered bank records—influence the perspectives and options he had mulled over the night before?

Attachment 1 Historical Recreation (HRC)

MEMORANDUM

January 25, 1987

To: Mr. David Woytek
From: John Beard
SUBJECT: Possible Irregularities at Enron Oil Trading

This memo intends to summarize our findings so far regarding potential financial irregularities at Enron Oil Trading (EOT) and to lay out the issues requiring further investigation.

On January 23, Internal Audit was contacted by an officer at the Eastern Savings Bank. The bank had identified unusual activity involving an Enron bank account and wanted to verify with company officials that certain transactions were legitimate.

The officer reported that Tom Mastroeni, treasurer of EOT, had recently opened an account at the bank. Mastroeni and EOT president Louis Borget are listed as signers on the account. Immediately following the account opening, transfers totaling $5 million flowed into the account from a bank located in the Channel Islands, a European tax-haven location. Subsequently, funds in excess of $2 million left the account and were transferred to another account registered in Tom Mastroeni's name. Eastern Savings has cooperated by sending us statements documenting both the account opening and the funds flows into and then out of this new account.

We have checked Enron's corporate registry of bank accounts and can find no evidence of the Eastern Savings Bank account having been recorded on the company's books.

We have interviewed Steve Sulentic and John Harding, EOT's contact executives in Houston. They advise that since 1985, EOT has, at their request, taken actions to move accounting profits from one reporting period to another. Apparently, the actions involved are twinned trades, i.e. simultaneously negotiated sale/buy oil trades having different time periods. In the typical transaction, EOT would sell oil one month forward at a price attractive to the buyer and contract to purchase the oil back two months forward at an equally attractive price. The net effect of the two trades is zero, but if done at the end of an accounting period, the first transaction creates a loss for EOT, with an offsetting gain recorded in the subsequent period.

It is unclear whether Messrs. Harding and Sulentic knew of the precise mechanism used by EOT to move profits between accounting periods. However, these executives indicate that such transactions are not unusual among oil traders. Sulentic and Harding now believe that the transactions that led to funds transfers into the Eastern Savings account may have resulted from EOT's entering into year-end 1986 twinned trades. They also indicate that Borget and Mastroeni are available to come to Houston to clarify this matter.

As of this moment, we do not know whether the funds transfers represent legitimate EOT business transactions, trades done solely for accounting purposes, or irregular activity. It is certainly a concern that funds flowed through the Eastern Savings account and into the personal account of a company officer; such activity involving an amount over $2 million is highly irregular. It is also a "red flag" that this activity took place in a new account set up in circumvention of clear corporate guidelines requiring the reporting of all new bank accounts to corporate headquarters. To the extent that these transactions are irregular, they may represent theft of corporate funds. To the extent that the transactions are found to be legitimate, their "off-the-books" nature could require restatement of financial records and reported results for 1986.

The issues requiring further investigation are thus the following:

- For what purpose was the new account at Eastern Savings Bank opened?
- Why was this account's opening not reported to Houston? Failure to do so is a direct violation of company control standards.
- Was there any substantive business purpose associated with the cash transfers that entered the Eastern Savings Bank account?
- What justification can be provided for corporate funds being transferred to the personal account of an employee?
  - o Are all corporate funds accounted for?
  - o When will the funds be returned? If not immediately, why not?
- If the underlying transactions were entered into solely for the purposes of altering EOT's reported earnings, do Enron's 1986 financial statements need to be restated?

In conclusion, the facts known to date are of grave concern and warrant a full investigation. The potential implications include loss of corporate funds as well as misstatement of records, deliberate manipulation of records, and the creation of fictitious losses with impacts on Enron's financial statements and tax returns for the year ending 12/31/86.

Attachment 2

Enron Corporation

Summary Financial Statements, 1985-86*

$ Millions

Year	1985	1986
Revenue	9,767	7,454
Earning Before Interest & Taxes (EBIT)	554	230
Interest Expense	(337)	(421)
Taxable Income	234	(191)
Income Taxes, net	(109)	565
Income from Continuing Operations Before Extraordinary Charges	163	374
Net Income	(79)	557
Total Debt	4,356	3,538
Net Worth	1,492	1,203
Debt/Total Capital	74%	75%
EBIT/Interest Expense	164%	55%
Operating Cash Generation	682	478
Investment/Acquisitions, net	(2,357)	756
Financing, net	1,641	(963)
Change in Cash	(35)	270

* Figures may not be additive because of other items, charges and rounding

Author's Note

This case relies principally on the accounts of the Valhalla financial control issues provided in *The Smartest Guys in the Room* (pp. 15-19) and *Conspiracy of Fools* (pp. 15-19). Both books treat the episode in detail and with minor discrepancies provide accounts that are consistent as to the facts.

Each book offers some details not provided by the other. For example, *The Smartest Guys in the Room* provides details of the trading limits in existence at EOT, the financial condition and bank covenants of Enron at that time, and the fact that David Woytek sent Ken Lay a memo describing the EOT twinned trades as creating "fictitious losses". *Conspiracy of Fools* provides a detailed account of the meeting of EOT's Borget and Mastroeni, Enron Internal Audit, and Enron management. This work also confirms that Lay attended that meeting and gave explicit instructions as to what remedial actions were to be taken.

The Smartest Guys in the Room (p. 18) identifies Steve Sulentic and John Harding as Borget's Houston-based nominal superiors. That work quotes "internal documents, court testimony and notes detailing these events" in describing how the two executives articulated a rationale for Borget to "move some profits from 1986 into 1987 through legitimate transactions". Sulentic's defense of the traders' actions as a "misunderstanding" appears in *Conspiracy of Fools* (p. 18).

Several portions of the case are created for purposes of surfacing the issues and options facing Ken Lay. Lay's thoughts on the night before the meeting have been crafted for these purposes. They do not represent any sort of historical record found in any published source. This applies also to the list of options he outlines while sitting in his office. The portrayal is, however, consistent with (1) the fact that he received a memo from David Woytek on the possible irregularities and (2) the actions taken by Lay at the end of and right after the meeting. It is also apparent from the content of the memo forwarded by David Woytek that Lay had heard at least a preliminary version of the "twinned trade to move accounting profits" story that Harding and Sulentic articulated at the actual meeting. Lay's options list has obviously been expanded beyond the actions he actually endorsed in order to provide students with a full range of choices to consider.

The account of the meeting with Internal Audit is based upon the two sources cited.

Attachment 1, Beard's memo to Woytek, is a Historical Recreation (HRC) intended to summarize the facts known to the auditors prior to the meeting with Borget and Mastroeni. However, it is factually based, being grounded in not only the general accounts provided in the sources but also in: (1) the fact that Woytek did provide a memo to Lay and other senior managers, (2) published comments from Beard's notes, and (3) a published quote from Woytek's memo describing the twinned trades as creating "fictitious losses".

Attachment 2 is drawn from Enron's restated public financial filings.

Notes

1. *The Smartest Guys in the Room*, p. 17.
2. *Conspiracy of Fools*, p. 18.

How to do an Ethics Case Study: Key Steps in Tactical Planning

Why Case Studies? The Need for Preparation and Practice

MOST INDIVIDUALS IN CORPORATE LIFE come to ethics issues largely unprepared. And then, when unlucky enough to encounter something unethical, people can find the deck stacked against them.

They are unprepared because they have had little training and even less practice in handling the complexities ethics issues bring. They may have their personal sense of morality as a guide but not much more. If they had liberal arts training, they may have discussed philosophy or morality but not in a concrete setting in which the personal consequence may be demotion or termination of employment. Their business or law school training my have provided a low-emphasis course on corporate governance but not much on what to do when your boss orders you to work around a law.

They will find the deck stacked against them because when they first encounter an ethics problem, they usually will be dealing with someone above them in management. This person or persons will have the advantage not only of senior position, but also more experience managing decisions through the organization and past its gatekeepers.

New employees are quickly socialized by their everyday business experiences into the real world of "gray zones". Firms don't violate accounting principles per se but use them adroitly to present their results in the best light. People often spin or withhold information internally or from customers or partners when they perceive an advantage in doing so. Tax departments work up almost-substanceless transactions to reduce taxes. Almost everyone comes around to a belief that pressing against-even bending-the rules is part of competing and succeeding in the real world of business.

So, most everyone is partially conditioned to unethical practices when suddenly something more substantial cuts across their radar screen. The first reaction may be a flash of recognition and an impulse to push back. And then the complexity of the situation and the personal risks come to mind. If there isn't a reliable financial control structure to look to for support, the challenge involved in resisting can seem overwhelming. For many caught in

S.V. Arbogast, *Resisting Corporate Corruption* (pp. 22–33)
© 2008 by M & M Scrivener Press

this unhappy situation, decisions to go along or avert one's eyes can come quick and easy.

The alternative answer is to practice in advance the spotting of ethics issues and the formulation of effective resistance plans. These practice situations have to be representative, realistic, and difficult. Suggested solutions have to draw upon lessons of what has worked in real situations that involved difficult ethics issues.

Practice will instill several valuable capacities. For one, it will sharpen the ability to distinguish a serious ethics issue from the more mundane boundary pushing that constitutes an accepted part of normal business. Real career-jeopardizing resistance should be expended only on serious ethics issues. For another, it will enhance understanding of the tactical options available for resisting, the personal risks involved in resisting, and ways to manage the two. This understanding can bring several advantages:

- It can improve one's thinking on how to win a more ethical outcome and thus bolster one's sense that resistance is both feasible and worth the risk.
- It can also sharpen one's sense of the varying personal risks posed by different courses of action. Not every act of resistance runs a termination risk. Much resistance can also be mounted in ways that minimize career hazards for the resister.
- Finally, practice in formulating tactical plans can help one improvise as necessary in a "live fire" situation. The more situations one has considered, the more tactical responses one has devised, and the more creative will be one's responses to real ethics dilemmas if and when they arise.

With practice on these cases, students should be able to react to a real situation with a sense that they've seen something like this before. Beginning resistance from that posture rather than one of shock or confusion is half the battle.

The Solution Framework: Defining the Ethics Issue:

As outlined in Essay 1, individuals have to formulate resistance plans that address each of four elements:

1. A clear statement of the ethics issue, including why it deserves to be considered exceptional. This statement also requires definition of a boundary condition—an ethically acceptable outcome to the concrete business situation.
2. Identification of the potential personal consequences for resisting successfully or unsuccessfully. Different things are likely to happen in each case. An initial assessment should be made as to whether these consequences can be accepted if worst comes to worst. Practical consideration of how to mitigate personal risk is then deferred until the end of the process.

3. An alternative business approach to the questionable proposed practices. The standard here is to identify the best alternative business option that is consistent with an acceptable ethical outcome.
4. Development of a tactical plan of resistance. Most times, this plan will be aimed at securing a decision in favor of the ethical business plan. Other times, however, the tactical plan will be aimed at containing damage and/or positioning for a later time.

When trying to define the Ethics Issue, it can be helpful to try to assign the problem to one of the following general categories:

- Potential violations of law or regulations with force of law.
- Potential violations of company policies.
- Actions that violate sound financial control practices.
- Actions that weaken the fabric of internal controls, potentially paving the way for specific subsequent abuses or legal violations.
- Conflicts between professional roles and a responsibility to resist illegal activities (e.g. an in-house attorney's predicament when serving a client with potentially illegal ideas).

The cases in this book pose ethics issues that fall into all of these categories.

Students can better determine which category best applies to each case by focusing on the possible consequences of allowing the questionable activity to proceed.

The next step is to conceive of an acceptable ethical outcome. Expect solutions to be difficult, and so temper one's target outcome with a necessary realism. Certainly, one may wish that a firm didn't use any aggressive tax shelters, but a realistic solution may be stopping those likely to result in IRS penalties or lawsuits. For some matters, such as those involving possible legal violations, realism may involve recognizing the clarity of the violation and the supremacy of the law.

One aid to finding the right balance between realism and doing the right thing is to conceive of ethical boundary conditions. Doing so means asking: What is the minimum outcome that could be considered ethically acceptable in this case? This defines the ethical line, on the other side of which you are admitting defeat. By defining this minimum acceptable outcome, ethics and realism will have to be reconciled, at least conceptually. Defining this boundary doesn't prevent one from striving for a solution well inside it. However, knowing this boundary does help clarify where no more compromises can be made.

Sometimes an acceptable ethical outcome is not politically achievable at that moment. These situations can be particularly complex as well as fraught with personal risk. Those caught in such cases may end up having to choose between a less-satisfactory outcome inside the firm or taking the matter to outside agents.

In terms of the internal options, resisters can target one of the following "next best" outcomes:

1. Containing the damage by surrounding the unethical practices with compensating controls and review procedures.
2. Making arguments and issuing warnings that set the stage for reversing the unethical decision later.
3. Relocating the issue from inside the firm's management structure out into the firm's relationship with regulators and/or markets.

When making this choice, resisters will need to consider the gravity of the unethical practice and the state of the firm's controls. For example, a decision that weakens controls but doesn't violate the law might well be treated as a fight- another- day situation.

At the other end of the spectrum, continuing to resist illegal activities from within the firm runs the risk of the resister becoming legally culpable. Such sober realities, along with the fundamental need to respect the law, can present compelling reasons to take matters outside. This issue receives specific treatment in Case Study 13 'New Counsel for Andy Fastow (B)' and also in Case Study 16 "Whistleblowing" before Imploding in Accounting Scandals'.

Finally, there is a "resolve reason" for defining the ethics issue first. It is important to see it clearly and to decide whether it is worth a fight before the matter becomes clouded by business issues and personal risks. Sherron Watkins's story is a case in point. Early on, she arrived at a clear sense of why Enron's Raptor accounting was not simply wrong but also fraudulent. Once word got around that she had written to Ken Lay, several people tried to convince her to give up the effort. Sherron was told that Ken Lay "gravitates to good news," was reminded that Arthur Anderson had signed off on the accounting, and was advised that others she trusted saw the accounting as "aggressive but not over the line". If she hadn't defined the ethics issue first, she might well have been put off by this onslaught of counterarguments; in the full light of day, her first reading turned out to have been the right one.

Tactical Planning and Alternative Business Plans

Once the ethics issue has been defined, the next step is to make a brief survey of the potential personal risks. Whether these turn out to be serious or minimal, potential resisters should then put them aside until they have thought through a tactical resistance plan. Having such a game plan will promote a calmer deliberation of the risks, and may also open up opportunities to mitigate personal risks that were not initially visible.

As noted, having an alternative business plan can be indispensable to a successful tactical plan. Tactical planning will however, vary markedly, depending on the firm's stage of ethics decomposition. Options available in the first two stages are usually closed by Stages 3 and 4. Accordingly, tactical planning begins with determining where the firm stands in terms of ethical decomposition. Because all the facts may not be known, potential resisters should consider the possibility that the situation is at least one stage worse than they think and plan accordingly.

Tactical Planning in Early Stages of Ethical Decomposition

For ethics issues arising in Stage 1, tactical planning should concentrate on convincing key decision makers to allow the established control system to work. At this stage, a variety of outcomes can be acceptable; these range from rejecting unethical proposals outright to ensuring that adequate controls surround the new aggressive course. The basic integrity of the controls environment provides a basis for believing that new "compensating" controls will function.

Students need a good grounding in the fundamental rationale for controls if they are to prevail in early contests that test controls systems. Those proposing various expedients will typically be articulate about their potential business benefits. Resisters will need to be well armed with potent counterarguments that include both the risks and the costs particular to the specific situation; these include the systemic effects—those longer-term ills that come with eroding controls. Essay 3 lays out multiple rationales for why sustaining good control is the best economic decision; several of these rationales are seldom wielded in business ethics discussions and can be used both to surprise opponents and lend weight to the pro-controls course of action.

In the early stages, management will tend to see business and ethics issues as intertwined. To convince senior managers to select more ethical approaches, a technical command of business issues is important. Many times, the technical details of the case hold important elements that can determine the outcome. For example, the technical details may reveal that a questionable transaction is going to unnecessary lengths to achieve a business outcome. The same outcome can be achieved in another, more straightforward manner, one that does not damage controls. It is only the transaction proponent's personal agenda that will suffer from taking the higher road.

Understanding transactions in detail may also hold the key to discovering risks that may be deemed unacceptable once they are brought into the open. Almost inevitably, unethical strategies display technical weaknesses—these are inherent in the nature of unethical behavior, which involves circumventing or ignoring policies, regulations, and law. Most of the cases in this book come with a plethora of technical detail about the underlying business problems/transactions. Students should practice spotting such technical vulnerabilities; from there, tactical planning can focus on how to use these flaws and the associated risks as ammunition to help an ethical outcome prevail.

This point leads directly to another: resisters need to take the time necessary to master both the technical details and obtain good information about the business issues. Thus, time management is an element in tactical planning. Often, the first reaction to discovering an ethics issue is outrage and an impulse to doing something "right now." Making a measured assessment of the situation instead often reveals that partial or misinformation is defining the situation; much that a resister needs to know simply is not known up front. This argues against immediately bringing ethics situations to a head. Students should instead note that there is a time zone within which an ethics situation can be worked. They will then want to pick the optimal time to bring matters to a head, taking into account their need to research issues. Tactically controlling the pace for working ethics issues is an undervalued advantage that takes practice to use.

Once they adequately understand the ethical and business issues, students should craft an alternative business course. It is vital to show management that they are not choosing between an unethical option and a business reverse. Sound controls can and should be defended as a business moral imperative—something that is simply right to do, regardless of the business consequences. However, human nature and corporate politics being what they are, it is much easier for the right-thing-to-do argument to prevail when management can see another way to move forward.

The alternative business course is a tactical element that vary widely with the particulars of the case. However, some general comments can be offered. First is the question of whether the unethical course actually is critical to the desired outcome or simply one of the following:

- Advancing the personal agenda of the proponent.
- Quicker, more convenient, less effort, etc.
- More certain to be achieved in the near term.
- Some particular cost or risk is eliminated, disguised or finessed.

These situations reveal an ethical tradeoff that is less than a necessity. Isolating and measuring this tradeoff can permit resisters to respond to management with one of the following:

1. Analysis showing that the true benefit is not the one advertised by transaction proponents and is less a matter of necessity than of preference; often, this shrinking of the transaction's rationale is enough to discredit the deal.
2. Attacks arguing that the proposal fails to address business fundamentals; consequently, it is unlikely to succeed over time and may promote the degradation of business capabilities.

3. A warning that whatever the true benefit, it pales in comparison to
the various risks involved. These risks may involve such outcomes
as overpaying third parties or driving away customers, legal or public affairs risks, or some combination.

When the business advantage of an unethical course is substantial, composing an alternative business course is particularly essential. Unethical
transactions with big impacts are by their nature going to bring big risks.
They can still be attacked using arguments 2 and 3 above. Such attacks and
warnings can cause even partially compromised executives to "take a second
look". They can also open doors to recruiting new allies. However, for the
second look to get to a different conclusion and for allies to sign on, there
must be available an alternative program for supporters to buy into.
Otherwise, attacks on an ethically questionable course are likely to fall prey
to the "so what do you propose?" challenge—to which silence is often a fatal-
ly flawed answer.

Though in Stages 1 and 2 one is still talking about normal companies, control systems can and do come under pressure. Consequently, resisters still need
to consider the tactical context surrounding ethics issues. Here, it matters
whether the pressure is coming from midlevel executives pushing their own
agendas or from a complicit senior management. Where midlevel executives
are free lancing, effective resistance is easier to mount. Mostly this involves
exposing the transaction's true nature, suspect gains, and ample risks. In some
cases, this exposure effort must ultimately persuade senior management. More
typically, it must persuade the internal control organization, which is still func-
tioning, and which will handle the review with senior leaders.

When senior leaders are involved and telegraphing support for a questionable course, the situation is much more difficult. Clearly, it matters
which senior leaders are involved. If it's not the very top management or if
this senior group is divided, resisters must focus their hopes on persuading
those with the "last word" to support an ethical outcome.

One important tactic to consider in such cases is to articulate the full slate
of risk warnings warranted by the facts. Here, the emphasis should be on
breadth of the warnings. This warning list should be articulated verbally
and then documented in a memorandum of what was said. Senior managers' caution instincts are triggered by documents that may put them in an
unflattering light if worst comes to worst. Possibly, this will trigger the take-
a-second-look impulse. Then, if the decision cannot be won outright,
resisters may still be able to achieve one of two other outcomes, either: (1) to
contain the current decision to the maximum extent possible or (2) to leave a
record of warnings which may serve as a basis for reversing course should
one of them prove prophetic.

Disbanding politically because "things didn't go your way" is likely to
reinforce the firm's slide into ethical decomposition. When one of the warn-

ings does come to pass, there will be a tactical opening both to clean up the mess and to propose structural reforms. This can also be the political opening to reconstitute the independence of the internal control function. Resisters will need to be ready with their proposals.

Many times, senior leaders regard questionable transactions as temporary diversions. They may be especially sensitive to short-term timing issues, such as quarter or year-end reporting dates. Resisters can benefit from paying attention to the calendar; whenever possible, ethics issues should be brought to a head away from such deadlines. Resisters can also use tactics of "revisiting" questionable decisions at less pressured times. Under the right circumstances, temporary expedients can be reversed or at a minimum, subject to enhanced controls.

In conclusion, the first two stages of a company's controls environment permit ethical business advocates to wage what might be regarded as a conventional internal struggle. Typically they can work through channels, find allies, fight to win decisions at higher levels, and fight again to reverse losses. During these stages, the most common mistakes involve the failure to offer alternate business courses and a well-formulated slate of broad warnings. Mistakes of this sort characterize controls organizations too willing to divorce themselves from the business and insensitive to the need to nurture the political support that preserves their function

Advanced Stages of Ethical Decomposition

Once a self-serving or corrupt environment takes hold, resisters can no longer think in terms of conventional corporate processes. Tactical planning now becomes an exercise in creating political options within the firm or of deciding whether to take issues outside the company. When making this inside/outside decision, resisters must devote much assessment to determining how far decomposition has advanced.

This assessment begins with two questions: 1. Is anyone in senior management still concerned enough about controls to overrule some expedient course? and 2. Is there an agent of corruption at work among senior management? Determining these situations will help indicate the political possibilities for still working an ethics issue inside the firm.

The executive pool just below the CEO/COO level is a place to look for potential champions to restore ethical behavior. Some executives may yet be untainted; others may be receptive to the argument that, should they advance to a top job, they will not want to become responsible for scandals created by others.

Because of the nature of their functional expertise, senior finance officers should be the most oriented towards reversing ethical decomposition. If a firm has become impaired, the top finance officer likely has been compromised. However, that person's rivals and replacements may contain candidates eager to reverse practices obnoxious to the core principles of their function.

Assuming that potential allies can be found in the senior ranks, how can they be enlisted? In the first two stages, developing an alternative business course was critical to influencing senior management; in the latter two stages, more is needed. While an alternative business course will still be essential, a damage-control plan must be added. By Stages 3 and 4, firms have accumulated vulnerabilities or even violations. Sound remedial action usually means disclosing uncomfortable-even incriminating-information. Senior managers will be loath to consider courses of action they are not sure they can survive.

Here, the alternative business course can provide a valuable context within which past mistakes can be corrected. Senior managers can become champions of restructuring and reform; typically they will be well regarded for ferreting out and correcting business problems. Suspect transactions can be unwound because they are declared bad for business. Needed control improvements can be embedded within process redesign. Agents of decomposition can be held accountable for exposing the firm to unacceptable business risks or for failing to achieve sound fundamental outcomes. This approach works best when the ethics problems reside in a particular organizational unit, one that can be isolated and fixed.

The important thing is to bring forward major controls issues within a context of broader business restructuring that then allows senior managers scope for damage control. This assumes that management is still open to such proposals. Advocates of ethical business should not dismiss this possibility, however. Self-preservation rightly understood can be a powerful motivator. Even at an advanced stage of ethical decomposition, senior leaders usually retain some sense that they and the firm are at risk; indeed, only two months before he resigned, Jeff Skilling forced Andy Fastow to step down as head of his LJM partnerships. The sense that one is exposed and might get caught can be a powerful motivator for senior managers to decide that things have gone too far. Although it was too little and too late, Ken Lay's message to employees on returning as Enron's CEO is instructive; even as Lay told them that Enron was in great shape, he also commented that Enron's "values had slipped" and needed to be restored.

The threat of outside discovery thus becomes the key tactical weapon of resisters in Stages 3 and 4. **One of the great lessons of Enron's story is that it is difficult for a "public company" to prevent a series of unethical transactions from becoming public.** Even when the gatekeepers have been neutralized, required public disclosure provided clues about questionable related party transactions. Enron's financial statements kept inviting skeptics to probe its opaque disclosures. Employees disgusted by the firm's behavior or embittered by being discharged found ways to direct information to the financial press, Wall Street analysts and even the Securities and Exchange Commission (SEC). By summer 2001, Enron was finding that its accounting was fooling fewer and fewer investors. The possibility of using this history and these risks to warn off senior management may be one of the few positive legacies from Enron's sad story.

That leaves the matter of deciding when and how to go to outside agents. Here, resisters enjoy more options than they may at first perceive. Resisters need not limit their tactics to trying to persuade a compromised management to reverse course. Especially for public companies, passing information to a host of official and unofficial watchdogs has become a potent option. It is clear from Enron's story that investigative reporters, such as Bethany McLean/Peter Elkind and John Emshwiller/Rebecca Smith, received tips from within Enron on what to investigate. Even more interesting is the role played by short sellers, by James Chanos and Richard Grubman, in exposing the business weakness underlying Enron's glowing financial reports.

It is also worth noting that such information passing can be done anonymously and still be effective. This is not to say that anonymous disclosure does not involve potential costs or ethics issues. Rather, Enron's story documents that this has become a potent–if dangerous and morally complex–option for resisters. The ethics of anonymous external disclosure are discussed further in Essay 3.

Personal Considerations

To touch on anonymous disclosure is to touch upon the matter of addressing personal risks within one's tactical plan. Nothing chills the impulse to resist like the sense that one may be "betting one's career." Then, the perception can take hold that resistance amounts to self-sacrifice. For this reason, resisters should defer detailed consideration of their personal risks until the end of their tactical planning. At this point, however, it is essential to address these concerns.

The opportunities to manage personal risks are often underestimated. Resisters typically draw quick conclusions about whether they can withstand the consequences of failing to reverse some unethical practice. For those who can proceed more deliberately, a planned approach to personal risk often reveals possibilities that make effective resistance possible; this approach involves the following:

- Summoning the emotional commitment to accept some possible consequences. Many employees operate from the premise that no damage is acceptable. This option often produces paralysis. Anticipating some career cost and then working to minimize it usually is more effective; this course creates both political operating room and a mindset more ready to do what is necessary to be effective.

- Carefully documenting one's cause of action and course of conduct. Having time to prepare this record is one of the advantages of not bringing matters to a head too soon. Once the issue is joined, this record can serve as ammunition, leverage, and even protection. At a minimum, it can be used to rebut misrepresentations of one's behavior. The record is also a source of potential public disclosures—which can be a source of considerable leverage for a resister when/if conditions become severe.
- Maneuvering room, especially for very senior people. These often feel they have much to lose, but the fact is, they also have the most freedom of maneuver. Typically, their past remuneration takes economic hardship out of the picture. They usually have contacts and options outside the company. They also know information that the firm doesn't want to see in the hands of competitors or the press. This gives senior executives leverage in ethics disputes and insulation from the worst sorts of consequences. It is often only the disturbance of what must be considered an enviable position that causes senior executives to shy away from facing ethics issues.

Those who are most at risk personally should still follow the preceding tactical planning recommendations. However, these individuals must add some things. For one thing, they should try to enlist someone with more career protection as an ally and, if possible, front man. The more vulnerable person can then step back into a supporting role as the dispute comes to a head. Second, they should consider whether there is a safe haven within the company. Knowing that there is some place to land other than on the street can bring the personal-risk assessment into clearer focus.

Finally, they must gauge the level of resistance they can mount without suffering unacceptable retaliation. If that level is insufficient to accomplish much, thought should be given to leaving the firm. Once safely lodged in a new location, consideration can then be given to pursuing the matter with oversight agents.

A Final Word About Financial Control

Most of this discussion about tactical planning is necessitated by the fact that when ethics situations arise, employees inclined to do the right thing often discover that they cannot count on support from the financial-control system.

When sound financial controls are in place, employees have recourse to professionals experienced in handling ethics issues. Procedures for working ethics cases are clear. Employees raising concerns are protected. Guidelines and precedents exist for determining appropriate discipline for violators. In short, when sound control structures are in place, an employee raising concerns has far less need to improvise in building political support for doing the right thing. Much of the preceding discussion of tactical planning seeks to address circumstances that don't offer employees this more straightforward path.

Sustaining a sound financial-control structure is thus critical to the maintenance of an ethical business culture. Employees interested in having an ethical workplace must see that they have a personal stake in preserving good controls.

Case Study 2

Enron Oil Trading (B): The Future of Enron Internal Audit

I'm not sure that there's a future in Internal Audit at Enron. I may need to make a career move.

D AVID WOYTEK STARED DOWN at an August 1, 1987 letter, that he had just drafted (Attachment 1). Addressed to Keith Kern, Enron's CFO, the letter expressed interest in moving onto a different career track within Enron's financial functions. What it didn't say was how discouraged Woytek had become about the ability of his current function, Internal Audit, to perform its job.

It had been a discouraging six months for Woytek. Alerted by Eastern Savings Bank to a possible fraud at Enron Oil Trading (EOT), Woytek and his colleagues had confronted its executives. They presented evidence that EOT executives failed to report the opening of a bank account, moved corporate funds into a personal account, and altered bank statements. A meeting with Ken Lay had resulted in the CEO's giving directions to EOT not to repeat its controls violations, to record its profits correctly, and to seek guidance from Houston when dealing with exceptional situations. However, neither Louis Borget (EOT's president) nor Thomas Mastroeni (EOT's treasurer) had been terminated or disciplined. Moreover, the meeting had not resulted in any guidance on restating Enron's financial statements. Shoring up controls and oversight at EOT had also been left unresolved.

As the meeting concluded, Enron CEO Ken Lay asked Woytek to remain for a private conversation. Lay told Woytek to take his best people to Valhalla, New York (EOT's location), and continue the investigation. Lay continued: "Make sure every penny of this money is returned to the company, even this bonus Borget was talking about. I want all of it back. And I want you to go today, now."[1]

That sounded pretty good to Woytek. It seemed that the gravity of EOT's controls breaches had registered with Ken Lay after all. Woytek promised to get on with the investigation right away.

After a couple of days, Woytek, his colleague John Beard, and Carolyn Kee from Arthur Anderson arrived at EOT's offices in the Mount Pleasant Corporate Center. It was then that the "fun" began.

S.V. Arbogast, *Resisting Corporate Corruption* (pp. 34–42)
© 2008 by M & M Scrivener Press

Stonewalled in Valhalla

Woytek's audit team had been greeted by Borget with an order not to speak to his traders, followed by this warning: "I don't want you stirring up and making me lose people."[2]   Woytek requested backup documentation for the twinned trades that had prompted the investigation. A minimum of paperwork was produced. The auditors did manage to uncover some additional disquieting findings. Proceeds ($7,800) from the sale of Borget's company car had also made its way into the Eastern Savings Bank account. Payments in excess of $100,000 were supposedly made from the same account to "M. Yass", described by Borget as a Lebanese trader for Southwest Oil & Commodities. The transactions were suspicious, but to make a definitive finding, Woytek and his team had to gain access to the documentary backup for the trades.

Eventually, Woytek confronted Borget and demanded all the trading records: telexes, wire transfers, and trade confirmations. Borget promised to produce them. However, no paperwork arrived. A few hours later, Woytek received a call from Enron president Mick Seidl. The senior executive came right to the point: "You guys need to pack up and come home. Borget is getting upset, the traders are getting upset. You need to pull out. We're going to turn this over to Arthur Anderson instead."[3]

Woytek and Beard returned to Houston. Carolyn Kee, supplemented by other resources from Arthur Anderson, continued the investigation. As Kee and her team went to work, Mick Seidl sent Borget a memo advising him of the issues Arthur Anderson would be pursuing, so that EOT could be better prepared with answers. Seidl later sent Borget a telex congratulating EOT on the quality of the answers provided to the investigators and affirming his complete confidence in Borget's personal integrity. It ended "please keep making us millions."[4] This memo was sent before Arthur Anderson presented its findings.

Before abandoning the field, however, Woytek had hired a private investigations firm, Intertect, to check into Borget and Mastroeni's backgrounds and to verify the existence of the companies and individuals with whom EOT had engaged in suspect trades. Intertect's report arrived in Houston in February 1987. Its findings were significant, if not dramatic. The three companies supposedly counterparty to EOT on the twinned trades—Southwest Oil, Isla Petroleum and Petropol Energy—did not exist. Telex numbers attributed to these firms by Borget and Mastroeni were false. On the matter of personal character, Intertect found that Mastroeni had been sued by banks for using fraudulent documents when applying for loans.

Woytek took his findings and the Intertect report to Keith Kern, Enron's CFO. Kern objected to Internal Audit's hiring of Intertect, noting that the EOT investigation was now assigned to Arthur Anderson. Woytek was ordered to drop the matter.

Dead and Buried in Houston

On April 29, 1987, Arthur Anderson delivered its findings on EOT to the Enron audit committee. The report contained more than a few indications of controls problems, including:

- Being unable to verify ownership or any other details pertaining to EOT's supposed counterparties for the suspect trades.
- The transactions lacked business purpose beyond affecting the timing of reported profits.
- The impossibility of determining whether EOT was complying with its own controls on trading positions, because the unit made a practice of destroying its daily position reports.

Thus, EOT could be exposed to much bigger losses than was commonly believed. However, Arthur Anderson refrained from drawing any conclusions on matters that might have required Enron to take action. The auditor did not opine on the legality of EOT's twinned trades, the legitimacy of such transactions from an accounting perspective, or their materiality. To have declared the transactions to be both material and without accounting substance would have pointed Enron toward having to restate prior-year financial filings. It might also have opened the door to SEC and/or IRS sanctions. Arthur Anderson instead indicated that Enron would need to make its own determination on the legitimacy and materiality of the prior accounting. The auditor noted that it had already received a letter from Enron chief counsel Rich Kinder declaring that: "the unusual transactions would not have a material effect on the financial statements…and that no disclosure of these transactions is necessary."[5]

The report did not comment on the altering of bank statements or Mastroeni's prior history of using false documentation.

The Arthur Anderson report was greeted with concern by some of Enron's directors, including Ron Roskens. Ken Lay then confronted the Audit Committee with a firm position:

"I hear your concerns and I understand them. But I've made the decision. I've got to put my CEO hat on and do what is in the best interests of Enron. We cannot afford to be disrupting our trading operations unnecessarily. It is too important to our financial performance."[6]

Lay was not going to fire anybody. Some changes would be made. Mastroeni would remain on the payroll but step down as EOT's treasurer. A new unit CFO would be named and moved to Valhalla. Moreover, all EOT banking and financial activities would henceforth report through Enron-Houston. After further discussion and some dissent, the Audit Committee, with reservations, backed Lay's position.

Steve Sulentic, previously involved in Houston's oversight of EOT and a defender of Borget and Mastroeni, was dispatched to Valhalla, replacing Mastroeni as EOT's senior financial officer.

Subsequently, Kinder forwarded an opinion from in-house counsel to the full Enron Board declaring that the twinned trades were "legitimate common transactions in the oil trading business" and did not "lack economic substance".[7] Since the transactions were thus considered legitimate and substantive, no accounting restatements or revised external disclosures were made.

During the summer of 1987, two other events relevant to EOT took place. Mike Muckleroy, an experienced Enron commodity trader, began to pick up indications that EOT had developed a large exposed position, one far in excess of its control limits. Muckleroy took his concerns to Enron president Mick Seidl on multiple occasions and eventually to Ken Lay. Both executives commented that Muckleroy must be jealous of Borget and otherwise dismissed the matter.

The second event involved Rich Kinder. Lay moved him out of the general counsel's position, naming him chief of staff. In his new role, Kinder would be expected to troubleshoot difficulties of the type that had materialized at EOT and to help raise the general financial performance level throughout Enron.

Internal Audit at a Crossroads

David Woytek monitored how the Valhalla incident played out and found himself sinking into an ever-gloomier state of mind. He was on the point of concluding that there was no point to staying in Internal Audit. If he was going to have any sort of career progression at Enron, he might have to get into a different financial function. It was in this mindset that he had drafted his letter to Kern requesting a transfer. Once the words were on paper, however, Woytek began to worry. Kern had been one of the parties to the Houston-based stonewall; he might take the letter personally, viewing it as an implied accusation. Such was not likely to foster Woytek's career prospects. On the other hand, David found himself uncomfortable that Internal Audit was "going down without a fight". He sometimes wondered whether the letter ought to be even more pointed, make more of an issue of the treatment handed out to Internal Audit.

Torn by conflicting thoughts, Woytek sought out a longtime mentor, a partner at one of the public accounting firms that competed with Arthur Anderson. Over drinks, Woytek showed him the draft letter to Kern and filled him in on the background facts of the incident. The partner reflected:

Well, it's no surprise that you are discouraged. Enron has given Internal Audit a big set of negative signals. I'm sure all the management teams out in the operating units have been paying attention. So far, the signals have been these:

- Acts of open dishonesty and clear violations of company controls uncovered by Internal Audit will be tolerated if the people in question are good profit generators.

- Internal Audit can be called off the case by complaining to people in high places.
- Arthur Anderson can be used to replace Internal Audit when it investigates aggressively.
- Arthur Anderson can then be "managed" as to the findings it produces.
- Financial-reporting standards can be pushed to the limit to justify taking no action on findings uncovered by Internal Audit.

It would be difficult, though not impossible, to come up with a more comprehensive repudiation of what Internal Audit is supposed to accomplish. So, from a strictly career standpoint, I can see why you want to move someplace else.

One question is whether that someplace else should still be at Enron. A company that views financial control and reporting in this light may not be much better to work for in a business unit as opposed to Internal Audit.

A second question is whether you want to go anywhere without making more of a fight for the future of financial control at Enron. One could make the argument that Internal Audit did a pretty good job of simply saluting and retiring from the field in this story.

David Woytek took strong exception to this characterization. He pointed out that matters were already at the most senior levels of management and that the corporation's chief financial officer had been the very person who rejected the Intertect findings. The very same Keith Kern then had told Internal Audit to drop the matter. What hope for a hearing could Internal Audit have when Enron's top executives were openly committed on the other side?

Woytek's mentor continued:

First off, a fight is different from a hearing. In a fight, you expect resistance and plan to attack it.

It has always amazed me that many financial- control professionals have difficulty thinking strategically and politically. They tend to think that controls are an "enclave" where performance of their duties should be protected from conflicting interests and politics. Ideally, that might be the case. In practice, relatively few corporations always insulate Internal Audit in that way. This means that Audit has to take some responsibility for looking after itself politically. That involves doing some strategic thinking about how Internal Audit fits into the company's broader economics, strategy, and plans. Internal Audit must be able to articulate its business rationale and keep it in front of management; that way, when conflicting pressures come, management will be less likely to see "rolling over" Audit as the low-cost solution to its immediate problem.

Second, there are different ways to raise an issue. For example, one way is to focus discussion on the damage done to Enron's financial controls by the way Valhalla played out. Many times, executives who make distasteful decisions worry thereafter about the fallout. Sometimes, the same executives can be open to trying to repair collateral damage after the fact. But if nobody brings them a plan, the matter slides off the radar screen as new issues come along.

Third, you sometimes have to play a longer-term game. The case for financial control has to be advocated continuously in the hope of being validated over the long run. In my experience, many senior executives have never heard the rationale for strong controls articulated in a bottom-line, dollars-and-sense fashion. Often, they think of it as a set of prudent rules for "normal times," to be waived or discarded in "extraordinary times." They have to hear how tightly the rationale for good controls is woven into achieving excellent financial performance over the long haul.

If you make this case, it has to be backed by a plan that can come to be seen as prescient in the light of later events. Sometimes, you have to position Internal Audit as having the answer to a situation that hasn't arisen yet but may well appear before too long.

Woytek responded that this all sounded good but that he saw no place to go with any controls initiatives. All of Enron's key executives-Lay, Seidl, and Kern- had bought in to what he felt to be a whitewash of the Valhalla incident. They were only likely to resent efforts by Audit to keep the matter open. That could only hurt Woytek's chances of salvaging some sort of career at Enron.

The mentor reflected further:

Well, give it some more thought. If you simply change jobs, what message does that send to the audit troops you leave behind? Think also about sorting out your priorities. You seem to be struggling with how to prioritize your career in general, your career at Enron, and what's the right thing to do for financial control at Enron.

Try to decide which comes first and whether the others can then be reconciled to that priority through some thoughtful plan of action. Also, give some thought to who in management may be more open to Internal Audit's message and/or who might benefit politically if controls issues loomed up again in the company. Try to position Audit to be part of the answer for these executives as they develop their own plans for the company.

And remember, companies that decide to live with weak financial controls often find themselves quickly looking for someone with a plan to clean up a mess.

Attachment 1 – Historical Recreation (HRC)

DRAFT

August 1, 1987

Mr. Keith Kern, Chief Financial Officer
Enron Corporation, Building

Dear Keith,

With the time approaching for completion of our annual Rating and Ranking process, I would like to schedule a meeting with you to discuss my performance and future career path.

One topic I would like to discuss concerns the recent controls incident involving Enron Oil Trading (EOT). It is my belief that Internal Audit performed well when investigating this matter. Evidence suggesting serious controls violations was discovered, and indications of potential fraudulent activity were identified. It is not clear that Internal Audit is receiving appropriate recognition for its performance. Particularly disturbing was the abrupt termination of its forensic fieldwork, which was turned over to public auditor Arthur Anderson.

These events have raised questions as to the future of Internal Audit within Enron, and by extension the career prospects of those who would make their career in audit. If Internal Audit is to be subordinated to Arthur Anderson on future high profile investigations, that in itself suggests an important career limitation for Enron's audit professionals.

The recent EOT matter was complex and may have been exceptional. It is also clearly within management's prerogatives to decide that audit services will be sourced from third parties. It is precisely because recent events have raised uncertainties about what is "one-off" and what will be future policy that I would like to meet with you and obtain clarification.

In all events, I would like to express possible interest in transferring from Internal Audit into a line financial position with a major business unit. My strong controls background would be an asset in such a position, especially if the business unit requires robust controls on trading positions. It is also my belief that a unit financial position may afford me more opportunity to employ other financial and accounting skills heretofore not often called on in Internal Audit.

My secretary will contact your assistant to seek a mutually convenient time when we can meet.

Thank you for your consideration of this matter. I look forward to talking with you shortly.

Sincerely yours,
David Woytek

Author's Note

The account of the guidance given to David Woytek by Ken Lay at the conclusion of the February 2, 1987, meeting is based upon the facts as reported in Conspiracy of Fools (p. 19). The description of what happened to Woytek's investigation of EOT is based on the accounts found in The Smartest Guys in the Room (pp. 19-'21) and especially, Conspiracy of Fools (pp. 34-'37).

Mick Seidl is identified by The Smartest Guys in the Room as Lay's number two (p. 19). The account of his writing to Borget in advance of Arthur Anderson's report is found on p. 20, along with the information that Woytek's team was recalled to Houston without completing its field-work. Conspiracy of Fools picks up the story and adds details. Seidl is identified as the individual who called Woytek's team home (p. 35); it also reports that Woytek's private investigators uncovered the fictitious nature of EOT's "trading partners" and that Mastroeni had a history of being sued by banks for submitting fraudulent documents with loan applications. CFO Keith Kern is then reported as dismissing this report because Arthur Anderson was pursuing the investigation (p. 36).

Rich Kinder is often presented as one of the more focused and disciplined Enron executives. Many believe that Enron would not have gone down the path it did if Kinder had succeeded Lay as CEO. However, the Valhalla investigation was not his finest hour. Kinder was general counsel at that point. The account of his providing the rationale for not restating Enron's financials appears in The Smartest Guys in the Room (pp. 20-'21). It is noteworthy, however, that Lay moved him into a key troubleshooting role right after the investigation was closed. From there, Kinder began to take a much tougher line on internal inefficiencies and in-fighting.

David Woytek's letter to Keith Kern is a Historical Recreation intended to capture the conflicts between career interests and fighting for the future of financial control at Enron. There is no record that Woytek ever produced such a letter or considered confronting Kern over the treatment of Internal Audit in the EOT matter. For this reason, Woytek's HRC letter is crafted as a draft. However, Woytek did leave Enron's Internal Audit function shortly after the EOT episode. In Conspiracy of Fools, he reappears in 1991 as CFO of Enron's liquid-fuels division (pp. 55-'57).

David Woytek's dialogue with his external mentor is also a creation intended to put certain issues in front of students. Foremost among these is the need for financial-control executives to take responsibility for sustaining political support for their function. Of similar importance is the need for Internal Audit's leadership to be able to articulate the business rationale for strong controls and to be able to plan long-run strategies for positioning Internal Audit successfully within the firm.

Notes

1. *Conspiracy of Fools*, p. 19.
2. Ibid. p. 34.
3. Ibid. p. 35.
4. *The Smartest Guys in the Room*, p. 20.
5. Ibid. p. 20
6. Ibid. p. 20.
7. Ibid. p. 21.

Case Study 3

Enron Oil Trading (C): An Opening for Enron Audit?

I thought we had those oil traders under control. Seidl wouldn't be getting on a plane unless they had done something that's a problem.

O N OCTOBER 9, 1987, KEN LAY was over the Atlantic, flying back from meetings in Europe. In mid-flight he was handed a message. Enron president Mick Seidl was getting on a plane and flying to Newfoundland, where Lay's plane would stop for refueling. This couldn't be good.

Within a couple of hours, Lay and Seidl met at the Gander International Airport. Seidl told Lay what he had just learned from EOT president Louis Borget. EOT was "short" some 84 million barrels of crude oil. This meant that EOT had sold but did not possess oil equivalent to that amount. More significantly, EOT had sold the oil at prices well below current levels. If Enron were forced to cover the position at current prices, the company would incur more than $1 billion in trading losses. Clearly EOT had hugely exceeded its authorized trading limits and in the process had put the solvency of debt-laden Enron in jeopardy.

Lay immediately rerouted his flight to New York, interviewed Borget, and terminated him. Lay then returned to Houston and began figuring out how to salvage the situation.

Mike Muckleroy and a group of Houston traders were sent to EOT's Valhalla, New York, office. Over a three-week period, they were able to shrink EOT's short position to a level where it could be covered with "only" a $140 million pre-tax loss. After taxes, this would result in an $85 million hit to Enron's 1987 earnings; this was an event that could not be hidden from investors. Enron eventually announced the charge to earnings but only after closing a financing transaction that had been in the works. Lenders were not informed of the news prior to closing.

Late in October, Ken Lay called an all-employees meeting at which he blamed the EOT incident on the now terminated Borget. Lay then made the following statement:

43

S.V. Arbogast, *Resisting Corporate Corruption* (pp. 43–44)
© 2008 by M & M Scrivener Press

"We became involved in a business with risks that we did not appreciate well enough...and I promise you, we will never again risk Enron's credibility in business ventures without first making sure we thoroughly understand the risks."[1]

With the immediate crisis managed, Enron faced a decision about what to do with EOT. The unit's management had been decapitated, and its image as a consistent profit generator was in ruins. EOT has also been positioned publicly as a rogue organization, so as to exonerate Enron management in general—and Ken Lay in particular—of responsibility.

Enron's Internal Audit personnel knew that a public scandal of this magnitude could lead to big changes within the company. Senior leadership positions might change. A clean-up program might be instituted throughout the company. EOT might be reconstituted or shutdown.

Would Internal Audit play any part in these changes? Would it actively seek to influence or shape how these future events would transpire?

Author's Note

The facts of this case, including the extent of EOT's short position, Lay's actions and the role of Mike Muckleroy, are as reported in *The Smartest Guys in the Room* (pp. 21-'24) and Conspiracy of Fools (pp. 37-'39). The latter work described Lay's presentation at the October 1987 all-employees meeting as follows:

"He [Lay] held himself up as a victim of Borget and Mastroeni, as someone who had no reason to suspect the problems in Valhalla."[2]

There is no public record of what Enron's internal auditors thought or did in the wake of EOT's trading scandal breaking. The case imagines the possibility that they reflected on the implications for their function, in order to pose the issue: What should Internal Audit do now?

Notes

1. *Conspiracy of Fools*, p. 39
2. Ibid. p. 39

Essay 3

Necessary Ammunition—
The Economic Rationale
for Financial Control

THIS ESSAY FOCUSES ON THE BUSINESS CASE for maintaining strong financial controls. Its thesis is that the economic rationale for controls is too seldom articulated, and when it is, important elements are left out. This essay describes the key structural elements that make up a sound financial control system. It also discusses the role of values in sustaining a good "controls environment" and how values can be instilled in the cultures of firms operating within the harsh world of the marketplace. Finally, this essay provides a broad economic rationale that justifies the investments of effort and money that good controls require.

People who wish to see business operate more ethically should have a strong interest in understanding what constitutes good financial control. They also should want to understand how the costs of controls are more than compensated for by their contribution to business success. Only then will resisters be able to argue persuasively for sound control practices and to summon the resolve needed to resist ethical pressures.

Financial Control at the Heart of Business Success: Personal Experience

Late in 1999, Exxon and Mobil merged to form ExxonMobil. Shortly thereafter, senior leaders from both companies were invited to a meeting in Dallas. There, Exxon chairman Lee Raymond joined with Lou Notto, his Mobil counterpart, to lay out key themes to guide the merged company. Raymond, the merged firm's CEO, spoke first. His remarks quickly delivered a message about priorities. His first point was expected. Both firms were great companies, and the merged entity would seek to combine their respective strengths. His second point was more unexpected. There was to be no mistake about one thing, Raymond said: A commitment to flawless safety performance and financial control was to be everyone's first priority. Executives who failed in these areas would not prosper, regardless of what they might contribute in other ways.

45

S.V. Arbogast, *Resisting Corporate Corruption* (pp. 45–64)
© 2008 by M & M Scrivener Press

For those members of the audience who were "heritage" Exxon, Raymond's emphasis was not too surprising. Lee Raymond and his predecessors had consistently asserted the supremacy of safety and controls within Exxon's hierarchy of values. More importantly, they had established without question that this was for real. Safety and controls were always Job 1. All of us had seen the consequences for business units and individuals who had failed to measure up in this way.

Reactions on the Mobil side were more mixed. Many Mobil executives knew of Exxon's controls mentality from working together in joint ventures and from industry scuttlebutt. Some probably thought that it had its virtues. Others thought that Exxon was over controlled, too tied up in procedures to be really agile in the marketplace. Mobil itself had deemphasized controls in the mid-1990s, the better to cut costs and push decision authority lower in its organization.

What the Mobil executives thought, however, wasn't going to matter. Safety and controls were going to be done the Exxon way. Raymond's speech was only the first salvo of a concerted effort that would quickly make this clear.

Watching this unfold caused a question to form in my mind: How had it come to pass that Lee Raymond's Exxon, a firm now famous for cutting overhead, had put safety and financial controls at the top of the firm's values structure? Why hadn't controls costs simply been lumped in with the rest of its overhead? Safety, perhaps, could be understood as an exception: After all, the Valdez accident had demonstrated that a bad safety incident could be frightfully expensive for a "deep-pockets" firm. But Exxon didn't give financial control less emphasis than safety. Clearly, something had convinced Exxon's senior management that good financial control was worth more than it cost.

Like many important things at Exxon, management's periodic comments provided a clue, but only a clue, as to the deeper philosophy at work. In the case of safety/financial control, the clue was this: Exxon management noted that those organizations that achieved excellent safety and financial audit results also achieved the best operating results. After years of reviewing safety and audit data, Exxon's management thought this correlation was unmistakable. But what was cause, and what was effect? After studying the matter further, Exxon's leadership came to the conclusion that accomplishing good safety and financial control also created the intangibles that allowed organizations to become "operationally excellent."

That was the basic idea put across to the employees. Usually, it was stated in the negative: Organizations that can't manage safety and controls won't be able to become good operators. Developing the specific intangibles that underpin both controls and operations was mostly left for managers to figure out.

That still left the question of identifying the intangibles. How these became clear to me over time can best be illustrated by specific examples.

Like most employees, I came into Exxon with only a limited understanding of financial control and the role it played in the business. My initial attitudes were probably typical of newcomers and more than a little cynical: Controls were a necessary evil to prevent the occasional theft or abuse; Exxon's approach seemed highly regimented and bureaucratized, which justified a certain going-through-the-motions approach when periodic audits turned up the spotlight. The corporate ethics policy was a piece of necessary boilerplate, which management could use as justification to punish low-level employees when the odd controls issue arose. These views turned out to be highly misinformed.

I joined the company in 1972. Shortly thereafter, a scandal broke involving Exxon's affiliate in Italy. The affiliate president was found to have been using unauthorized bank accounts to funnel contributions to Italian political parties. This became known as the Cazzaniga affair, named after the affiliate's president. Exxon's auditors discovered the misappropriation of funds, and management took strong corrective measures, including dismissing Cazzaniga. Of more lasting impact, however, was another result from the scandal: Exxon rewrote its ethics policy.

The popular story is that CEO Ken Jamison did not like the multi-page product a committee had worked up. Consequently, he took one sheet of paper and wrote his own. Whether the story is true or not, the one-page ethics policy survives in that form to this day (see Attachment 1). It is noteworthy for distilling corporate ethics down to bare essentials:

- Employees will obey the law of whatever jurisdiction in which they operate; this includes the laws of all non-U.S. locations.
- Employees are responsible for the integrity and accuracy of company information, especially financial information published in the company's reports.

The Exxon Ethics policy is also distinctive for one addition: its "highest course of integrity" provision. Discussing the nature of applicable laws, the exact wording of this provision is: "Even when the applicable laws are permissive, employees are to adopt the course of highest integrity."

These words got many people's attention, including mine. What exactly did course of highest integrity mean? I assumed that this was language of the moment intended to impress external readers in the wake of the recent scandal. Certainly, it set a high standard of conduct. I and many other employees would be interested to see what this meant in practice as our careers progressed.

There was one other major piece of fallout from the Cazzaniga affair. Sometime around 1977, Exxon entered into a consent decree with the SEC. Despite having discovered and corrected the Italian affiliate's issues, Exxon had been taken to task by the commission. This occurred in the aftermath of the Church Committee Senate Hearings on Multinational Corporate behavior and prior to the passage of the Foreign Corrupt Practices Act (FCPA). Whether this represented the commission's making an example of Exxon is not really the point. Rather, the concern is what Exxon agreed to observe and its enduring effects on the company's controls environment. In essence, Exxon consented to follow the provisions of the FCPA, which had not yet become law. Knowledgeable company insiders identify this decree as the beginning of an ever-greater Exxon focus on controls and proper conduct in foreign countries. If so, it underscores the synergy between a good internal controls culture and the reinforcement provided by law and regulation.

I was soon to see the effects of Exxon's new controls focus. My first test came in the early 1980s. I was sent as finance manager to a major Latin American affiliate. The country was then going through a major financial crisis. Foreign exchange was short, and the central bank refused to provide U.S. dollars to firms like ours to pay dividends. So, I developed a "cross-border" swap with a European firm; it would provide U.S. dollars to Exxon outside of Latin America in return for local currency in my location. Thinking this a clever approach to creating a dividend-in-substance, I sent it to regional headquarters and was surprised to be told that it would also need to be submitted to the Central Bank. This was duly done. Only then did the transaction proceed. The residual lesson for me: Exxon cares how it gets results and does not favor methods that circumvent laws or regulations. You will have to design solutions whose fundamental soundness allows them to withstand public scrutiny.

This same Exxon affiliate also suffered from the illegal behavior of local independent competitors, which bought and sold fuel products without paying excise taxes. Frequent lobbying efforts were mounted against their activities. Little was accomplished, as these parties were too well connected politically. Through all this, I noted, there was never any discussion of attempting to buy the political influence necessary to secure effective law enforcement. The lesson for me: The company will pay a price in business terms rather than resort to questionable means; therefore, operating management will have to develop competitive advantages that can overcome political disadvantages. If it cannot, Exxon will either find management who can or reconsider whether it can do business in that location.

Ethics and legal issues got more interesting when I went to Asia in 1989 as an affiliate finance director. In this capacity, I was functionally responsible for the condition of financial control throughout the operation. The location in question was considered high risk from a financial-control standpoint.

This assignment introduced me to the full panoply of features in Exxon's financial-control system. I now worked closely with both Internal Audit and the affiliate's financial controls advisor. Audit preparation, design, conduct, and interpretation became matters of importance. So did controls training, business practices reviews, and the conduct of the annual Representation Letter process. Controls training made sure that every employee was familiar with the ethics policy and such other policies, such as conflict of interest, as might be relevant. Periodic business practices reviews showed employees examples of recent ethics/controls issues that had arisen elsewhere within Exxon. They also encouraged employees to raise concerns about any practices they might feel were questionable. The Representation Letter process occurred annually. It asked sequentially higher levels of managers to verify that all controls issues in their area had been addressed and that all material information had been accurately reported through the appropriate channels and so reflected in the company's accounts.

"Irregularity" investigations were another form of involvement. There were episodes of service station dealer tank trucks with false compartments and a major incident involving maintenance workers colluding with outsiders on the sourcing of replacement parts. The investigation of this last incident took months and ultimately involved death threats and the local police authorities. This was my first real look at how sizable sums of money could walk out the door if the company was not paying attention. Those involved in the collusion were sure that they wouldn't get caught and that if by some chance they did get identified, were sure that they could somehow wiggle free. They were wrong.

The message delivered by this incident to the affiliate's workforce was important. Exxon had decided to invest close to $US 1 billion for a major expansion of this affiliate's refinery. This was to be accompanied by other large sums for logistical and marketing investments. In such a context, the opportunities for stealing funds would have been considerable if controls were weak. This episode's lesson really started my education in the economics of financial control. Exxon's attention to detailed controls, its insistence that procedures be followed and documented, its thorough audit process, and responsiveness to audit findings: these characteristics were not simply about managing the occasional irregularity, but about creating an environment in which billions of dollars could routinely be spent with an expectation that theft or waste was unlikely.

The politics surrounding the refinery expansion were also educational. Local authorities granted licenses for refineries to be built or expanded. A tender had been conducted awarding the rights for a new-build refinery. Rumors abounded that the firms competing had "played the game" to secure influence in the right places. Meanwhile, Exxon's request to expand its refinery had been turned down. There was no discussion of "playing the game" to reverse this decision.

As events played out, government political conflicts produced a reversal. A reform government came to power and decided that approving Exxon's project was consistent with its reform agenda. The fact that Exxon's project was also the most economical and the quickest to completion provided ready-made justifications for this government.

The lessons for me here were complex. Again, one message was that proper means counted: We would not pursue business success by means in conflict with U.S. and foreign law. Even more significant, a reputation for ethical dealing is itself a real business asset. Over time, it can help overcome reverses and even open up opportunities. This long run must continually be kept in mind. Finally, sound business fundamentals reinforce this high-road approach, making it easier to harvest the opportunities from changing political fortunes when they arise.

Following my Asian tour, I returned to the United States as vice president, finance, of a troubled affiliate. This company was then a major exception among Exxon's operations. It had a poor safety record relative to other affiliates. Its union was unhappy and presented a myriad of labor issues. Its business was undoubtedly shrinking. Exxon decided that a complete change of top management and a major reorganization were required to restore this affiliate to acceptable performance levels.

I again was in charge of the overall financial-control environment. Moreover, I participated in the company's Safety Committee. It was there that the next "intangible" materialized. Studying the affiliate's safety data raised an issue: How good was the reported safety-incident information? Part of the culture of that affiliate involved arguing that minor safety incidents were not material and should go unrecorded. It quickly became clear to the revamped Safety Committee that at least two things were wrong with this mentality. First, since cumulative minor incidents are a lead indicator of major incidents, not reporting them distorts the warning signals to management. Second, when the employees concentrate on arguing away incidents, the risk increases that focus on improving operating practices will be lost.

Allowing either or both of these effects to progress eventually causes management to lose touch with safety performance. Corrective action then increasingly comes too little and too late.

This affiliate's Safety Committee decided that the first order of business was to end the haggling over incident reporting. Managers were drilled on the reporting rules. "Borderline" incidents got reported. Focus then went into changing behavior that eliminated even minor incidents. Accountability for this was established "in the line". This meant that business unit managers were clearly the first responsible for the safety performance of their units. They could not pass this responsibility to anyone else: not their safety adviser or the auditors from the Safety organization.

Major incidents consequently disappeared. Minor incidents dropped to very low levels. Over the subsequent decade, the affiliate won safety award after award and came to be recognized as the best operator in its industry.

The parallel lessons from safety to financial control were unmistakable. Good information is unequivocally linked to effective accountability. So long as the data was a subject for debate, it would be debated. Addressing fundamentals would then take a back seat. While the managers debated, nothing effective in terms of fundamental procedures made it down to the working level. Absent effective focus on fundamentals, people at the working level would take liberties as events occurred. Meanwhile, management increasingly lost touch with what was occurring at the working level. Actual performance deteriorated. Increasingly, managers and operators would lose confidence in each other, feeding a downward spiral. This was as true with audit results and irregularity investigations as it was with safety incident data and incident investigations.

My experience at this operating affiliate contributed another lesson, one of paramount importance. Exxon's financial-control system had one other signal characteristic; its internal audit function was independent of affiliate operating management. As part of the Controllers organization, Internal Audit reports to a general auditor who reports directly to the Exxon Management Committee and the board's audit committee. Operating managers know that they will have their chance to argue about audit findings, but they will not be able to impose any outcome they wish.

This troubled affiliate was under consideration for divestment. Its senior manager had strong views about which firm should be the buyer and close relations with the senior management of that potential acquirer. My presence within the management team was intended in part to ensure that this potential conflict of interest remained latent. It did, barely. Throughout much intensive jockeying, I was aided by being able to communicate with a completely independent financial function. Affiliate management knew this and tempered its actions accordingly. A sale proposal to another party ultimately was developed.

Drawing upon such examples, the contributions of sound financial control to business success become clearer.

Summarizing the Controls/Business Success Intangibles

Sound financial control does more than prevent theft and abuse. It lays the foundation for a culture that stresses business fundamentals as the key to both corporate and personal success.

It does this primarily by protecting and promoting a culture of accountability. It demands the collection of information that measures performance and then protects the integrity of that information. By insisting that financial audits be high priority, that controls issues be addressed immediately and fundamentally, and by ensuring that information reporting failures is not compromised, it creates a general culture characterized by:

- Complete and accurate information about results, be they good or bad.
- Clear accountability at the operating management level for results, with consequences, good and bad, in line with the reported results.

Finally, sound financial controls backing a clear ethics policy cut off managers' recourse to expedient means. Problems cannot be solved by cutting corners. Instead, they have to be solved by fixing problems. Often, this process is uncomfortable, pressure filled, and even career threatening. It may take time and require new managers with new approaches.

For the organization, however, it is extraordinarily healthy. It breeds an aversion to "getting behind the curve" on problems. There will be no easy escape via expedient means should this happen. Consequently, managers pay attention to preempting problems and managing risks for real. As this becomes the organization's standard practice, a general operating excellence spreads. This becomes both a source of pride and a new element of identity. You wake up one day and discover that your business is a place where values govern, and everyone quietly knows that this is a better place.

The value of achieving such a culture is enormous in business terms. Plants run longer and better. Problems are spotted sooner and fixed for good. Strategies and capital projects are based on real numbers. Creative approaches are focused on fundamentals and must respect legal and ethical boundaries. Employee grievances and external lawsuits diminish and their costs by incident also decline. This list of benefits only scratches the surface.

Good financial control (and its safety cousin) doesn't create all this. It does, however, lay the foundation for a broad culture of accountability. Recognizing this contribution makes it possible to articulate a much broader economic rationale for financial control, one whose economic contribution clearly justifies the effort and cost of maintaining good financial control.

The Economic Consequences of Sound Financial Control

The economic consequences of sound financial control are both preventive and promoting in nature. The preventive effects are more commonly known. The promoting consequences relate to this broader culture of accountability.

These consequences will now be examined by type.

Preventive Consequences

1) Preventing Theft. This is the most straightforward of financial control's economic benefits. After all, control systems are explicitly designed to prevent company funds from being stolen. Such standard procedures as duplicate signatures for funds disbursements, levels of authority matched to expenditures of different sizes, and special resolutions governing the opening/closing of bank accounts clearly aim to forestall theft of company cash.

Since cash is not the only asset that can "walk out the door", theft prevention ends up applying to a other classes of assets. Near monetary assets, like receivables and customer loans, must be watched carefully. Physical assets that can be monetized must also be controlled. Obvious examples include maintenance items such as tools and stores, and certain types of product inventory, such as fuel products or easily marketed finished goods. Company computer equipment, software, and peripherals make especially tempting theft targets. Intellectual property can also be stolen and sold to competitors or used by the thief in some new venture.

Employees can also steal from the company by abusing expense accounts, company policies, and benefit plans. Employees can collude with customers, suppliers or competitors to sacrifice their employer's interests in return for rewards paid "on the side." Employees can cheat in what they indicate they have accomplished, either by misrepresenting facts, reporting misleading data, or gaming incentive compensation systems.

This list of theft possibilities barely scratches the surface. Employees repeatedly demonstrate their capacity to devise creative ways to pilfer their employers. The point here is this: Weak or ad hoc controls usually fail to contain this employee "creativity." Conversely, strong controls create an environment that becomes largely self-governing. It reinforces the basic honesty of most employees and recruits them as willing allies of the formal controls structure. Together, they form a system that is strong everywhere, because it is inbred and voluntary.

Thus, a strong controls environment preempts what would otherwise be a bewilderingly diverse set of asset losses by a firm. Employee theft becomes highly exceptional; when it does occur, it usually is discovered and ended quickly.

Theft is not usually highlighted as one of Enron's major problems. On closer inspection, however, a staggering amount of theft went on. Employees spent expense money extravagantly. Human Resources policies on travel and expenses were often ignored. More serious was the widely reported practice of closing poorly conceived deals for the sake of achieving personal bonus targets. Risk controls and approval authorizations were evaded; dubious projections were served up—all of in the name of closing transactions whose size would directly bear on individual annual bonuses.

The breaching of trading limits almost destroyed Enron shortly after its inception. In 1987, Enron discovered that oil traders were more than $1 billion in the hole. Enron held its breath while it traded the position back to a pre-tax loss of "only" $140 million. That sum alone could probably have funded a good controls system at Enron for decades.

Finally, there were Andy Fastow's related-party transactions, which netted Fastow more than $30 million and certain colleagues over $12 million–money that the Powers Committee Report labeled shareholder value that would not have been surrendered in arms-length transactions.

Of course, the ultimate cost of Fastow's thefts turned out to be far more than the cash he took from Enron's shareholders. This point brings up the next preventive benefit of sound controls.

2) Avoiding Administrative and Judicial Judgments. Many employee theft schemes directly or indirectly involve breaking the law. Sometimes, laws or regulations, such as those prohibiting price fixing, stand directly in the way. Sometimes, employee schemes run afoul of disclosure rules that would expose dodgy practices to public scrutiny.

The first point here is that the questionable practices often add legal risks on top of the problem of misappropriating company assets. These risks accumulate in parallel with the misappropriation activities; this creates the possibility that the illegal activity will be discovered by agents outside the firm, thereby exposing the company to the full weight of the legal system. External discovery multiplies by orders of magnitude the company's potential for losses.

The legal thicket surrounding public companies creates litigation possibilities on multiple levels. When a scandal breaks out, many actors declare open season on the company. Depending upon the particulars, the criminal justice system can prosecute. A wide variety of regulatory agencies enjoy jurisdiction over some portion of a firm's activities; these agencies are experienced in discovering a "cause for action" whenever a scandal becomes public. Shareholder litigation has become a developed and lucrative activity for the legal profession. Customers and suppliers may sue because they have been injured, because it will advance their own strategies, or because they want to see what they can get. Individuals can and do sue for similar reasons.

The cost associated with defending and resolving such disputes is often enormous. Suits attack both the firm and its responsible executives. Depending on the incident, both compensatory and punitive damages can result. Litigation can drag on for years, driving defense costs into the tens of million of dollars. Adverse judgments can impose not only monetary penalties but also new restrictions that hamper the business going forward.

Although Exxon's Valdez debacle can be characterized as a safety incident, the ensuing litigation turned on a controls matter: Did Exxon exercise proper control in permitting a former alcoholic to resume his duties as ship's captain? The merits of this matter are not the issue here. What is of interest is the nature and cost of the litigation. Exxon was fined $150 million, agreed to criminal restitution of another $100 million, and settled civil liability with the federal and state governments for another $900 million. Private compensatory damages of several hundreds of millions came on top of these governmental settlements. Finally, Exxon was assessed $5 billion in punitive damages, an award that has been litigated in the appellate courts for more than 10 years.

Enron's bankruptcy prevented the full weight of litigation from bearing down on the company. One wonders what a solvent Enron would have ended up paying out for its California electricity market manipulations or to shareholders for its deceptive accounting. However, one can get a sense of these potential losses by looking at the class-action judgments assessed against some of the banks that funded Enron's accounting manipulations: Citigroup, $ 2 billion; J.P. Morgan, $ 2.2 billion; Canadian Imperial Bank of Commerce, $ 2.4 billion. These amounts of course do not include each firm's defense costs, SEC settlements, or damage to current business or reputation.

From an economic perspective, if sound controls forestall even one major legal scandal, this can pay for many years of running the internal control system. Depending on the size of the firm, a well-organized internal control function will cost anywhere from several million dollars to perhaps $10 million to $20 million annually for a large multinational. One $200 millionsettlement avoided is going to fund such a system for a generation. Moreover, sound controls don't typically forestall just one incident. As Enron demonstrates, weak controls eventually yield multiple scandals with multiple litigants, defense costs, and settlements/awards.

This rationale for sound controls highlights monetary costs. A close reading of this material should also identify another, potentially greater, cost of avoidable scandals. This is:

3) Preventing Disruption of the Normal Course of Business. When irregularities are discovered, considerable disruption is inflicted on the business. Should a scandal break, the disruption is far worse. Costs from distraction and lost opportunities can multiply on so many fronts that they become difficult to quantify.

Anyone who has gone through a significant irregularity knows that the business suffers. For some period, management must shift focus away from existing business objectives. Irregularities force organizations to give priority to repairing the controls breach. It must be investigated and evaluated. Responsible parties must be identified, dealt with, and replaced. Often, new procedures must be put in place. The reconstituted organization must then be monitored to ensure that it functions as intended. All this takes the time and attention of business unit management, which must also satisfy higher management that the repair job has been done right.

When scandal and litigation break out, the disruption is orders of magnitude worse. Now senior management must divert attention into managing a whole new set of risks. Litigation risks are difficult to quantify and cap. Consequently, managing these risks can consume huge amounts of management time in disclosure, discovery, deposition, trial planning, and settlement negotiations. This is all time that senior managers won't have available to devote to strategy or operations.

Meanwhile, suppliers, partners, and customers all recalibrate their relations with the firm; their instinct will be to hedge those what-we-don't-know-yet risks. Financial markets do the same. Stock prices typically suffer.

Financing transactions under development will see delays, higher costs, and even cancellations. Business opportunities can be similarly affected.

Such distraction can have a devastating effect on strategy implementation. Strategy typically depends on achieving milestones within a timetable. Managing scandals and their fallout often puts deals and timetables on the shelf. When a scandal is finally put to bed, management returns to find it faces that a new business situation.

With adverse consequences mounting on so many fronts, the total costs of a scandal can climb in a fashion that is both difficult to define and open ended.

One need not look at Enron's ultimate meltdown to encounter the disruption costs of weak controls. Enron's manipulation of the California electricity markets provides a dramatic earlier example. Enron booked huge profits from dubiously named schemes, such as Fat Boy, Death Star, Get Shorty, and Ricochet. It also began to anticipate being sued. A large litigation defense team was mobilized in October 2000. Enron retained Brobeck Phleger, a trial firm experienced in complex business litigation. Shortly thereafter, this firm wrote to Enron's internal counsels, noting that six investigations of events in California's electricity markets were already under way and warning:

> "If Enron is found to have engaged in deceptive or fraudulent practices, there is also the risk of other criminal legal theories such as wire fraud, RICO, fraud involving markets, and fictitious commodity transactions…In addition depending upon the conduct, there may be the potential for criminal charges prosecuted against both individuals and the company…We believe it is imperative that Enron understands in detail what evidence exists with respect to its conduct in the California electricity markets as soon as possible"[1]

From there, both Ken Lay and Jeff Skilling would become personally involved in managing the California fallout. Lay would meet multiple times with Governor Gray Davis and federal officials. Skilling visited the state, attempting to manage the public relations fallout. Both devoted major time to internal consultations on legal defense and public affairs strategies. This was all time taken away from managing the failure in Broadband, preventing trading losses at EES, selling off non-core assets, and reversing the general deterioration of Enron's financial condition. When the final crisis hit in October, a depleted, distracted management reacted clumsily to events.

Avoiding the loss of focus that comes with scandals is often ignored as a benefit of good financial control. The good habits that characterize productive corporate cultures take time and focus to inculcate. Sound financial control not only avoids the disruption of immediate business operations and planning, but it also enables the process of inculcating positive intangibles to proceed apace.

It is to these 'promoting' consequences that we now turn.

Promoting Consequences

4) Accurate information for Running the Business. Large organizations can be managed effectively only if management possesses comprehensive and accurate information about the business. Without such information, senior management cannot spot problems in the making or impose coordinated strategies across the firm. When crises arise, management is surprised and has no choice but to go into reactive mode.

Management information systems (MIS) can be put in place, but the value of such systems depends on the controls culture that surrounds them. Temptations to withhold or distort information are ever present. A weak controls environment can allow a culture of "managing the numbers" to take root; then, executives will receive only the information that people lower in the organization want them to see. Needless to say, opportunities and successes will be emphasized while problems are hidden.

One pillar of a sound controls system is management's insistence that all transactions be recorded completely and accurately on company books. This principle sounds elementary but is in fact continually challenged. When it succeeds in imposing this culture on the organization, senior management establishes the foundation for much else:

- It establishes that both good and bad news must be reported accurately.
- Management can then run the business, based on an accurate understanding of how it has and is performing.
- Management, including senior management, can then be held accountable for results. Subordinate management is accountable to senior management, and top executives are accountable to investors who react to the firm's published reports.
- A culture of honesty even when it's inconvenient is thus established, with spillover effects into the firm's "go-forward" culture, i.e. the planning of strategy and investments.

One of the less-recognized causes of Enron's demise was the gradual but steady decline in the quality of the information available to make decisions. Many have pointed to the large amounts of capital expended on uneconomic international projects. These failed projects burdened the balance sheet with massive debts while failing to generate the cash needed for repayment. What allowed these projects to be approved? Certainly, the fact that project developers could submit economics based on whatever assumptions were needed to secure approval was a major contributing cause. This disregard for realistic project-planning assumptions was undoubtedly encouraged by the firm's adoption of mark-to-market (MtM) accounting. Employees saw the reasons for MtM's adoptions—the immediate magnification of reported revenues and profits. They then saw MtM deteriorate into what came to be labeled mark-to-model. Reacting to these internal signals, other business units found their own ways to secure convenient and quick results.

Of course, what ultimately brought about Enron's bankruptcy was the financial markets' loss of confidence in its reporting. As the Powers Committee Report put it:

> "On October 16, 2001, Enron announced that it was taking a $544 million after-tax charge against earnings related to transactions with LJM2...It also announced a reduction of shareholder's equity of $1.2 billion related to transactions with that same entity. Less than one month later, Enron announced that it was restating its financial statements for the period 1997 through 2001 because of accounting errors relating to transactions with a different Fastow partnership...and an additional related-party entity, Chewco Investments L.P...
>
> These announcements destroyed market confidence and investor trust in Enron. Less than one month later, Enron filed for bankruptcy."[2]

These announcements were quantitative expressions of the extent to which Enron's MIS had lost touch with Enron's reality. Only two months before, when Jeff Skilling retired, he and chief accounting officer Rick Causey assured Ken Lay and the board that there were no "unknown problems." It's possible that they weren't intentionally lying. Rather, they had gotten used to viewing Enron's numbers through the lens of their own devices. They thought, for example, that because Enron accounted for tens of billions of dollars of debt as 'off the balance sheet', Enron wasn't really responsible for its repayment. This turned out to be fundamentally wrong; there were also items buried in the details of certain deals (e.g. Chewco) that they didn't know about. When the truth came out, it set off an avalanche of investor flight which an unprepared Enron management could not handle.

As noted, comprehensive and accurate MIS lays only a foundation for a culture of management accountability. To build on this foundation, other components are needed to contribute other intangible assets. We thus now turn to these components and the last and most significant intangible contributed by effective financial control.

5) Accountability and Continuous Improvement. Maintenance of sound financial controls requires managers to embrace two elements: (1) acceptance of accountability by operating line management; and (2) a continuous cycle of review, appraisal, and improvement. Controls responsibility "in the line" stands in contrast to relying on the internal audit or controls advisers to bear the primary responsibility. When controls accountability resides in the line, operating management must focus on the details of control structures/procedures. Breaches will be for their account when performance review time comes around. Thus, they focus on controls for real as opposed to performing last-minute fixes to pass an audit.

Internal audits can then be conducted for their real purpose, the evaluation of current controls and identification of improvements. Although audits always have an adversarial aspect, line management usually becomes receptive to legitimate audit findings when it has accepted responsibility.

The results of achieving these twin elements are the inculcation of precious intangibles. The entire organization comes to accept that controls cannot be faked but have to be worked at fundamentally and continuously. It also understands that failure to do so cannot be hidden and will have personal consequences. Finally, it comes to regard the entire preparation and audit process not as make-work, but as an opportunity to upgrade the organization.

It doesn't take much stretch of imagination to see how these attitudes can be carried over into other work processes. Sound preparation, appraisal for real, and the ethic of continuous improvement take root, become habit, and set the standard for performance of all work duties. The fact that maintaining and improving controls is never finally accomplished also combats tendencies toward complacency that materialize in successful organizations.

Enron never valued the detailed work necessary to sustain good control. It didn't really appreciate the long-term dividends that this work would pay. Enron's initial failure to fire those Valhalla oil traders who grossly breached bank account controls evidenced a clear preference for near term gains over long-term operational excellence. The then-president's telex to head oil trader Louis Borget said it all. Sent before Arthur Anderson reported its findings, it read in part: "Your answers to Arthur Anderson were clear, straightforward, rock solid. I have complete confidence in your business judgment, and ability and your personal integrity...Please keep making us millions."[3] Borget would later plead guilty to three felonies and serve jail time.

For all its flashy conceptual brilliance and trading acumen, Enron never became a good operator. Its safety record was spotty, marred by incidents, such as the San Juan gas explosion that killed thirty-three and injured eighty. The week before he resigned, Jeff Skilling had to fly to Teesside, United Kingdom, where a massive explosion during routine maintenance had killed three. Enron built plants in poor locations, such as the Dominican Republic facility that collected city garbage in its water intake. A new Chinese plant never operated commercially. It bought others, such as the Buenos Aires municipal water system, at inflated prices and without the due diligence that would have discovered the absence of a headquarters, customer records, or the ability to collect receivables; there was, however, $350 million in deferred maintenance and investments to address. And, then there was Dahbol.

Jeff Skilling's "asset-lite" strategy was not simply a strategic preference; it was a reflection of Enron's demonstrated inability to grow and operate a successful hard-asset strategy. This failure was rooted in the same distain for detail, process and integrity that was visible early on in Enron's approach to financial control.

Summing Up

This essay has argued that the economic rationale for sound financial control is often undervalued. The economic benefits go far beyond avoiding an occasional misappropriation of funds. The benefits include the avoidance of damaging litigation, penalties, and judgments that tend to arise when disregard of rules, policies, and the law becomes entrenched. Financial consequences from such suits can be huge. However, even more damaging than any eventual judgments is the disruption of normal business, the damage inflicted by litigation risks that partners and investors can't quantify, and the diversion of senior management into crisis control.

Second, this essay has argued that even these preventive benefits do not capture the complete rationale for sustaining sound controls. Good financial control can be achieved only by line management accepting responsibility and accountability for this task. It can be sustained only by maintaining focus on the details of control structures and procedures, by inculcating habits of truthfulness and attentiveness into all employees, and by participation in an open-ended cycle of appraisal and improvement.

Accomplish this, and the foundation is laid for extending these values into all aspects of the business. This will bear fruit in the form of complete and accurate information, operating excellence, and an ethic of continuous improvement.

This essay makes the point that any one of these economic rationales can pay for the cost of controls. This equation, though valid, perhaps understates the challenge encountered in the workplace. Often, the tradeoff is seen as a huge profit payoff versus allowing controls to operate. The aforementioned president's note to Borget expressed this very equation: "...please keep making us millions." Enron's California gamesmanship also illustrates this test. Enron booked more than $1 billion in profits from its market manipulations. Quite possibly, there was an expectation that regardless of what litigation ensued, Enron would not pay out more than a fraction of this sum.

Because the immediate comparison between profit opportunities and adherence to sound controls can appear lopsided, those who would defend good controls need to be able to articulate the full slate of controls rationales. They need to combat the idea that the organization is somehow immune to the perverse effects of embracing questionable practices. These individuals need to assert that management's making a conscious decision to ignore controls "over here" is likely to lead to someone else making a similar decision "over there"–perhaps for reasons not in the company's interests and perhaps without making it evident in company accounts. Such people need to make tangible the reality that senior management's acceptance of weak controls amounts to their risking loss of control over the business, via increasingly suspect MIS, the need to manage future litigation scandals, or because operations never seem to measure up to expectations.

Finally, it needs to be recognized that an immediate argument over some ill-gotten scheme is not the best moment for deploying the full slate of controls rationales. These need to be inculcated into management and employees alike as part of the normal course of business. The foundational excellence that flows from good controls must come to define normal. Enron's example of what can happen when controls are sacrificed may then emerge as one of its few positive legacies.

Notes

1. *The Smartest Guys in the Room,* p. 276.
2. *The Report of the Special Investigation Committee of the Board of Directors of Enron Corporation,* pp. 2-3.
3. *The Smartest Guys in the Room,* pg. 20.

Attachment 1

ExxonMobil Standards of Business Conduct: Ethics Policy

The policy of Exxon Mobil Corporation is one of strict observance of all laws applicable to its business.

The Corporation's policy does not stop there. Even where the law is permissive, the Corporation chooses the course of the highest integrity. Local customs, traditions and mores differ from place to place, and this must be recognized. But honesty is not subject to criticism in any culture. Shades of dishonesty simply invite demoralizing and reprehensible judgments. A well founded reputation for scrupulous dealing is itself a priceless company asset.

Employees must understand that the Corporation does care how results are obtained, not just that they are obtained. Employees must be encouraged to tell higher management all that they are doing, to record all transactions accurately in their books and records, and to be honest and forthcoming with the Corporation's internal and external auditors. The Corporation expects employees to report suspected violations of law or ExxonMobil policies to company management.

The Corporation expects compliance with its standard of integrity throughout the organization and will not tolerate employees who achieve results at the cost of violation of laws or who deal unscrupulously. The Corporation supports, and expects you to support, any employee who passes up an opportunity or advantage that would sacrifice ethical standards.

Equally important, the Corporation expects candor from managers at all levels and compliance with ExxonMobil policies, accounting rules, and controls. One harm which results when managers conceal information from higher management or the auditors is that subordinates within their organizations think they are being given a signal that company policies and rules can be ignored when they are inconvenient. This can result in corruption and demoralization of an organization. The Corporation's system of management will not work without honesty, including honest bookkeeping, honest budget proposals, and honest economic evaluations of projects.

It is ExxonMobil's policy that all transactions shall be accurately reflected in its books and records. This, of course, means that falsifications of its books and records in the creation or maintenance of any off-the-record bank accounts is strictly prohibited.

Attachment 2

Enron Code of Ethics (July 2000): Business Ethics

Employees of Enron Corp., its subsidiaries, and its affiliated companies (collectively "the Company") are charged with conducting their business affairs in accordance with the highest ethical standards. An employee shall not conduct himself or herself in a manner which directly or indirectly would be detrimental to the best interests of the Company or in a manner which would bring the employee financial gain separately derived as a direct consequence of his or her employment with the Company. Moral as well as legal obligations will be fulfilled openly, promptly and in a manner which will reflect pride on the Company's name.

Products and services of the Company will be of the highest quality and as represented. Advertising and promotion with be truthful, not exaggerated or misleading.

Agreements, whether contractual or verbal, will be honored. No bribes, bonuses, kickbacks, lavish entertainment, will be given or received in exchange for special position, price or privilege.

Employees will maintain the confidentiality of the Company's sensitive or proprietary information and will not use such information for their personal benefit.

Employees shall refrain, both during and after their employment, from publishing any oral or written statements about the Company or any of its employees, agents, or representatives that are slanderous, libelous, or defamatory; or that disclose private or confidential information about their business affairs; or that constitute an intrusion into their private lives; or that give rise to unreasonable publicity about their private lives; or that constitute a misappropriation of their name or likeness.

Relations with the Company's many publics—customers, stockholders, governments, employees, suppliers, press, and bankers—will be conducted in honesty, candor and fairness.

It is Enron's policy that each "contract" must be reviewed by one of our attorneys prior to its being submitted to the other parties to such "contract" and that it must be initialed by one of our attorney prior to being signed. By "contract" we mean each contract, agreement, bid, term sheet, letter of intent, memorandum of understanding, amendment, modification, supplement, fax, telex and other document or arrangement that could reasonably be expected to impose an obligation on any Enron entity. (Certain Enron entities utilize standard forms that have been pre-approved by the legal department to conduct routine activities; so long as no material changes are made to these pre-approved forms, it is not necessary to seek legal review or initialing prior to their being signed.) Please bear in mind that your conduct and/or your conversations may have, under certain circumstances, the unintended effect of creating an enforceable obligation. Consult with the legal depart-ment with respect to any questions you may have in this regard.

Additionally, it is Enron's policy that the selection and retention of outside legal counsel be conducted exclusively by the legal department. (Within the legal department, the selection and retention of legal counsel is coordinated and approved by James V. Derrick Jr., Enron's Executive Vice-President and General Counsel.) In the absence of this policy it would not be possible for our legal depart-ment to discharge its obligation to manage properly our relations with outside counsel.

Employees will comply with the executive stock ownership requirements set forth by the Board of Directors of Enron Corp., if applicable.

Laws and regulations affecting the Company will be obeyed. Even though the laws and business practices of foreign nations may differ from those in effect in the United States, the applicability of both foreign and U.S. laws to the Company's operations will be strictly observed. Illegal behavior on the part of any employee in the performance of Company duties will neither be condoned nor tolerated.

Case Study 4

Enter Mark-to-Market (A):
Exit Accounting Integrity?

I know mark-to-market isn't the right accounting answer. It's too bad that Jeff Skilling doesn't care about the merits of the case.

S ERGE GOLDMAN WAS NOT LOOKING FORWARD to tomorrow's meeting. It was May 1991. Goldman, Arthur Anderson's (AA) "engagement partner" on the Enron account, was being pushed by his client to allow mark-to-market (MtM) accounting at one specific Enron unit: Enron Finance (EF). EF was a new business unit, formed in just the last year. Its head, Jeffrey Skilling, had been an Enron employee only since August 1, 1990. Skilling had made it known that he wanted MtM for his unit. In fact, he told Enron chairman Ken Lay and president Rich Kinder that using MtM in EF was a condition for Skilling's agreeing to leave McKinsey & Company to join Enron.

Goldman had several problems with Enron's requested change. For one thing, he wasn't that familiar with MtM. Mark-to-market accounting, a relatively recent development, was used largely by Wall Street investment banks that traded marketable securities. Use of MtM was nonexistent in the Texas oil patch. Oil and gas accounting, on the other hand, was both well established and understood by accountants like Goldman. Serge felt uncomfortable being the first public accountant to approve using MtM in the oil and gas business.

Moreover, Goldman had concerns about the technical appropriateness of Enron's using MtM. True, EF was a unit that resembled investment banks in some ways. EF lent money to gas producers in return for an interest in their future production. EF then sold the future production thus acquired to utilities and industrial customers under long-term supply arrangements. Skilling called Enron's intermediary role the "Gas Bank". In its fully developed state, EF was not only banking producers and supplying consumers but also "securitizing" both the producers' financing and the customers' sales contracts. A complete outline of EF's Gas Bank concept is provided in Attachment 1.

Much of this origination/securitization resembled what Wall Street firms were doing with real estate mortgages and financial derivative contracts. Hence, Goldman could not simply dismiss EF's MtM request as being inap-

65

S.V. Arbogast, *Resisting Corporate Corruption* (pp. 65–77)
© 2008 by M & M Scrivener Press

propriate to an oil and gas business. But there were issues. For one thing,
the contracts EF was signing were not marketable securities; they did not
have readily discernible values. Yet, Enron wanted to account for them as if
they were like Treasury securities.

Upon signing a contract, Skilling wanted EF to book the deal's entire
expected net present value as profit. This would produce large reported
accounting income, the cash for which would materialize only over the long
life of the contract. Moreover, Skilling was not content just to book a deal's
present value as profit. He also wanted EF also to record the present value of
each sales contract as revenue while treating the present value of loan/pro-
duction payment obligations as "cost of goods sold." Using this approach
would ensure a huge rate of growth for EF's "top-line" revenue.

Goldman was not at all sure that such an approach would improve
investors' understanding of Enron's financial reports; he rather suspected
that it might confuse investors, serving up impressions of dramatic growth
in revenue, lesser but still impressive growth in reported profits, and a large
disconnect between accounting profits and cash flow.

But more than accounting questions were adding to Goldman's discom-
fort. Jeff Skilling would certainly attend tomorrow's meeting. Skilling had
hit Enron like a force of nature. Described as "incandescently brilliant," he
was known not to take no for an answer. Skilling had assembled a team-all
of them very bright-who took their cues from his lead. Goldman knew that
he could expect to be browbeaten by all the Skillingites if he refused to
approve MtM. Indeed, he could expect to be browbeaten if he gave any sort
of answer other than "let's do it."

Delay tactics and/or asserting AA's technical prowess also didn't look
like promising approaches. Skilling had quickly developed a reputation as a
hands-on manager. When he wanted something done, he got personally
involved to ensure that it got accomplished.

A final consideration was Enron's emerging importance as a client. It
was becoming clearer by the day that Enron was prepared to spend large dollars on consulting help. Indeed, Skilling had come on board after consulting
for Enron for three years. In fact, Skilling had developed his Gas Bank
scheme while working as a consultant. The problem this posed for Goldman
concerned his own firm's appetite for consulting business. Arthur Anderson
increasingly viewed consulting as the growth engine for the firm; indeed,
Goldman had heard the view expressed internally that the most important
aspect of AA's being retained as a public accountant was the possibility that
engagements would open the door to consulting work. Enron looked to be
a prime prospect. Not only was it likely to use consultants, but in hiring
managers like Skilling, Enron was clearly signaling its intent to innovate.
That would mean a continuous search for new ideas and for top consultants
who could generate them. How would the increasing importance of consulting impact AA's traditional commitment to public accounting? Would AA

still be able to summon the wherewithal to say no to accounting clients if that put consulting engagements in jeopardy?

With an eye to figuring out how best to respond to Skilling's expected salvos, Goldman reviewed his file's brief history of Skilling's career.

Jeff Skilling's Association with Enron

Jeff Skilling started working on Enron issues in 1985. By that time, he had been at McKinsey for five years. The big Omaha pipeline company, Inter-North, was an established client. When Inter-North merged with Houston Natural Gas to form Enron, Skilling was asked to work on a politically sensitive question: Should the headquarters be in Omaha or in Houston? He gave the politically incorrect but substantively correct answer of Houston, catching Ken Lay and Rich Kinder's eyes in the process. Lodged in McKinsey's Houston office, Skilling continued to consult for Enron after the company's headquarters moved to its soon to be famous 1400 Smith Street location.

Skilling worked on several issues but all were connected in some way with Enron's central preoccupation: How could a gas pipeline company make money under deregulation in a low natural gas price environment? Skilling's eventual answer was the Gas Bank.

Skilling first pitched the idea to Rich Kinder in December 1988. In classic Skilling fashion, the pitch consisted of one chart scrawled on a piece of notepad paper. The industry's basic problem, Skilling argued, centered on the gas producers. Those with reserves were reluctant to sign long-term contracts at the rock-bottom prices then prevailing. Producers also lacked internal funds to finance new drilling, and in the wake of Houston's oil price bust were finding it difficult to get financing from banks. Meanwhile, industrial consumers were reluctant to build new gas-fired power or manufacturing plants when they couldn't obtain term supply commitments with firm prices. The natural gas industry was thus stalemated; producers weren't growing production and consumers weren't growing demand. This meant depressed volumes moving through the pipelines of companies like Enron and poor prospects for growth any time soon.

Skilling's chart was based on the fact that in such an environment an intermediary could buy natural gas reserves for a low dollar/thousand cubic feet price and then commit to sell the future production to end users at a significant premium. Potential consumers were prepared to pay that premium to obtain supply and price commitments against which they could then run their own economics for generating power or producing aluminum or chemicals. Skilling saw Enron playing this intermediary role. It would be the "bank", taking gas deposits from producers and providing ensured supply to consumers in return for a mark up. Kinder saw the economic spread that had attracted Skilling and also saw that performing this intermediary role might get Enron's pipelines full again. Any resumption of demand growth for natural gas had to be positive for transportation providers. Kinder encouraged Skilling to develop his concept more fully.

Although Kinder and Ken Lay liked the Gas Bank, much of Enron's existing organization was opposed or indifferent. The concept languished until Lay became convinced that the Gas Bank would never get off the ground without Skilling's being in charge of execution. Kinder agreed. In April 1990, Lay and Kinder set out to persuade Skilling to leave McKinsey. Skilling was a partner at McKinsey, which implied that he made more than $1 million per year. Enron was not able to match such a salary. Enron could, however, offer Skilling an incentive scheme whereby he would share in the profits generated by his new business unit: Enron Finance. Bored with McKinsey's internal workings and eager prove the viability of the Gas Bank, Skilling eventually agreed to a $275,000 annual salary plus the incentive scheme. EF would have to become nicely profitable for Skilling to match, let alone exceed, his McKinsey remuneration; on the other hand, if EF became a homerun profit generator, Jeff Skilling could reap an altogether different level of compensation.

Since coming on board, Skilling had refined the Gas Bank and built a team to roll it out. The initial problem had been the reluctance of producers to commit gas volumes under long-term contracts. Skilling overcame this by offering financing for their new drilling. The lure of up-front money to fund drilling proved enough for producers to agree to grant Enron long-term "production payments" as the means to repay their financing. What looked to the producers to be loan repayment was to Skilling a committed supply of gas at a fixed price. The Gas Bank now had the long-term gas supplies it needed to extract the premium that gas customers were willing to pay.

A second problem concerned Enron's limited supply of finance capital. In 1990, Enron had barely recovered from its 1987 near-death experience of weak financial results and the Valhalla trading scandal. The company still carried a junk bond rating. There would not be enough Enron capital available for EF to build the Gas Bank as rapidly as Skilling thought the opportunity demanded.

Skilling's answer was to securitize both sides of the natural gas trades done by Enron's Gas Bank. Production payments acquired by Enron from gas producers would be pooled and interests sold to outside investors. The same could and would be done with the supply contracts Enron signed with gas customers. This approach freed the Gas Bank from Enron's internal-funding constraint. It also paid another enormous dividend: It opened EF's eyes to the fact that it could originate and then trade components of its long-term contracts; these components would be useful to other gas market players as hedges of their different positions. Skilling and his new team—Gene Humphrey, Lou Pai, George Posey, Amanda Martin, and new "securitization hire" Andrew Fastow—were mesmerized by the potential. Through origination and securitization of natural gas contracts, Enron could do more than rejuvenate its pipeline business. It could create and then dominate an entire new industry activity: the trading of natural gas futures contracts.

As Skilling saw the trading potential of his original Gas Bank scheme, his resolve to use MtM only intensified. It hardened even more when Oil and gas accounting (OGA) turned out to pose a specific problem. When it sold interests in its sales contracts to third parties, EF would not, under OGA, be able to match the gas acquisition price embedded in production payments against the sales price embedded in customer supply contracts. Instead, the sale of interests in a gas-supply contract resulted in an immediate gain or loss, depending on how the term sale contract price compared with the spot gas price then prevailing. In theory, Enron could end up realizing an initial accounting loss if spot prices happened to be high when a term sales contract was securitized. The fact that this same contract was already hedged by a fixed-price production payment would be recognized only down the road when gas was actually produced.

This mismatch further irritated Skilling and led directly to the scheduling of the meeting for which Serge Goldman was now preparing.

Serge Goldman prepares to meet Jeff Skilling

When news of the OGA mismatch problem reached Goldman, he had asked his young associate, David Duncan, to contact AA's Professional Standards Group (PSG) to discuss the matter. PSG was an elite group of AA's best accounting technicians; its writ was to assist AA accountants when client engagements posed especially difficult technical issues. If there was conflict between the engagement team and PSG, the latter was to have the last word. Goldman had asked Duncan to secure both a pros/cons discussion of using MtM at EF and any specific ideas PSG might have on the OGA mismatch issue. PSG's response is provided in Attachment 2.

To better prepare, Goldman divided up the issues into major baskets. In the first, labeled Technical Accounting, the challenge was to enumerate the specific issues under scrutiny and to discern the best technical accounting answers. Goldman expected that Skilling and his team would try to reduce the accounting issues to a simple "MtM: yes or no?" As PSG's memo makes clear, EF was seeking a variant of MtM, one that went well beyond that used by Wall Street firms. Goldman felt that each of the issues broached by PSG deserved its own discussion. He wondered how he could achieve such a conversation as opposed to having the discussion polarize quickly over whether AA would say yes or no to MtM.

This conundrum led directly to a second basket, which Goldman labeled Achieving the Client's Business Objective. The title contained an implicit assumption—namely, that the client's objective could be obtained in a fashion consistent with a sound accounting approach. Goldman knew that he must explore such possibilities. An acceptable solution might mean that AA would not demand use of the "best" technical accounting approach. However, the method chosen would still have to satisfy several tests, including being technically sound, comprehensible to the financial markets, and satisfactory to regulators. Obviously, if there was a way to use the best accounting method to achieve the firm's business objectives, so much the better.

Over the years, Goldman had learned that how AA orchestrated a client meeting often determined the outcome of the accounting discussion. Generally, it was better to start with positive news—what AA could agree to—before getting into what was still under review or, worse, what could not be accepted. Here, Goldman felt nervous. He did not yet have any good news to offer up. He did not have a technical fix for EF's mismatch problem and had not been authorized by AA to agree to MtM. Once all that bad news got out on the table, he doubted that Skilling and his team would want to sit still for a detailed discussion of the reasons.

As the thought of Jeff Skilling's likely reaction flitted through his mind, Goldman grew even more apprehensive. He could easily imagine Skilling starting to scream denunciations and then retreating to his office to call AA in Chicago. Doubtlessly, Goldman would be portrayed as a bean-counting dolt who didn't "get it." That wasn't what bothered Serge the most. Rather, it was the risk that if/when Skilling's call hit Chicago, Goldman's superiors, eager to placate this important and lucrative client, would cave on the substance of the matter. MtM "in principle" might be conceded. Goldman would be told to work out the details with George Posey, EF's CFO. Once Chicago showed that it wasn't standing behind Goldman, those details would end up being pretty much whatever Posey would settle for. Goldman might also receive a quiet black mark for not having managed the client, such that an Enron "rocket" didn't land on AA Chicago.

Was there a better way to manage the client and the meeting? Goldman went back over his file on Skilling and his Gas Bank. How much of Skilling's passion for MtM concerned its playing an essential role in making the Gas Bank work? Would the Gas Bank remake EF into the equivalent of a Wall Street firm? Did Skilling believe that a trading-oriented accounting system was needed to recruit and reward the type of individual needed to succeed at such activities? Was it more a matter of Skilling, the former high-flying consultant, believing that design/origination of the idea was the true value-creating event? Or, was it all about Skilling's personal compensation: his need to cover his former McKinsey's remuneration and eventually to move well past it?

Goldman reflected that if he could pin down Skilling's MtM motives, he stood a better chance of holding his own at the meeting, keeping the discussions "localized" in Houston, and eventually developing an answer that might also be acceptable from a technical accounting standpoint.

He poured another cup of coffee and turned back to the PSG memo.

Attachment 1

Enron Finance's Gas Bank Concept

EF's Gas Bank involves the following participants: 1) gas producers, 2) Enron Finance, 3) a special purpose entity (SPE), 4) institutional investors, and 5) term gas customers.

A standard Gas Bank transaction, as shown in the diagram below, would unfold as follows:

1. EF agrees to loan money to gas producers in return for an ownership interest in a portion of future gas to be produced: a production payment. The volume of gas committed in the production payment is sized to generate ample cash to pay interest and principal on the loan.

2. EF forms an SPE, meeting the tests of 3 percent minimum independent capital and an independent "mind and management" determining the SPE's commercial decisions.

3. (a) SPE sells ownership interests to institutional investors, using the proceeds to (b) buy EF's production payment. EF is now "whole" as regards cash, and the SPE is "long gas".

4. EF repurchases the SPE's gas over time under long-term, fixed-price contract. The SPE now expects to realize the cash flow from EF's original producer loan but paid in the form of sales proceeds from gas it delivers to EF.

5. EF enters into long- term gas sale contracts with end users at prices that carry a premium over the acquisition price paid to the SPE.

As additional steps, EF can sell off portions of either its gas repurchases from the SPE or its sales to end users. EF can also cover the open position so created by buying or selling gas from/to other third parties. These operations allow EF to benefit from (1) being a market maker in natural gas purchases and sales for all terms and regional markets, (2) from "customizing" coverage for specific counterparties, and (3) taking a speculative position if its senses that gas prices are likely to move in a particular direction. Diagrammatically, the Gas Bank looks as follows:

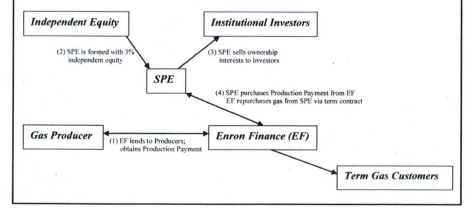

Attachment 2—Historical Recreation (HRC)

MEMORANDUM

June 15, 1991

To: Mr. Serge Goldman

From: Professional Standards Group

Subject: Adoption of Mark- to-Market Accounting by Enron Finance

You have asked that the PSG consider three questions:

1. What is the general suitability of using mark-to-market' (MtM) accounting for the oil/gas financing and trading business under development at Enron Finance (EF)?
2. What are the pros/cons of having EF shift from using conventional Oil/Gas accounting (OGA) to MtM?
3. Is there a technical fix for the asymmetric treatment OGA affords to EF's acquisition of production payments versus its sale of interests in term contracts with end users?

Below please find specific answers to these questions and some general observations on whether this is a matter that EF and AA may settle between themselves.

General Suitability of MtM for E

MtM is a recent development in financial accounting and is used by a variety of banking and commodity trading firms. As of this moment, its use is not mandatory. A draft FASB Statement is being developed; its focus is financial assets that have readily ascertainable market values, including stocks, bonds, and market-traded futures and options.

MtM's focus concerns the treatment of marketable securities and financial contracts. When MtM is used, these assets must be reported on the balance sheet on each statement date at their ascertainable current market value rather than historical acquisition cost. Any change in value versus the prior period gives rise to gain or loss to be reported on the firm's income statement.

The principal rationale for MtM is that it updates valuation of a financial firm's assets. This process more accurately reflects a firm's current worth. For firms that continuously buy and sell marketable securities, using MtM thus represents an improvement in recognizing the results from trading. MtM also reduces a firm's ability to manage earnings by selling appreciated assets while holding on to assets that are worth less than their historical cost.

In terms of suitability for use at EF, there are some parallels between that unit's activities and businesses that already use MtM. EF seeks to create value via financial structuring. In this sense, it is different from an oil/gas business concerned with the discovery, production, and physical movement of hydrocarbons. More specifically, EF intends to create tradable futures instruments in natural gas purchases and sales. This, EF can plausibly argue, is analogous to what Wall Street firms do when they originate and securitize financial instruments, such as collateralized mortgage obligations or "synthetic" zero coupon bonds. EF may also argue that it will be looking to attract professional traders away from Wall Street firms; undoubtedly, EF feels that to compete for such resources, it will need to recognize and reward trading performance. The use of an MtM accounting approach, it can be argued, is thus consistent with EF's trading business model and incentive systems for key personnel.

There are also several aspects of EF's business model that don't fit well with using MtM. These include the following:

- Most, if not all, of EF's assets will not involve widely traded instruments. As such, they may not have readily ascertainable market values. This causes such instrument's valuation to become a function of assumptions and analysis done internally at EF. Technically, the valuing of these instruments will be challenging. Of even more concern, there will be serious potential for objective valuation to be compromised by other agendas. Without adequate and sustainable controls, the risk of accounting abuses at EF would be high.

- Should EF use MtM, a large and growing variance will develop between reported profits and cash flow. Investors will need to puzzle through reports of large "unrealized" gains/losses to figure out the extent to which EF is contributing cash to parent Enron. The problem will not be dissimilar to that encountered some years back on foreign exchange translation accounting; there unrealized gains/losses swung earnings and earnings per share back and forth without materially influencing near-term cash flow. Ultimately, unrealized foreign currency effects were consigned to a cumulative translation account (CTA) in the net worth portion of the balance sheet to eliminate this confusion.

- For Wall Street firms, this gap between reported earnings and cash flow is less of an issue; the assumption is that their assets are readily salable into liquid markets. Should it face a cash flow crunch, the firm can be expected to liquidate some assets at values reasonably close to those reflected in its most recent financial statements. This assumption cannot be made for EF; its unique and nonstandard assets cannot be assumed to be easily liquidated at prices near to values on the books, especially if accounting values reflect internal assumptions that become skewed over time in an optimistic direction. Thus, the risk of EF's being unable to generate cash resembling its value on the books is substantially higher than for most firms currently using MtM.

We conclude from this that although EF has some arguments that could justify adoption of MtM, there are equally weighty, if not stronger, arguments suggesting that serious problems could arise.

Accordingly, the pros/cons of any EF decision on MtM must be weighed in terms of (1) the specific form of MtM that EF proposes to adopt and (2) such modifications of MtM, measures of control, and additional disclosure that EF would undertake to address the identified risks.

Specific Pros/Cons of an EF Switch to MtM

If we correctly understand what you have told us, EF's proposal goes beyond adoption of conventional MtM. Indeed, it seems that EF is intent on combining certain features of MtM with others of OGA into a hybrid system. This approach appears to magnify the potential for aggressive, potentially abusive, accounting and for the distortion of published statements.

EF's version of MtM involves the application of "merchant investment" accounting to its origination or trading of purchase and supply contracts. This differs markedly from how MtM is used by the financial firms that EF supposedly is seeking to emulate.

Financial firms that use MtM typically do not reflect expected cash flows from purchased or sold instruments in either revenue or cost of goods sold. Instead, such firms simply put purchased assets on the balance sheet, reflect changes in value on statement dates while these are held, and then reflect any gain or loss versus the last updated value when said assets are finally sold. Even when it originates and retains an instrument, a financial firm does not book expected revenues or costs immediately. **Stating things more simply, financial firms book their "trading spreads and fees" into income and then reflect market fluctuations on financial assets held in inventory.**

Under EF's version of MtM, the expected net present value (NPV) of originated/acquired customer supply contracts is to be booked immediately as revenue and the NPV of materials purchase contracts as costs of goods sold.

EF's intended approach appears to magnify a distortion discussed earlier and to create two entirely new issues. The magnified distortion concerns the discrepancy between reported income/losses and cash flow. Under EF's approach, it will not simply be recording profits that will be realized only years hence; it will be reporting current revenues that in fact will materialize only years into the future. EF talks in terms of natural gas supply/sales contract with tenors of ten years or more. This means that the magnitude of the discrepancy between reported current revenues and revenue as "earned and collected" will be substantial.

One new issue concerns the conditions typically applied to justify recognition of revenue. Traditionally, revenue recognition has required the service that generates the revenue to have been rendered and that cash collection has either occurred or is highly probable. EF's approach departs from both of these principles on the grounds that it will be dealing in financial instruments whereby underlying service and credit risk are minimal. However, EF's basic concept is tied to the purchase, sale, and physical delivery of gas. To the extent that the instruments EF will be creating and trading are not divorced from underlying production, delivery, and credit risk, its version of MtM unduly minimizes the risks facing the firm.

The second issue involves a wholly new distortion to EF's business model. By immediately recognizing all expected future revenues at the time of contract signing or acquisition, EF commits itself to start over at zero revenue at the outset of each new accounting period. There will be no "book" of already contracted business ready to generate revenues into the future. This will put pressure on EF to generate at least as many contracts or trades as in prior periods just to match the revenues already booked.

These multiple possibilities for distorted financial reporting and the abuse of basic accounting controls imply considerable potential for deterioration in the quality of EF's financial reports; quite possibly, this reduction in quality would exceed whatever would be gained via having updated valuations of contract assets on the balance sheet.

Technical "Fix" in Asymmetric Treatment

More details are needed about the specifics of the transaction you described as having upset the client. However, two things are already clear from the brief outline provided to date.

First, a full-scale switch to MtM is not needed to address asymmetric treatment that current rules may be applying to one portion of EF's planned business model. Any decision on whether to let EF adopt MtM should not be driven by this issue alone.

Second, there are a variety of precedents for addressing asymmetric treatments of two-side transactions. Examples include hedge accounting and "integrated financial transactions." With more details, PSG may be able to suggest an approach that could alleviate the objectionable asymmetric treatment. Be advised, however, that developing and implementing such an approach may require time and involve obtaining approval from regulatory authorities.

Comment on Resolution of Client's Request

As indicated, serious technical and financial-control issues exist about the advisability of EF's adopting its preferred version of MtM. The client may be able to resolve some of these issues by agreeing to modify its approach.

The adoption of any form of MtM by a unit of a publicly traded oil/gas firm, such as Enron, is likely to attract the attention of regulators. We therefore suggest that you advise EF that the consent of the SEC may be required.

If, after your next discussion, the client still wishes to pursue a change to any form of MtM, PSG will make a definitive assessment as to whether SEC approval of the change will be necessary.

Author's Note

This case captures Enron at a pivotal early moment. At this point, Enron is still a conventional company from an accounting perspective. Oil and gas accounting is still used throughout the company. Arthur Anderson still has a powerful voice, even a veto, in determining what accounting methods are acceptable and how difficult technical questions will be resolved. However, a powerful force for change has entered the picture. The case explores how AA can defend its convictions in the face of Jeff Skilling's determination to have his way and against a backdrop of AA's having a major commercial interest in preserving good relations with the Enron client.

Conspiracy of Fools identifies the AA engagement partner with whom EF and Jeff Skilling held discussions on switching to MtM. Serge Goldman is a fictitious name given to this real person. Since few details are public about his interaction with other partners at AA, it was deemed prudent to fictionalize this person. Also, this case does not intend to imply that it is a historical account of discussions within AA on the topic of Skilling's request. Neither does it intend to offer a historical account of Goldman's pre-meeting strategizing. Indeed, the published sources rather imply that Goldman did not come to this Skilling meeting with a well-orchestrated plan in mind. Rather, the case attempts to present the dilemmas-technical and otherwise—which Skilling's demand to use MtM posed for AA, a story that is a matter of the public historical record. The pre-meeting planning thoughts projected into Goldman's mind are an effort to begin the issue identification for students.

Skilling's background, his decision to join Enron, and his approach to EF are as outlined in *Conspiracy of Fools* (pp. 40–45, 53–58) and *The Smartest Guys in the Room* (pp. 32–39). The former outlines Skilling's Gas Bank concept, providing the basis for the description in this case.

The analysis of MtM accounting issues draws on the two texts just referenced and also *Enron: Corporate Fiascos and Their Implications,* edited by Nancy B. Rapoport and Bala G. Dharan, in which Dharan and William R. Bufkins provide a detailed discussion of the distortions and risks associated with EF's version of MtM (pp. 97–112). Peter C. Fusaro and Ross M. Miller's *What Went Wrong at Enron* (pp. 33–37, 62–64) highlights how the discrepancy between reported earnings and cash flow helped undermine Enron's spending discipline, which in turn reinforced Enron's insatiable appetite for financing, putting pressure on Enron's investment-grade credit rating. Investment-grade status was essential to

Enron's lucrative trading businesses. The resulting collision between Enron's "need to feed the beast" with fresh capital while also avoiding a credit downgrade pushed the company toward off-balance sheet financing and the use of special purpose vehicles. It was on this playing field that Andy Fastow would operate.

Dharan's and Bufkins' article (pp. 101–123, especially pp. 102–105) and Dharan's testimony before the House Energy and Commerce Committee highlight Enron's adoption of the "merchant investment" model and its resulting inflation of accounting revenues. Professor Dharan's work is a significant contribution, underscoring how Enron aggressively reached beyond conventional MtM. This impression coincides with the account of David Woytek's conversation with EF CFO George Posey, described in *Conspiracy of Fools* (pp. 55–57). In that discussion, Woytek points to the issue of inflating revenues:

"You're saying you want to recognize revenues from twenty-year contracts in the first year. I don't know what that is, but that's not mark-to-market."[1]

This text suggests that EF adopted the "merchant investment" version of MtM from the outset. It is clear from Dharan and Bufkin's article (p. 103) that by the time Enron On-Line came into operation, Enron was using this aggressive interpretation more broadly; this led to staggering increases in reported revenues between 1998 and 2000. For the sake of crystallizing the full slate of accounting issues latent in EF's request, the case assumes the "merchant investment" model to be embedded in EF's approach from the beginning.

Although it is likely that Goldman discussed EF's request with AA's PSG, there is no evidence that he received detailed written advice prior to his planned meeting with Skilling. Attachment 2 is thus an HRC intended to lay out the technical issues and provide certain warnings on the control and transparency issues at stake in the upcoming meeting. *Conspiracy of Fools* indicates that Goldman received advice that any switch to MtM would require SEC approval (p. 55). When he tells Skilling that SEC approval is needed, Goldman makes clear that his advice "came from Chicago". Attachment 2 has thus been crafted to mention this as a possibility so as to encourage students to use this fact in developing their strategy for managing the meeting with Skilling.

Note

1. *Conspiracy of Fools,* p. 56

Case Study 5

Enter Mark-to-Market (B): Accounting & the Aggressive Client

The meeting had not gone well.
In fact, the casual observer might call it a disaster.

SERGE GOLDMAN CLOSED HIS OFFICE DOOR, sat down, and leaned back in his chair. Straight ahead on his desk lay the phone. In a few minutes, Goldman, as Arthur Anderson's (AA) engagement partner on the Enron account, would have to call AA's Chicago headquarters. There a group of senior partners sat awaiting a report on Goldman's meeting with Jeff Skilling. On the face of things, Goldman would not have good news to report. As expected, Skilling had pressed AA hard to agree that Enron Finance (EF) could switch from Oil and gas accounting (OGA) to mark-to-market (MtM). Somewhat unexpectedly, the meeting had turned ugly. Near the end, one of Skilling's lieutenants had turned on Goldman and his colleagues, accusing them of just being stupid. Moreover, Skilling had made it clear that he would carry his battle for MtM past Goldman to AA-Chicago.

Clearly, Goldman's meeting strategy had not worked. Now he would have to scramble to reconstitute his approach. Before picking up the phone, Goldman would have to piece together a strategy to regain the initiative. AA's having the final say over Enron's accounting decisions was at stake. Although his partners were waiting, Goldman decided that they could wait a few minutes longer. He would take a moment, reflect back on the day's meeting, and then compose an approach that would allow AA to manage this client and this accounting decision. Only then would the conversation with his partners be anything other than a disaster report.

The Meeting with Skilling

The meeting had convened like a summit conference, complete with advisers from Bankers Trust and lawyers from Vinson & Elkins. Goldman brought along several colleagues, including the young David Duncan. The immediate issue prompting the meeting was the inconsistent treatment afforded by OGA to different sides of a Gas Bank transaction; however, everyone in attendance

78

S.V. Arbogast, *Resisting Corporate Corruption* (pp. 78–85)

knew that the real agenda concerned EF's proposed adoption of MtM. Skilling immediately took over the meeting, presenting EF's rationale for using MtM.

Skilling launched into a broad argument asserting MtM's superiority to OGA as an accounting treatment. First, he analogized EF to Wall Street trading houses. These, he argued, used MtM as common practice. In doing so, they more accurately reflected the current worth of their business. MtM was obviously the superior accounting system for a trading business.

As described by Skilling, MtM had the following desirable attributes:

- The full expected value of a transaction would be recorded at inception.
- Any change in the value of the transaction prior to final liquidation would be recorded as profit or loss.
- The risk of a matched or unmatched position would be reflected more accurately.
- Firms could not "manufacture" earnings by selling profitable positions and retaining losers.

Skilling used a brokerage transaction to illustrate. If a brokerage firm owned a stock and the daily trading price rose, the firm recorded a gain. Should the stock price drop the next day, the firm booked a loss. This, he implied, made MtM both a more accurate and a more consistent accounting system for a trading business. MtM would, for example, eliminate the asymmetric treatment of integrated transactions like those characteristic of the Gas Bank. MtM would simply integrate both sides of the transaction and record the total profit or loss expected from the position over its full life.

Skilling then summarized: "That is the beauty of mark-to-market. It reflects market reality"[1]

It was at this point that Goldman responded. Skilling had touched on the Gas Bank transaction, the specific issue under discussion. Goldman tried to bring the debate back to the fundamentals of this deal: "Wait. But this is an oil-and-gas transaction. You need to use oil-and-gas accounting."[2]

Goldman thought that putting this position on the table would accomplish two goals. First, it would pin the discussion down to the transaction in dispute. The general matter of MtM might be put off while the group focused on whether the problem of asymmetric accounting could be resolved. More fundamentally, Goldman was setting up his major message. Enron was an oil and gas company, not a Wall Street firm dealing in financial instruments. Virtually all Enron transactions involved oil and gas assets underlying the deal. It would be a major departure for any unit of Enron to shift away from OGA.

Goldman didn't plan to play his "high card" at this meeting, but assuming that Skilling continued to push for MtM, he'd eventually be told that the Securities and Exchange Commission (SEC), and not AA would make the final accounting determination. Enron was a publicly traded firm. Each quarter, it filed financial statements with the SEC. Goldman and his AA colleagues were virtually certain that the SEC would not permit an Enron unit to completely alter its accounting system without securing the commission's prior approval

It was at this point that the meeting spun out of control. Skilling and his lieutenants insisted that it made no sense to continue OGA for a unit whose business involved buying and selling both sides of a transaction. Goldman maintained that the transactions in question were rooted in oil and gas valuations and that OGA should apply. At last, Lou Pai, one of Skilling's favorites, threw up his hands in frustration: "You guys are just stupid. You're "frigging" stupid."[3]

Goldman realized that his meeting plan was in disarray. The discussion had not settled down to the particulars of the disputed Gas Bank deal. Goldman had failed to establish that EF was not comparable to a Wall Street firm; he also had failed to make clear that EF could not unilaterally be carved out from the rest of Enron for purposes of choosing an accounting method. Skilling and his team continued to argue that EF was different and to push for MtM. The best that could be said was that Goldman had drawn a line over OGA and not yet conceded any ground on MtM. With the meeting stalemated and tempers rising, Goldman tried to diffuse the situation.

The opportunity came when Skilling pushed Goldman to consult with AA's technical experts in Chicago. Goldman readily agreed to do so. Telegraphing his determination to get the result he sought, Skilling emphasized that he was ready to go to Chicago and present his arguments in person. He also pushed several PowerPoint slides (Attachment 1) across the table and told Goldman to send them to Chicago.

With this as a go-forward plan, the meeting broke up.

Goldman Plans to Brief his Partners

Once his head cleared a bit, Goldman took stock of the situation. Some things were instantly clear. Goldman was now personally at risk of seeming to have mismanaged the client. EF and AA were at loggerheads. EF's top executive had not only refused to accept the engagement partner's advice, but also made clear his intent to appeal over Goldman's head. Unless Goldman simply capitulated, his senior partners would have to become involved. At a minimum, they would wonder why their involvement was necessary.

Tempting as capitulation now seemed, it was a recipe for long-term trouble. If Goldman simply rolled over, EF would have established that AA could be pushed into unchartered territory by hard charging plus some huffing and puffing. Word would spread rapidly within Enron. AA already regarded this client as among its more aggressive managers of accounting results. Few AA accountants with Enron experience had forgotten that the Valhalla oil trading scandal had roots in the firm's attempt to manage quarterly earnings. Any quick "give" on MtM would surely encourage other Enron units to press for their preferred accounting positions. AA's position as Enron's accounting gatekeeper could be fundamentally compromised.

Moreover, the real issues involving EF's switching to MtM had not gotten out on the table. Goldman had hoped to use the Gas Bank transaction to illustrate the risks associated with MtM. However, Enron's line of attack had never given him the chance. This posed a complication. Goldman was guessing that his senior partners would not want to lead a technical accounting discussion. EF seemed not to be interested in having one. How, then, to get the risk and abuse issues buried in EF's detailed version of MtM out on the table?

This point was especially bothersome. EF's version of MtM went well beyond that practiced by Wall Street firms. EF's transactions were also less transparent, less easy to value than anything traded at Morgan Stanley or Lehman Brothers. It was precisely in the accounting details that the potential lurked for Enron to distort financial statements and manufacture profits. Somehow, AA had to make EF see its concerns and hold to a position that avoided the pitfalls of EF's approach.

Talking accounting theory or even financial control with Skilling was not likely to work. He appeared to be both impenetrably confident and utterly determined to have his way. Nothing about the way Skilling behaved in the meeting suggested that he was open to a discussion on the merits. Goldman suspected that Skilling had another, perhaps several, agendas. It would take some rock that Skilling couldn't move with a slick presentation to force him to consider another perspective.

As Goldman mulled over the debris left by the meeting, he came to an especially awful realization. It was going to take a near flawless communications strategy with his partners to salvage the situation. If he simply dialed them up and began to recount the meeting, they instantly would conclude that a disaster had occurred. At that point, they might stop listening to Goldman's point of view and start thinking about what they would have to do to salvage the situation. Some would start thinking about how to placate a valued client. Others might begin thinking about replacing him as the engagement partner. Most likely, the discussion would turn toward finding an answer to satisfy Skilling before he came to Chicago. Some partners might try to minimize the damage by visualizing how AA might retreat from the position Goldman had staked out during the meeting. In the face of Skilling's determined and confrontational style, it was not clear that mere tactical retreat would salvage much of AA's gatekeeper role.

Somehow, Goldman was going to have to position the meeting's outcome within the context of a strategy for managing both the client and the issues. The meeting's outcome was going to have to appear anticipated, a necessary stage to pass through on the way to a sound answer Goldman had worked out in advance. If Goldman could convey to his partners that he had such a plan, that it anticipated hardball tactics from the client, and that he still remained two or three steps ahead of the client, there was a chance that the Chicago partners would be willing to play their roles; any such plan would also need to reroute Skilling away from Chicago and back to Goldman and his team.

But did he have such a plan? If so, was it still intact, and would it withstand Skilling's presenting his arguments, charts, and implied threats in Chicago?

Goldman decided that his partners could wait a few minutes more while he attempted to sketch an outline of how AA might manage this particular client.

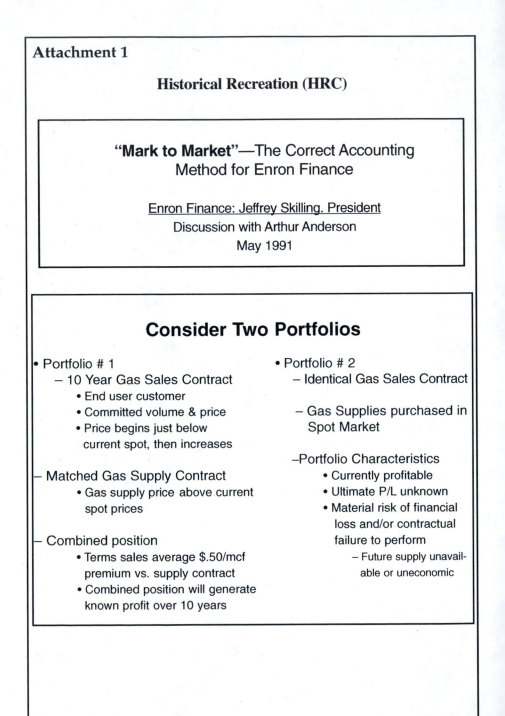

Attachment 1

Historical Recreation (HRC)

"Mark to Market"—The Correct Accounting
Method for Enron Finance

<u>Enron Finance: Jeffrey Skilling. President</u>
Discussion with Arthur Anderson
May 1991

Consider Two Portfolios

• Portfolio # 1
  – 10 Year Gas Sales Contract
    • End user customer
    • Committed volume & price
    • Price begins just below
      current spot, then increases

– Matched Gas Supply Contract
    • Gas supply price above current
      spot prices

– Combined position
    • Terms sales average $.50/mcf
      premium vs. supply contract
    • Combined position will generate
      known profit over 10 years

• Portfolio # 2
  – Identical Gas Sales Contract

  – Gas Supplies purchased in
    Spot Market

  –Portfolio Characteristics
    • Currently profitable
    • Ultimate P/L unknown
    • Material risk of financial
      loss and/or contractual
      failure to perform
        – Future supply unavail-
          able or uneconomic

Accounting Results for Two Portfolios

- Portfolio # 1

  - Under '0/G' Accrual Accounting
    - Combined position shows current loss

  - 'Mark to Market' Accounting
    - Combined position worth present value of all cash generated over contract life
    - Known value of combined contracts reflected immediately
    - ANY changes in expected value reflected as soon as known

- Portfolio # 2

  - Under '0/G' Accrual Accounting
    - Positive margins booked as current profit
    - Risks of supply/price exposure ignored

  - Mark to Market' Accounting
    - Portfolio worth less than matched position when valued using forecast that spot prices will rise

Some Comments and Observations

- O/G Accounting reinforces reckless industry behavior
  - Encourages mismatched positions that produce short term gains
    - Where have we seen this before?—THE S/L INDUSTRY!
  - Allows creation and sale of mismatched positions for purposes of managing quarterly earnings
    - Portfolio # 2 could do this by contracting 3 years of supplies at slight premium to spot, average price below that of Gas Sales Contract
    - Firm 'sells off first 3 year position, records immediate gain
    - Price/supply risk for back-end 7 years retained

Accrual accounting lets you create the outcome you want by keeping the bad and selling the good...MtM doesn't let this happen

Leading to This Conclusion

- Natural Gas Supply Business is changing radically
  - Formerly a fixed structure
  - Rapidly becoming a traded commodity

With this radical change, the accounting also has to change

Author's Note

Many ethics issues come to a head at meetings. This case
depicts such an instance. As is often the case, those advocating a
questionable change are not debating the matter on the merits.
They are interested only in getting the result they desire; verbal
browbeating and going over the head of AA's engagement partner
are permissible tactics in this cause. AA, as Enron's accounting
gatekeeper, must decide how to manage this client eruption, the
technical accounting matters at issue, and its own role as the arbiter
of acceptable accounting methods.

This case relies on the account of the MtM controversy as provided in Conspiracy of Fools. Pages 54–61 of that work offer an
account of: (1) the meeting between AA and Skilling and his team,
(2) a subsequent conversation on MtM between David Woytek and
Skilling's then CFO, George Posey, and (3) Skilling's presentation to
the SEC on September 17, 1991. The case's back-and-forth arguments at the Skilling/AA meeting are as presented in this
Conspiracy of Fools account. Lou Pai's quote has been altered to
sanitize the obvious obscenity.

While Goldman held a line on using OGA at the EF meeting, it
is not clear whether this was the result of any planned approach.
The flavor of the account in Conspiracy of Fools suggests more of a
meeting that quickly polarized because the client was interested
only in getting the answer it wanted and AA was not ready to say
yes. There is no historical record of what Goldman thought about
or communicated after the meeting. Goldman's post meeting
reflections are thus a creation intended to lay out possibilities for
managing both the meeting's fallout and his AA partners.

However, Goldman was an engagement partner for a major
client. To reach such a position, he likely would have had considerable experience managing meetings with aggressive clients and his
political position in the firm. It is therefore reasonable to assume
that as such, he would have sought to align his senior partners
prior to turning down an important client's request. To help illustrate the challenges aggressive clients can present to gatekeepers,
the case attributes to Goldman considerable post meeting reflection. To sharpen his dilemma, it also presents Goldman as doubt-
ing the resolve his senior partners would muster. Given AA's subsequent very accommodating stance toward Enron, such doubts
were probably not unrealistic.

Attachment 1 is an HRC. However, it accurately reflects the
key arguments Skilling used in his meeting with the SEC (see
Conspiracy of Fools, pp. 59–61). There is no evidence that Skilling

gave these graphs to Goldman at the conclusion of their meeting, nor is it clear exactly what materials Skilling used when he did subsequently visit AA-Chicago. It is unlikely, however, that his line of argumentation was materially different from what's in the attachment. Since the SEC arguments are recounted and are the ones that ultimately carried the day, they have been incorporated here to allow students to analyze the case using Skilling's final position.

Note

1. *Conspiracy of Fools,* p. 5
2. Ibid.
3. Ibid.

Case Study 6

Enter Mark-to-Market (C): The Disease Spreads to Enron Clean Fuels

Jeffrey Skilling can be a persuasive SOB. He also seems to have his own team planted inside Enron's financial functions and even within Arthur Anderson.

K EN RICE COULD ONLY SHAKE HIS HEAD and smile at his own thoughts. It was the middle of 1993. Earlier in the year, Rice had been called to Skilling's office. Skilling offered Rice, a resourceful and proven marketer, the chance to run his own business: Enron Clean Fuels (ECF). ECF manufactured natural gas-based liquid fuels/additives, such as methanol and MTBE. ECF was also losing serious money, which was detracting from the success that Skilling's team was achieving in gas trading. Skilling was determined to stop the bleeding.

At first, Rice was reluctant to take the job. He knew ECF to be a mess. The unit had a couple of lucrative long-term contracts, term deals whereby Enron's plants fed product directly into pipelines tied to dedicated customers. However, the vast bulk of ECF's sales were either spot transactions or term deals with thin margins. Spot prices for both methanol and MTBE were weak and volatile. There was plenty of competition from large producers with low unit costs; to cap everything off, MTBE had a shaky regulatory regime. Gasoline-product specifications favored oxygenates, of which MTBE was a current favorite. That status could change with simply a modification of the rules or with any event that might cause public policy to shift its preference to a competing oxygenate such as ethanol.

So, Rice told Skilling that he didn't know anything about the business. Skilling didn't accept the excuse. He had a plan in mind and wanted a trusted lieutenant to execute it. Referencing the unit's several profitable contracts, Skilling commented: "If we can create a market and renegotiate these contracts, maybe we can get mark-to-market earnings on them"[1]

It wasn't clear to Rice why, if the contracts were so attractive, they needed to be renegotiated. However, he told Skilling that he'd think about the job and asked for a couple of days to do so.

86

S.V. Arbogast, *Resisting Corporate Corruption* (pp. 86–92)
© 2008 by M & M Scrivener Press

As Rice mulled over the job offer, he thought he saw more clearly where Skilling was coming from. Together, they could replicate in Clean Fuels what Skilling had accomplished in natural gas. ECF could create a trading market in methanol and MTBE. Better yet, it could become the market maker. As the trading market deepened, term contracts would multiply; then, term prices would become more firmly established and more transparent. Eventually, a "forward curve" would materialize in both commodities, with ECF running a book and transacting on both sides of the buy/sell. With a market thus established, it would be valid to adopt mark-to-market accounting. EF had already created the precedent for Enron trading operations, so it was likely that ECF would not have to go to the SEC–this one could be settled between Enron and Arthur Anderson (AA).

Excited, Rice informed Skilling that he would take the job. Then, he began working to outline a strategy for building a trading market for methanol/MTBE (Attachment 1).

Within days of arriving on the job, Rice was confronted with a more aggressive approach. In recent years, Rick Causey, one of the accountants who had played a role in winning SEC approval of MtM, had migrated from AA into Enron. He was now Jeff Skilling's top accounting officer. In that capacity, he had assigned a controller to ECF and given her marching orders.

She arrived in Rice's office bearing copies of the profitable term contracts Skilling had first mentioned. These involved two customers that Enron served via direct pipeline feed. Placing the contracts on the desk, she told Rice: "Let's talk about how we can make these mark-to-market."[2]

Rice listened with some amazement as the new controller laid out a plan for short-cutting the clean fuels market-development project. In quick succession, she ticked off the necessary steps to renegotiate the contracts with the two customers:

1. The party supplying the customers would be a new entity, a joint venture company containing some independent equity; however, this new company would remain controlled by Enron/ECF.
2. The new contracts would contain a clause permitting the new SPE entity to source methanol/MTBE from any source, not only from Enron.
3. All other contract terms and conditions would remain unchanged.

With these changes, the controller assured Rice, ECF could be considered to have established the necessary trading market: "All we need to show is two or three independent deals. Causey says that will be enough to get Arthur Anderson's approval."[3]

Rice was stunned. Was that all it took: a little "corporate entity" shuffling, some innocuous contract clauses, and a little renegotiating with customers? That constituted the creation of two to three independent deals? Do that, and millions of profits could be booked immediately? He took a deep breath, marveling at the audacity of it all.

Thinking a bit further, Rice expected little difficulty from the contract customers in implementing such a plan. The proposed changes would pose no difficulty for the customers. ECF could package it as legal housecleaning having no downside for the clients. In fact, there was a theoretical improvement. Should there ever be a problem with ECF's plants or the opportunity to source cheaper/better supplies elsewhere, Enron's new entity would already be legally free to buy from other suppliers. In practical terms, Rice wasn't worried about this flexibility. ECF would still control decisions at the new entity, and the customers were still bound by their contract to buy from an Enron-controlled entity. ECF's pipeline connection to the customers also guaranteed that it could retain the end-use customers under virtually any contingency. Still, the flexibility would look good on paper and apparently gave the accountants the comfort they needed to satisfy the requisite independence test.

Rice had to admit that the proposal was tempting. He noticed, however, that several doubts were nagging at him. The proposal was a crass artifice. Did "market valuation" and "independence tests" mean nothing in substance? Were accounting rules meant to be circumvented that easily? What was that going to mean for the "quality" of Enron's reported earnings going forward? Would they come to resemble an ever-growing mix of traditional "as earned, cash in the till" profit and these aggressive bookings of expected future income? How much of these unrealized, non cash earnings would be real, and how much would be purposefully manufactured by the assumptions made internally? With no real market in existence, ECF would do its own contract valuation. How objective would that process be or stay over time? Rice looked over at the young controller sitting across from him. With accounting advice like this— and apparently over at AA too—would anybody in Enron's financial functions even care about earnings quality?

Rice could also see that ECF's results would quickly appear very different. Despite a fundamental business that was still losing money, ECF, with MtM in use, would immediately appear to have pulled off an impressive turnaround. Of course, no such business event had occurred. This was the tempting part. For a time, Rice would be the beneficiary of this seemingly miraculous improvement. But there was a catch. What would save ECF during the subsequent financial reporting periods? Stripped of the earnings that would normally accrue on these contracts, ECF would look even worse down the road. What then: savior to goat in twelve months?

His business and political instincts told Rice to be careful about jumping at the accountant's proposal. Then another thought went through his mind. Would this accountant be in his office, saying these things, if Jeff Skilling was not already on board with this approach? So, it was not a simple matter of deciding what was best and following one's own best judgment. If he decided not to convert these contracts to MtM, Rice might well be going against the wishes of the man who had given him the job. What would he say to Skilling when he was called in and confronted for not adopting the obviously preferable course of action?

His new controller was looking at him. She had finished laying out the plan. What was Rice going to say and do?

Attachment 1—Historical Recreation (HRC)

Turnaround Plan for Enron Clean Fuels:
Strategy for Market Development
June 1993

Overall Plan
o   Transform a "manufacture/supply" clean fuels business model to a "trading/hedging" market-maker model
- Objectives:
  - ➤ Become the creator of traded futures/derivative products in methanol/MTBE.
  - ➤ Become the primary market maker; provide liquidity on both sides of buy/sell transaction while pushing term out from 30 days to 10 years.

Rationale
- ECF cannot compete on plant scale, feedstock, or financing with the lowest-cost clean-fuels manufacturers; hence, current business model is non viable.
- Divestment would be justified but involves significant cash losses and accounting write-offs.
- Existing assets do, however, provide a platform for understanding business economics, pricing, and valuation.
- ECF has access to unique Enron know-how on creating and trading financial instruments derived from underlying business contracts.
- First mover in clean fuels will design industry-standard instruments and set up trading to its specifications.
- Thus, trading-business model has potential for ECF to enjoy competitive advantages unattainable under current business model.

Operational Plan
- Add contract origination and financial instrument development group of 5, recruited from EF.
- Add 2 initial traders, and grow as contract volume and trading potential justify.
- Once the appropriate trading market is developed, ECF should be able to adopt mark-to-market accounting, following Enron Finance precedent.
  - ➤ Superior knowledge of contract design and recognition of trading opportunities, plus role as principal liquidity provider should ensure rapid growth in Clean Fuels contract origination.

➤ Rapidly growing contract origination under mark-to-market should generate earnings that rise quickly to levels that overcome losses from the current manufacturing business.

➤ Once ECF is profitable from ongoing trading activity, unprofitable contracts and/or underlying assets can be divested and unavoidable write-offs absorbed.

Immediate Action Steps

1. Identify and recruit contract origination, instrument development, and derivative teams from within EF.
2. Identify supply/demand imbalances, degree and shape of price volatility and unsatisfied contractual demands/requirements in methanol/MTBE industries.
3. Design initial contract/hedge product offerings and identify target customers.
4. Identify ECF ability to back product offerings with own supplies and needs to acquire supplies from third parties.
5. Plan messages and offering content of marketing campaign.

- Timetable to complete Immediate Action Steps:
  o Complete steps 1-3 in 3 months
  o Remainder completed by year end

Author's Note

This case is drawn from the account of Enron Clean Fuels' adoption of MtM as provided in *Conspiracy of Fools* (p. 68–70). None of the other major works on Enron provides any information on this migration of MtM into ECF.

Conspiracy of Fools provides background on Ken Rice and covers his initial conversation with Jeffrey Skilling. It also makes clear that Rice had a plan to develop the Clean Fuels trading market when Rice arrived on the job and that Rich Causey sent over a unit controller who laid out the plan for converting existing contracts to MtM. The specific elements of the controller's plan are as specified in this account.

Attachment 1 is a historical recreation intended to lay out what a plan to develop the Clean Fuels trading market would entail. It is clear from the Conspiracy of Fools account that Rice had a plan in mind sequenced as follows: (1) develop an authentic trading market in the ECF commodity products, and (2) apply MtM to the contracts, both old and new. The account further makes clear that the controller's proposal conveyed to Rice that his plan "was backwards": that MtM can and should be applied to existing contracts immediately and then efforts made to expand trading. Attachment 1 is a partly fleshed out version of what Rice may originally have had in mind and provides students with a more concrete sense of the alternatives Rice would be weighing.

The case places Rice right at the instant when he must respond to the controller's proposal. At that moment, he had the options of accepting the controller's ideas, sticking to his original plan, or deferring decision to weigh his options more carefully. The *Conspiracy of Fools* account credits Rice with having some recognition of the aggressive nature of the young controller's proposal. He is, for example, reported to have registered surprise at how easily a market that would satisfy AA could be created. Whether he ever actively weighed doing anything other than accepting the accountant's proposal is unclear. This case study gives him the benefit of the doubt in order to give students the chance to stand in his shoes at the moment when there was a decision to make.

This, of course, is one point made by this case: At the moment when Rice was confronted with his decision, it was increasingly going to take a difficult personal choice by individual Enron employees to raise ethics or legal issues. Such employees could no longer count on Enron's gatekeepers to perform that task. The migration of MtM into ECF may not have seemed like a big deal at the time. However, the episode makes clear that after the MtM decision for EF, AA adopted a much more accommodating position toward Enron; increasingly AA set low bars for what would meet critical tests of form versus substance. Far from fighting to maintain its gatekeeper role, AA, at the engagement-partner level, was increasingly focused on helping Enron achieve what it wanted in a technically complaint way.

Notes

1. *Conspiracy of Fools,* p. 68.
2. Ibid.
3. Ibid., p. 69.

Case Study 7

Adjusting the Forward Curve in the Back Room (A)

What do you mean the interest rate swaps don't work any more?
What has changed? I'm not aware of any major new developments
in the gas market. The basic parameters under which
they were negotiated are still in effect.
There is no reason for the swaps to be adjusted.

R AY BROWN, A NEWLY HIRED MANAGER of Derivatives Risk
Analysis (DRA), was stunned by what he was hearing. Hired in July
1995, Ray had taken charge of Enron's thirty-man group responsible for
analyzing and structuring complex derivative-based hedge positions. As the
year wound down, DRA had built up a substantial interest rate swap position.

At 9:00 am on November 11, Ray had been visited by Tom Hopskins, assistant manager of the Natural Gas Trading Division (NGTD). Tom had brought
unsettling news. Upon further review, NGTD had determined that its forward-
purchase transactions were not as profitable as first assumed. Expectations of
future natural gas prices had been revised to lower levels. This change reduced
the expected differential between the projected forward curve and the contract
price at which some gas had been bought. Based on this revised outlook, Tom
asked Ray to adjust the interest rate swaps associated with the deal:

Your swap position is too large now. There isn't the same level of expected profits anymore. You probably need to readjust "notional principal" by about
$70 million, spread over years five to ten.

Ray immediately reacted with incredulity. Tom did not offer a good
response. He just reiterated that the NGTD experts had revisited their projections, and, unfortunately, future prices had been overestimated. Everyone
would have to adjust, including DRA.

Ray's mind cast back over the various NGTD transactions that DRA had
hedged. Over the course of the year, Enron's natural gas traders had bought
and sold gas for long-term forward delivery. This combination of purchases and
sales aimed to capture an economic margin, or spread, thereby producing a
stream of expected long-term cash inflows. Sometimes, the purchases and sales
would be exactly matched; in other transactions, traders would "go long or

93

S.V. Arbogast, *Resisting Corporate Corruption* (pp. 93–102)
© 2008 by M & M Scrivener Press

short", leaving their positions unbalanced. Under the mark-to-market accounting, the present value of these expected cash flows was immediately reflected
in operating profits; subsequently, however, these booked profits would have to
be adjusted to the extent that the expected value of the flows fluctuated.

Interest rate variations were one factor that could cause booked trading
profits to require adjustment.   When trading profits were first taken to
profit/loss, an interest rate was assumed in order to calculate the present value
of expected gains. Frequently, the commodity traders would ask DRA to execute interest rate hedges locking in the rate assumed for booking profits. This
helped insulate recorded gains from subsequent adjustment. In the case at
hand, DRA had entered into five to ten year swaps under which Enron would
pay fixed and receive floating interest payments over the period. Attachment 1
outlines the essential features of the hedge and its underlying transaction.

Although new at Enron, Ray already possessed ten years of experience in
the evaluation of derivatives. Much of this time had been spent at a leading
Wall Street firm where aggressive trading of complex instruments was the daily
rule. Ray felt that he knew the difference between an honest mistake and
moves driven by a hidden agenda. Something here didn't feel right. Ray decided that he needed time to dig deeper.

Well, what you say doesn't make sense to me. Possibly I've missed something. Give me a day or two to look into the transaction and think about what to
do. I'll be back to you before the week is out.

Tom departed after a final comment that other deals were in the pipeline
and time was of the essence. As the door closed, Ray reached for his company
directory. A call to T. J. Malva would help clarify matters.

Conversation with T.J. Malva

NGTD had its own risk assessment group, RAC, whose charge was to assess
the accuracy of the traders' price assumptions and estimates of trading profitability. Although RAC reported to the senior vice-president in charge of NGTD,
strong informal ties had developed among the executives in RAC and DRA.
Thus, Ray knew that when he called, he would get a straight story from T.J.

This is a funny one, Ray. Tom brought it to us yesterday. He said that his
traders had reconsidered the natural gas forward price curve and were convinced that it needed a major downward adjustment. We couldn't see what had
changed since they cut the deals last month. It is true that spot prices have
moved sharply higher. This winter is turning out to be abnormally cold, and a
number of big traders have been caught short. Spot gas has rocketed up. The
same is true for the near term futures market out to six months. However, the
long-term gas futures have barely moved. Yet these earlier deals Tom is talking
about are long term; suddenly, he's saying that the traders see the long-term forward curve moving lower. If anything, it has moved up, if only fractionally. It
doesn't add up.

Tom took the adjustment to Bette Patucka in our group. As an aside, it seems that whenever NGTD needs a signoff on something questionable, they take it to Bette. Anyway, this was a bit much even for Bette. My understanding is that she initially refused to sign off. However, Tom apparently told her that the adjustment was going to get made whether she signed off or not. Tom also told her: "If your name isn't on the approval sheet, it will look bad for you. She signed off. Tom must have come to you next.

T. J.'s comments told Ray a lot. This transaction was definitely being steered by Tom Hopskins. That tended to happen when there was something questionable about the deal. Second, Bette Patucka had had exactly the same initial reaction as did Ray. This confirmed that no adjustment was warranted on the merits of the deal. Finally, it appeared that Tom had threatened Bette to get the approval he needed.

One needed to understand Enron's Performance Review System (PRS) to fully appreciate the import of Tom's words to Bette. One thing that had surprised Ray upon joining Enron was the manner in which compensation was determined. Under PRS, all executives were rated annually and grouped into quartiles. Rankings were fiercely, even bitterly contested; a two-quartile ranking difference could mean a six-figure differential in annual bonus. None of this was particularly unusual, however. Many firms employed such systems, especially those that emphasized trading and financial services, where annual revenue generation was a key driver of firm profitability.

What had surprised Ray was who sat on the PRS committee. Senior executives from the major trading departments regularly participated in ranking the risk-assessment managers who reviewed their deals. This sounded alarm bells for Ray; the opportunities for retaliation were obvious. Trading executives could consign a conscientious risk manager to the bottom with a few damning generalities, as in "not cooperative, not bottom line oriented, or can't tell the difference between risk assessment and obstructionism." Worse yet, the mere knowledge that this could happen was enough to make risk managers cautious about who they crossed; the more aggressive traders counted on this and became ever bolder in attempting to "roll" deals through RAC. T J's account of Tom's threats to Bette only demonstrated that Ray's fears were well founded.

All this strengthened the case that Tom's request was linked to a hidden agenda. However, Ray was still in the dark as to what that agenda might be. He spent the rest of the morning touching other bases without success. Finally, he placed a call to Max Anstadht in Accounting. Max handled the booking of NGTD's trades and its quarterly profitability statements. Max told Ray that NGTD was in the process of producing a record quarterly profit. Just as T. J. had said, near-term natural gas prices had made a run and were now up 35 percent versus the end of 1994. NGTD had gone long on gas for delivery during the 1995-'96 winter and beyond, correctly anticipating the price run up. As spot prices had moved higher, NGTD began to sell, booking huge gains in the process. NGTD's interest in lowering the long end of the forward curve developed shortly thereafter.

But, Max, why would NGTD be maneuvering to lower the profitability of its group? Usually when there is questionable dealing, it's in the opposite direction—guys trying to pretty things up, bury losses. And why are they putting so much political heat behind doing this revision? I don't get it. What's going on here?

Max adopted that careful tone of voice often used when someone ventures into dangerous territory.

I can't answer that definitively. Nobody has told me anything official. However, I did hear some discussion between Tom and another trader to the effect that the record quarterly profit was going to be a problem. Apparently, Ken Maddox-the COO, to whom NGTD reports- is known for adjusting next year's forecast profit upward when current-year results greatly exceed expectations. Perhaps Tom and his colleagues are concerned that they might end up with an impossible profit target for fiscal year 1996. Theirs is a volatile business, and NGTD may feel really challenged to repeat 1995's performance. That could mean disappointing bonuses next year.

For Ray, all the pieces suddenly fit. What Max had said about Ken Maddox squared with what Ray had heard from numerous other sources. Thus, NGTD was engaged in adjusting seasoned transactions after the fact to lower reported profits. This adjustment would create an offset to some of its recent gains from spot gas sales; the net effect would hopefully be to avoid Ken Maddox's imposing a higher NGTD Corporate Plan objective for 1996. But now the problem came back to Ray. Would he agree to adjust his interest rate swaps? If not, what would he tell Tom Hopskins later in the week? Ray went back to his office and shut the door so he could deliberate in private.

Ethics Assessment and Tactical Options

Ray didn't like Tom's request, but that wasn't good enough. Ray had to be able to identify—definitively and with precision—what was objectionable. Otherwise, his objections would be rebutted with half-truths backed by the same veiled threats that Tom had used on Bette.

Was the ex post facto adjustment illegal? Ray decided that the answer was potentially yes, but it would be hard to prove it so. Enron is a public company. Manipulating the booking of transactions to move profits from one period to the next was potentially a violation of SEC disclosure rules. However, a large amount of judgment was involved in the setting of commodity forward curves when marking forward sale contracts to market. Price discovery is limited at the long end of the gas trading market. Relatively few long-dated trades are concluded, and little or nothing gets published on deal terms. Thus, the traders themselves become the source of information for long term prices on the natural gas futures curve. Assuming that NGTD was smart enough not to leave retrievable detailed worksheets of its original forward curve estimates, the revised curves would survive as the one and only expression of NGTD's professional judgment. This "fact pattern" would likely make it difficult to prove that NGTD was manipulating its reporting.

Ray thought about gathering a file of the original booking and discussing the matter with Accounting and Law. He noted this thought as option 1 on a list of objections and options that he began to compile (Attachment 2).

Was the adjustment unethical—unethical in a way serious enough to justify efforts to stop it? Ray soon found himself navigating between a complex set of "yes" and "not really's." Companies moved reported accounting profits and losses around all the time. The options for doing so were numerous; many were openly taught in business school, such as managing year-end inventories or taking/reversing reserves for litigation, accidents, or credit losses. What NGTD was attempting-a smoothing of reported profits over a multi year period-was no different in spirit from what other companies did routinely using other tools. Inevitably, the true profitability of the deal would have to be recognized in a subsequent adjustment.

What bothered Ray, however, was the damage this adjustment would do to good procedure for pricing future forward contract deals. If deals could be re-priced without reference to external benchmarks, no price-discovery' process with integrity would exist. Instead, deals could be reshaped after the fact for any reason. Today's reason might be to move profits from one period to another. Tomorrow's might be to hide divisional losses from management or stock market analysts. Once the moorings of external reference points were uprooted and the internal checks provided by RAC and DRA overrun, what was to stop a business-line management from going rogue or covering up any unpleasant results?

The consequences of such an environment for Ray were painful to contemplate. As manager of the group responsible for hedging the underlying gas transaction, DRA would always be the last to know about re bookings in NGTD. DRA would be routinely asked to provide after-the-fact adjustment to the hedges. At a minimum, this could put DRA repeatedly in the position of often appearing to get the hedges wrong. Ray wondered what a string of restructured hedge positions, with Enron having to pay money to break up existing deals, would mean for him and his group. It couldn't be good for performance appraisals and job security.

Ray also feared this problem of "incrementalism". Typically a first test case has some reasonableness about it. Ray knew that if he confronted Tom Hopskins and turned down the request, that would not end the matter. There would be meetings at higher levels. Tom would accuse DRA of overreacting or being uncooperative. Tom would also argue that DRA should respect NGTD's judgment on the forward curve. NGTD's experts studied the curve every day. Who was DRA to second-guess the gas traders' judgment? Hadn't RAC signed off? If anyone had the right to dispute the traders' decision, it was RAC, and it was on board.

With RAC already compromised, Tom feared that he would lose this debate. The consequences of such a loss were potentially worse than quietly conceding the matter. Openly losing at higher levels would only establish a precedent that traders could and would use to silence DRA on future cases.

Despite all these ambiguities, bureaucratic politics, and personal risks, a decision was still required on the fundamental principles at stake. Ray feared that it would be seen as huge overkill to accuse NGTD of illegality; however, the damage to the internal control system and the implications for future trans-actions were serious enough that DRA needed to resist. What form should this resistance take? Ray seriously considered letting the transaction go forward as a one-time exception, documented as such, with a warning sent to NGTD stating that similar future transactions would not be accepted. Would that be strong enough?

Ray looked for other options. One was to consider whether potential allies in the organization might find the re booking as objectionable as Ray did. One such potential ally was the controller, Don Cooke. Don had no organizational role in reviewing the booking of NGTD transactions. However, his writ did involve more general matters of financial integrity, such as internal control. Don also was well respected for his expertise, fairness, and ability to explain complicated accounting to senior management. Don might be persuaded to see the "thin edge of the wedge" aspect of NGTD's re-booking. If so persuaded, Ray thought that Don might be able to turn NGTD around. At a minimum, Don could prove a valuable ally if discussions moved to higher levels. However, Don would need documentation to support the contention that the transaction had been fairly booked the first time and was being re-booked without cause.

Another option was to take the matter directly to Ken Maddox. Ken would have an interest in knowing what was transpiring, in order to avoid the profit-target adjustment he would otherwise decree. Ken would also have the clout to stop it and to protect DRA in subsequent PRS reviews. The risk in this approach lay in how NGTD could respond. NGTD would undoubtedly argue that this was their call, RAC was on board, and DRA was out of bounds. NGTD would try to make it a my-people-versus-those-other-people decision for Ken. If NGTD succeeded, serious retaliation against DRA would follow in the next PRS review. Tom Hopskins had a reputation for vicious retaliation when openly crossed.

A final option was to negotiate with NGTD on technical grounds. For example, Ray could insist that responsibility for the mishedged position lay clearly in NGTD's original forward curve and pricing. Ray could demand that any and all adjustment costs on the swaps be borne by NGTD. Once this point had been conceded, Ray could make the swap-adjustment costs expensive or drag out a discussion with Accounting on the mechanics of transferring the cost from DRA to NGTD. Through some combination of such actions, he could make the adjustment process painful for NGTD in the hopes that this would discourage future such initiatives on its part. Ray recognized that none of this contested the principle of what NGTD was attempting. It also depended upon its conceding absorption of the adjustment costs. NGTD might instead just try to muscle DRA to go along as it did with RAC.

Lastly, Ray turned to the matter of his personal situation. Employed at Enron less than six months, he was not eager for another job change. Still, he had to be prepared for that eventuality if matters escalated. As a risk-assessment veteran, Ray was confident that he could find other work and probably quickly, too. Such was not the case for his staff. Accordingly, Ray determined to involve no one else from his department in the matter, regardless of which course of action he selected.

Attachment 1

A Forward Commodity "Buy/Sell" Position with Integrated Interest Rate Hedge
Economic Profit and Accounting Gain/Loss

Underlying Transaction

- Forward Buy/Sell transactions can be profitable when a trader either buys a commodity forward at a price below the forward price curve or sells gas forward at prices above the curve. This illustration is based upon a forward sale transaction."

- The underlying driver for the transaction is to capture a market arbitrage. A trader sees an opportunity to sell a commodity at a price that is either above current prices in the forward market or that the trader expects will be above forward prices as the market adjusts. As the forward sale moves into the money versus the forward curve, the trader may either leave his or her position open or may hedge by purchasing forward contracts to cover the short (sale) position. The former action leaves the economic result of the sale open to change. Covering forward locks in the economic profit, or trading gain.

- An actual deal might unfold as follows. To capture a gain, traders begin by entering into an over-the-counter sale transaction with a gas customer. This contract will specify a sale price higher than that of the current futures market forward curve, or where the trader expects the forward curve to move. To give a simple example, assume that a trader expects forward natural gas prices to start weakening. Assume also that the trader sees an opportunity to sell gas equivalent to 1000 Nymex (New York Mercantile Exchange) contracts per year to a customer seeking delivery six to ten years out. The trader thus begins by entering into an over-the-counter contract to deliver such gas volumes at prices either already higher than the Nymex forward curve or higher than where he expects the forward curve will shortly be.

- Once the over-the-counter contract has moved into the money versus the forward curve, the trader has an economic gain. The trader then decides whether to leave it open to further gain (or loss) or to buy Nymex contracts to offset the trade sale and lock in the trading gain. For the moment, we assume that the trader leaves his position open.

Accounting for the Gain

- Enron followed the somewhat controversial practice of marking-to-market commodity forward sales or purchases. Although this practice was common among Wall Street financial firms, they deal in financial securities that trade in transparent, liquid markets; as such, pricing is judged to be efficient and easy to observe. These conditions don't always apply in commodity markets, especially at the long end of the forward curve. At the time the events of this case took place, the Nymex forward market for years 6-10 may have been thinly traded or even indicative. To illustrate using the facts of our example, the Nymex forward price may be based on only 100 traded contracts in the target years. Thus, it becomes Enron's judgment call as to whether that price reflects what would be the case if it sought to purchase 1,000 forward contracts equivalent to the gas volumes just sold to the merchant buyer.

- Thus, in marking its trading transactions to market, Enron's traders have considerable discretion to give reasons why the prices used for accounting purposes should be higher, lower, or the same as the Nymex forward curve. The traders can exercise this discretion objectively or in the service of other agendas.

- Once the forward price to be used for mark-to-market accounting has been set, it establishes a theoretical spread: a gain that the firm would harvest if it covered its short sale at the assumed forward price. This 'theoretical spread' must be converted into a present value booked as current operating profit.

- To convert the theoretical spread into current profit, an interest rate must be assumed for discounting purposes. Typically, this interest rate is the current U. S. Treasury rate-possibly with a spread added-for the period in question.

- Once the profit is booked, if the underlying transaction is still open, the accounting gain is susceptible to two forms of variation: (1) changes in the forward commodity price and (2) interest rate changes that would alter the discounting factor.

- It is to eliminate this second source of variation that Enron's traders ask DRA to put interest rate hedges in place. These hedges must match the size of the assumed commodity price gain in each of the periods. Thus, if Enron's traders expected to make a gain of $1 million on their position in year 6, DRA would execute an interest rate hedge with a notional principal amount of $1 million in year 6.

- A decision by the traders to adjust their forward price curve, thereby reducing the expected gain in year 6, would thus require DRA to adjust its interest rate hedge to the new, lower notional principal amount.

Attachment 2

Reasons to Object	Counter-Arguments	Options to Resist	Pros/Cons
1) Violates reporting/ disclosure laws	Not a 'bright line' test; crucial factor is NGTD's judgment	1) Accept as exception, with explicit warning to NGTD	Pro: lowest risk for DRA maybe future cases deterred; if not, fight harder later with more ammunition Con: damaging precedent set; low resistance invites next case
2) Fatally weakens internal risk control	RAC's call, and they signed off. DRA is overreacting	2) Document original terms; take to Law/Accounting	Pro: Strong allies; sound principles in play Con: Ensures high profile and big fallout; will they play?
3) Positions DRA to incur cost unrelated to DRA's decisions	This is a one-off event Part of DRA's business is risk that NGTD will re-do forward curves sometimes	3) Document original terms; take to Ken Maddox	Pro: Has motive and stroke to stop it now and for the future Con: Assures NGTD will fight/retaliate with all they have
4) Unsustainable in terms of DRA organization and morale	DRA is exaggerating the likelihood of recurrence Manage it	4) Document original terms; take to controller Don Cooke	Pro: Strong allies; sound principles in play Con: Can he get it changed?
		5) Negotiate terms to make DRA's approval as painful as possible to discourage future cases	Pro: Could deter future cases without political fight Con: Doesn't sustain principles

Case Study 8

Adjusting the Forward Curve (B): Managing the Showdown Meeting

Things had not gone as well as I'd hoped.
However, the current situation is not unexpected.

R AY HAD DECIDED TO NEGOTIATE with Tom Hopskins, hoping that this form of resistance would prove the least provocative and yet still serve to discourage NGTD from simply "making it up" when it wanted to adjust forward commodity price curves in the future. Tom, however, was not prepared to deal. Instead, he told Ray that he'd better get on board, or there could be serious consequences.

You are a newcomer, Ray. You don't know how things work here yet. Don't pick quarrels with folks you hardly know. This company is built on trading. Don't make the mistake of getting crosswise with our group before you've even had your first performance review.

When Ray persisted in demanding that NGTD absorb the "breakage costs" from adjusting the interest rate swaps, Tom got even more emphatic:

Alright. Don't say I didn't warn you. You are making a big mistake. Nobody outside the trading group has the right to second-guess our indications on the forward curves. That is our business. NGTD is not going to pick up your breakage costs. That's final. I also think we'll need further discussion as to how decisions are made on these matters.

With that, Tom departed. The next morning, Ray received a call from Gene Halsey's secretary. Gene was vice-president of Trading and was Tom's direct supervisor. Gene's secretary advised Ray that there would be a meeting at 1:30 that afternoon in Gene's office. The subject would be the division of responsibilities and delegations of authority between NGTD and DRA. The attendees would be Gene, Tom, Bette Patucka, and Ray. If he wished, Ray was welcome to bring his boss, Ted Hanson, head of Fixed Income.

Before talking to Ted, Ray called Don Cooke and gave him a detailed account of the situation. Don said little but indicated that he would contact Halsey and advise that he too would be attending the meeting. Ray then brought Ted up to speed. Ted was not pleased to hear the story. Neither was he happy knowing that a meeting with Halsey and Hopskins was scheduled for two hours hence.

S.V. Arbogast, *Resisting Corporate Corruption* (pp. 103–107)
© 2008 by M & M Scrivener Press

I really wish you had brought me in on this sooner, Ray. These are not nice guys to mess with. I understand why you did what you did, and I support you in principle. However, Trading makes the money in this company, and that usually means that it wins any escalation wars that occur when issues flash up to higher management. We should have found a way to negotiate this out at lower levels.

Ray indicated that he had been trying to do exactly that but that Tom just tried to roll over his position.

Ted then advised:

When we go to the meeting, NGTD will probably make all its arguments and insist that DRA (1) agree that it has no right to second-guess NGTD's price discovery and (2) has no right to transfer any costs to NGTD's P/L. You make your counterarguments. See whether NGTD offers any compromise. I'll sit and observe, and if I see an opportunity to propose some alternative solution, I'll chime in.

Meeting in Gene Halsey's Office

Gene Halsey opened the meeting:

Thank you all for coming on short notice. The reason for this meeting is to make sure that NGTD and associated departments, such as DRA, are aligned going forward. Tom Hopskins came to see me yesterday afternoon. He was very surprised and very concerned about what he was hearing from Ray Brown. If I understand this correctly, Ray, you are second-guessing NGTD's assessment of the forward price curve for natural gas. Let me be very clear about this. DRA in general and you, Ray, in particular have no role to play in setting forward price curves: none, nada. I know that you are new here and that perhaps where you worked before, commodity price determination was a collaborative thing. Here it is not. The forward price curve for natural gas is a matter of expertise and judgment, which makes it a matter for the experts who make their living trading the stuff every day. Now, are we clear about this?

Ray had decided to bring out the real issues in stages over the course of the discussion.

Gene, I think you've been misinformed or at best gotten only part of the story. The real issue is why Fixed Income should be incurring breakage costs on actual swaps in place because NGTD chooses to revise its forward price curves. More to the point, these revisions must have some other agenda driving them, because nothing has changed. The long end of the curve has not moved in weeks. So, I would summarize the issue this way: Should Fixed Income specifically and Enron in general be incurring cash costs because NGTD has some other reason to revise its former assessment?

Gene started to get more agitated:

What exactly are you insinuating? What is this "other agenda" that you're talking about? Unless you can be more specific and can really back it up, I suggest that you quickly retract what can only be interpreted as an allegation of inappropriate behavior by NGTD.

Ray had anticipated this hard line and responded:

Gene, it's all over the company at working levels that NGTD is making windfall profits on spot and short-term gas right now. What has happened could be easily interpreted as an effort to offset some gains with losses elsewhere: losses being manufactured by a revision of the forward price curve. I've seen the year-to-date P/L numbers for NGTD. They have taken a large blip upward. Unless Ken Maddox decides to discount a large portion of your profits as a "nonrecurring gain," NGTD will have a hefty stewardship target for next year. Coincidentally, the losses generated by this forward curve revision bring NGTD back into reasonable proximity with where profits were trending before this late run-up occurred.

Tom quickly jumped in at this point:

Look, NGTD has an issue with non experts second-guessing our price determinations. DRA has an issue with having to eat breakage costs on the swaps due to our revisions. Why don't we have Accounting book these breakage costs in the General Corporate Expense account, seeing as it has little to do with the primary activity of either group and is essentially the result of coordinating hedging activities designed to stabilize reported earnings?

This thought was quickly endorsed by Ted Hanson, who then turned to Don Cooke for his reaction. Don looked up from his notes and delivered what appeared to be well-considered thoughts:

The first thing that strikes me is that there has been no discussion of the process and mechanics by which NGTD makes its forward curve price determination. Presumably, NGTD does something more than just collect opinions from one or two traders. So, if we really want to get into the facts of this particular case, my auditors can come and have a look at (1) NGTD's written procedures for setting price curves, (2) the extent to which those procedures are routinely followed, and (3) what these procedures show in terms of a justification for a revised curve in this case. With those facts in hand, we should be able to determine whether the revised curve was justified. If so, DRA will have to bear its adjustment costs, since that's how we've operated up to this point.

I don't believe that setting up a separate account or stashing expenses in General Corporate is a good idea. These practices tend to become habit forming and encourage other, more aggressive, parties to try to hide their troubles in such places.

Gene did not like the new direction that the conversation was taking and intervened to restore its former focus:

I'm afraid that there isn't a big, complex price-setting process here, Don. That's the problem with forward trading of long-term commodities: There's no exchange market volume or reliable price survey to provide transparency. We've little more to go on than the judgment—let me emphasize that word, judgment—of the two traders who make this market for us. Recognize, however, that Enron accounts for almost 50 percent of market trades in long-term natural gas. Our judgment is pretty seasoned. That is why it needs to be respected by those who have no role or experience in this specialized market, and that's why we can't tolerate the kinds of attitudes Ray here has been displaying.

Don paused and then spoke again:

Gene, I appreciate your views, but I'm afraid that it is not as simple as that. Whether you realize it or not, what you are admitting is that these two traders can manufacture gains or losses by simply revising their judgment. This is a powerful capacity, and like other powerful capacities, it can be readily abused. Today's traders might be calling them the way they see them. Tomorrow's traders could have entirely different motives, including manufacturing profits to boost bonuses or to cover up losses from unauthorized trading. If one doesn't already exist, a more robust process for price curve determination will have to be created, and it will have to include a paper trail covering the trades used as reference inputs.

One other thing: We need to be concerned about our financial-control practices for very practical reasons. Arbitrary and unjustified adjustments that distort financial reporting can put the company at risk. They can contravene SEC rules, opening the door to investigations by that body and to the inevitable shareholder suits that follow. The distraction to business focus and the damage to our reputation with investors can be enormous. Precisely because it is hard to assess forward curves, it will be easy for outsiders to critique, and sue, if it is not done with defensible process and personal integrity.

Gene then acted to conclude the meeting:

I hear you, Don, but frankly, you are making a mountain out of a molehill. This was a forward curve adjustment like many others NGTD has made. It became an issue only because a newcomer in DRA tried to avoid some relatively small breakage costs and thus questioned our right to do what we've been doing all along. We are not going to allow that, and we are not going to allow DRA to ship its costs across the fence. That's all that's going on here; let's not inflate it into an attack on Enron's whole system of financial control. Frankly, I'm surprised that you're so exercised here. I think that management will be amused. Here is NGTD penalizing itself, lowering its profit performance, and we're suddenly being cast as a bunch of rogue traders. Save that for real culprits, should they ever show up. We've made our position clear. That's the way it's going to be. If anybody wants to discuss it higher up, go for it.

Author's Note

As noted earlier, meetings on proposals with ethics implications are not always conducted as debates about the merits of the proposal. Instead, they often become set-piece battles. As such, they usually unfold with pre-positioning of key attendees and displays of bureaucratic muscle. Case Studies 7 and 8 provide students with an opportunity to see how capable maneuvering within the bureaucracy can be essential to sustaining an ethical business environment. The cases also provide insight into the role that performance rating systems can play in these bureaucratic political struggles.

The two cases are based on an incident that occurred during the second half of 1995. A reference and brief description of these events can be found in Power Failure (p. 88). This account dates the incident at year-end 1995, gives the earnings impact in question as $70 million, and implies that this sum ultimately was moved from 1995 to 1996's results.

The incident has also been described in detail to the Author by one of the key participants, who wishes for the moment to remain anonymous. He has reviewed the facts of the case as written, including the description of the role played by interest rate swaps in hedging mark-to-market profits.

The account of the NGTD traders' desire to reduce their reported profits by adjusting their forward curves is historically accurate. So too is the resistance of DRA to the demand that it reopen and adjust its interest rate swaps. Ray Brown's conversations with various parties and the meeting discussions all are historical creations. These dialogues were created to convey the internal political dynamics associated with resisting a powerful business unit and the tactical options for resisting.

All names in the case are disguised. Since the case involves none of the Enron public figures and the story is heavily fictionalized, no point is served by using actual names of persons who will not be familiar to case readers. Ray Brown's character is loosely based upon the participant who provided details of the case. Organizational units, such as DRA, have been fictionalized from their Enron counterparts.

This case departs in an important way from what happened at Enron. Don Cooke is an invented figure with a specific purpose. His character is intended to illustrate the importance of having an executive concerned about sound financial control heading the financial functions. There is no evidence that such a figure operated at Enron during the time when this incident occurred. This character has been included to give students an opportunity to examine the resistance options that an independent finance function makes possible. Students are specifically encouraged to consider the implications of Don's support for Ray Brown's conduct and for his protection against retaliation. Finally, they should pay particular attention to the ways in which Don Cooke attacks Gene Halsey's position.

Case Study 9

Enron's SPE's:
A Vehicle too Far?

Will this still work?   What else don't I know here?

B EN GLISAN'S DESK WAS COVERED with draft documents. It was December 17, 1997. Glisan, the lead accountant on a transaction to be known as Chewco, shifted uneasily in his chair. He had come across a document indicating that Michael Kopper was to transfer part of his ownership interest in the Chewco Investments partnership to Bill Dodson, his domestic partner. A question crossed Glisan's mind, followed quickly by another: Will this still work? What else don't I know here?

Glisan opened his collar and loosened his tie. It was 7.00 pm, and there was no prospect that he could leave any time soon. The pressure of this deal was building and was already unbelievably intense. Chewco was a deal that had to be closed by year end. The major building blocks of the deal were still not it place. Two weeks minus holidays did not seem to leave very much time for lining things up. Did it leave any time at all for making sure that all the pieces still worked?

Enron was no stranger to year-end deal closing. Indeed, each year end seemed to bring a cascade of transactions designed to boost reported net income, strengthen the look of the balance sheet, and/or dispose of underperforming assets. To a neutral observer, however, there was an increasingly problematic trajectory to recent deals. Successive deals seemed less substantive, more artificially crafted to satisfy the technical requirements of the accounting rules. Even worse, there was a more recent trend of Enron executives' getting involved in deals as independent investors. The plan for Michael Kopper to be a Chewco owner was a case in point. Was there a line here that Enron shouldn't be crossing? Would it be able to spot such a line? Glisan wondered whether maybe the unenviable task of discerning that line might be falling into his lap.

Glisan reminded himself that pulling off creative deals under tough deadlines was something he had sought when leaving Arthur Anderson to join Enron. Creative structures using aggressive accounting were practices that had helped make Enron one of America's most-admired companies. Still, the news about Enron employee Kopper's being a Chewco owner made him pause; did bringing Kopper's domestic partner into the deal improve things? Where did the line between creativity and trouble fall? Ben Glisan glanced again at the documents as his mind drifted back over how the Chewco deal had reached this point.

108

S.V. Arbogast, *Resisting Corporate Corruption* (pp. 108–126)
© 2008 by M & M Scrivener Press

Enron and Special Purpose Entity (SPE) Vehicles

Enron found itself with the need to employ SPEs as a result of Jeff Skilling's Gas Bank. In the late 1980s, Skilling had spotted a way to arbitrage the natural gas market. Skilling noticed that gas users would pay premium prices to secure long-term supplies at fixed prices. Customers would pay this premium precisely because natural gas producers were not then willing to sell long-term, fixed-price gas. Producers were expecting that prices would rise from the rock-bottom levels then prevailing.

Skilling, however, spotted the fact that producers also couldn't find financing to drill for new reserves. Texas banks had taken a licking in the oil bust of 1986; those still operating were loath to back drilling for natural gas when spot prices were below $2/MBTU. Skilling saw that by offering producers financing, Enron could persuade them to supply term gas at fixed prices. Enron then resold the same volumes to utility and industrial customers at a premium, pocketing the difference.

One problem with this nifty scheme was that Enron didn't have much money to lend. The company's lackluster financial performance combined with a heavy debt burden to produce a borderline investment-grade debt rating. Most of the time, Enron sported a Baa or Baa– rating from Moody's and a comparable S&P rating. On a couple of occasions, downgrades dropped Enron below investment grade. Indeed, Ken Lay had spent considerable time consorting with Mike Milken, the junk bond king, in an effort to keep Enron liquid.

Skilling needed more funding to make the Gas Bank work. Eventually, he thought, Enron might be able to get it by securitizing the loans it made to producers. Skilling brought in Andy Fastow, a structured finance specialist from Continental Illinois Bank, to test out the idea. Fastow's first effort was called Cactus and it was a success.

The basic idea behind Cactus was to pool a group of producer loans and sell them off to investors. By pooling the right combination of loans, an aggregate cash flow could be created that resembled a large conventional loan. Enron's version of these producer loans involved something called a Volumetric Production Payment (VPP); under this type of agreement, gas producers committed to deliver physical natural gas, not cash, to repay their loans. Enron's challenge was to monetize this physical product stream so that the investors got repaid in cash.

Fastow's structuring approach was to sell the pool of loans and associated VPPs into an SPE created expressly for the transaction while simultaneously selling the SPE to investors. These connected sales generated cash that reimbursed Enron for its prior loan to gas producers. Enron then contracted to repurchase the physical gas over time from the SPE. Enron's payments thus provided the cash that the vehicle needed to pay its new owners their investment return.

Looking through the arrangement, the SPE's investors were funding Enron's producer loans and getting repaid by Enron. However, Enron's payment obligation was embedded in a sales contract rather than a debt instrument. Moreover, the arrangement was secured by the SPE's right to receive physical gas from the producers. Accordingly, the deal was not booked on Enron's balance sheet as a debt obligation. Instead, it was treated as a sale of partnership interests and a purchase of physical gas.

This accounting treatment also ensured that Enron could grow the Gas Bank without adding debt to its balance sheet. Once Cactus was up and running, it would borrow on its own to buy new VPP loans originated by Enron. In this way, Cactus became an ongoing fund-raising center for the Gas Bank. Attachment 1 outlines the Cactus SPE structure and cash flows.

Cactus was a success for several reasons. First, Enron wanted to be in the natural gas trading rather than the financing business; making loans was simply a means of attracting the supplies it needed to put together the rest of the package. Cactus enabled Enron to accomplish this without further burdening its already leveraged balance sheet. Second, Cactus worked technically and for solid reasons; the vehicle and all its debt were considered to be the property of its owners and not of Enron. Its owners were substantive investors, a list that included GE Capital. Its management was independent and looked after the interests of its owners. The pricing of Enron's VPP sales into Cactus was a market price negotiated among independent parties. All this was possible because the margins available to Enron on the gas arbitrage were robust. Said differently, Enron could extract a sufficiently low purchase price from the producers that it could let the owners of Cactus earn acceptable returns on their VPPs and still clear an attractive margin when Enron bought back/resold the gas to the ultimate customers. So long as producers couldn't get loans and customers couldn't get long-term, fixed-price supplies elsewhere, Enron could afford to pay real returns to real third parties.

Shortly after Cactus got going, a similar deal literally fell into Enron's lap. By 1993, Enron was seeing increasing competition from the banking community. VPP deal flow was starting to dry up. Fortunately, a household name investor, the California Public Employees' Retirement System (CalPERS), was impressed by Enron's creativity. CalPERS contacted Fastow, proposing a deal. CalPERS indicated that it was willing to invest $250 million in a joint venture to be run by Enron. The idea was for Enron to contribute comparable capital and to use the combined proceeds to make energy loans and acquisitions.

Fastow eagerly seized the opportunity and developed the Joint Energy Development Investors partnership (JEDI). In the structure ultimately implemented, Enron contributed $250 million of its stock to match CalPERS's cash. This gave each partner a 50 percent stake. Fastow then had the venture borrow $500 million; this capitalized the partnership with $750 million in cash to invest. Over the next several years, JEDI did exactly that, making a series of loans and acquisitions, most of which turned out well.

Before the end of 1997, CalPERS indicated that it wanted to sell its share of JEDI in order to invest in another Enron deal. Enron then estimated that the value of CalPERS's JEDI stake had climbed from the original $250 million to $383 million. Attachment 2 details the JEDI structure and some of the merchant investments made.

Like Cactus, JEDI also worked. Enron had a real partner in the form of CalPERS, and its deals were done with other third parties that looked after their own interests in the various negotiations. Consequently, JEDI qualified as a deconsolidated subsidiary of Enron. As such, JEDI's debts were not combined with those of Enron on Enron's published balance sheet.

Things began to change shortly thereafter. Enron's financial team started to view structured financings as an open-ended arena for creative development. Fastow and his team were widely praised for Cactus and JEDI. Skilling and others were interested to see what else they could dream up. This context coincided with the emergence of a real problem for Enron: The company's business strategies were voraciously consuming capital. Giant international power projects, such as Teesside and Dabhol, cost billions of dollars and took years to build before any cash flowed in. When problems occurred, as they did at Dabhol, the cash hole just got deeper. Acquisitions also required major cash outlays. Enron bought utilities in Brazil, Argentina, Columbia, and the Philippines. It also bought Portland General in the United States. Meanwhile, Enron's handsome reported profits were not bringing in comparable cash flow. Mark-to-market accounting was making Enron look like a profit machine. However, Enron's financial reality was one of producing negative net cash generation year after year.

This reality meant ongoing pressure on the finance team to fund the deficit with new financing. Insiders called this "Feeding the Beast." This basic challenge then combined with a second, more complicated one: How could Enron keep raising new capital without scaring off its existing lenders?

In fact, even at the peak of its success, Enron was a fragile financial entity. This fragility had many contributing causes, the four most important of which were:

1. A starting position characterized by a lower investment-grade debt rating.
2. The dependence of its lucrative trading business on maintaining an investment-grade rating, so as to avoid having to cash collateralize trades—this meant Enron had little maneuvering room. It could ill afford to "leverage up" and temporarily surrender its investment grade rating.
3. A reluctance to scale-back new investment to levels more in line with actual cash generation.
4. Poor internal cost control in many business units.

These four points combined to constrict Enron's financial flexibility. Enron didn't generate the cash needed to pay for its investments, it didn't have the balance sheet room to finance the shortfall, and it didn't dare give up its investment-grade rating for fear of strangling its lucrative trading business.

Enron sought to solve this conundrum by presenting a relentlessly positive profile to the capital markets. Hitting quarterly earnings targets became a necessity. Maintaining Enron's image as the generator of brilliantly conceived investment opportunities was equally important. Difficulties and failures, if acknowledged, would invite unwelcome doubts from rating agencies, analysts, and lenders. Step by step, Enron developed a deep commitment to managing the information it shared—and didn't share—with investors. As part of managing its information, Enron worked harder to keep the full extent of its indebtedness from appearing on its balance sheet.

This called for less straightforward ways to feed the beast. These methods would have to put cash in Enron's coffers but not be identifiable as debt or as an obvious "debt equivalent." Enron's next-favorite tool of choice became the "Pre Pay" (Attachment 3). This transaction was designed to be treated as a set of commercial transactions: one a forward sale of gas; the other, a forward purchase. However, the timing of payment was different for the two sides of the deal. For the forward sale, Enron would collect a discounted cash lump sum up front. On the forward purchase, Enron would pay the supplier over time. Netting out the two transactions, the surviving cash flows resembled a loan: cash received upfront and repaid with interest over time. However, because these flows were tied to underlying commodity transactions, Enron chose not to net them out; the residual "loan in substance" thus remained disguised. Enron booked the forward sale as revenue; the forward purchase went on the balance sheet as an account payable. Neither transaction entered into traditional measures of indebtedness, such as interest coverage or debt/total capital. Enron did many of these Pre Pays, usually to bolster reported cash generation prior to financial statement dates.

A further expansion in the use of SPEs came with the 1997 Whitewing transaction (Attachment 4). This deal started as a way of raising some $1 billion in new debt and then having this financing "converted" from debt to equity. In reality, however, the conversion was more accounting optics than substance. In Step 1, Enron's treasury borrowed $579 million from Citibank and set up Whitewing Investments, an SPE partnership. Whitewing then borrowed another $500 million, also from Citibank but funneled through a bank-controlled SPE. Enron next assigned to Whitewing the debt it owed to Citibank but leaving an Enron guarantee in place. Enron then delivered $1 billion of new-issue preferred stock to Whitewing, receiving in return $420 million of the cash that SPE partnership had raised from Citibank.

The net effect of these back-and-forth flows was as follows:

- Enron raised ~$1 billion in cash.
- Enron's new debt and preferred stock were now lodged in a severable SPE, along with another $500 million of subsidiary debt.
- All the $1,079 billion in debt would be off Enron's balance sheet and onto

that of the now "stand-alone" SPE. Enron would retain a guarantee on the $579 million, but that would be consigned to a financial statement footnote if it appeared anywhere at all.

- What would show on Enron's balance sheet was the issuance of $1 billion of preferred stock to a third party and the cash it received in return. From an accounting perspective, it would appear that Enron had completed a private placement of preferred stock to an outside investor.

Fastow's team accomplished this accounting severance by having outside investors contribute a sliver of equity to Whitewing. Early in Fastow's career, Arthur Anderson had advised on the conditions required for an SPE to be viewed as independent.

- At least 3 percent of its total capitalization had to come from genuine third parties.
- Management decisions at the SPE had to be in independent hands.
- Enron could not agree to compensate the SPE for its losses[1]

Examined from another perspective, these rules implied that 97 percent of the capitalization of an SPE could come from the party with which the vehicle would be doing business. Upon hearing this, Fastow reportedly had been incredulous. Supposedly, Fastow commented that his gardener could probably raise the 3 percent equity required to create an "independent" entity.[2]

Although the equity in Whitewing was small in dollar terms, it was crafted to exceed Enron's equity in that vehicle. Thus, the net effect of outside investors putting up a sliver of equity was to convert Enron's Whitewing stake into a minority interest. Whitewing's assets and liabilities then disappeared from Enron's balance sheet, taking all the Citibank loans along with it. Enron did disclose Whitewing in its financial statements but as a minority-interest entry that showed up in Enron's equity accounts. Debt had indeed been converted into equity through the mechanism of selling preferred stock to a debt-laden affiliated entity and then severing that SPE from Enron for accounting purposes.

Creative as Whitewing may have appeared, it was open to the allegation that the vehicle's sole purpose was to mislead outside investors. What substance was there to the transaction? With Whitewing, Citibank made a guaranteed loan to Enron and another loan to a subsidiary whose principal asset was Enron preferred stock. Yet Enron booked this transaction as if it had made a minority interest investment in a third-party company. Enron's appearance and reality were getting farther apart.

Enron later answered the Whitewing "substance issue", although not in the most straightforward way. Enron had Whitewing buy over $1 billion in assets from various Enron businesses.

A further "step-out" occurred with the RADR transaction, a small deal that used financial engineering similar to Whitewing. The business problem here was straightforward. Early in 1997, Enron had acquired the Zond Company, an owner of wind farms. Zond's wind farms qualified for federally mandated benefits, including higher prices on electricity sold to utilities. To maintain these benefits, Zond could not be more than 50 percent owned by an existing utility. That was not a problem for Enron when it acquired the company. Later in 1997, however, Enron bought Portland General, an electric utility. With this acquisition, Enron became a utility for regulatory purposes, and thus Zond would no longer qualify for its special benefits.

Enron's solution was to divest 50 percent of Zond into an SPE that would be independent for regulatory purposes but that Enron would still control economically. Attachment 5 describes of the structure used and the associated cash flows. Only $17 million—50 percent of the valuation placed on Zond—was involved. Raising 3 percent of this sum as independent equity was not a daunting task.

The actual raising of this equity had first proved problematic, then mysterious. Andy Fastow's original approach had run into trouble with Enron's accountants and lawyers. Fastow and Michael Kopper had formed an investor group, Alpine Investors that included a personal friend, Patty Melcher, Fastow's wife's family, and themselves. The accountants and lawyers indicated that the involvement of Enron executives and family members would not meet the independence requirement. Alpine Investors, as originally devised, didn't work.

Then things got murky. Patty Melcher and the Fastow family disappeared from the deal. Two entities—RADR ZWS and RADR ZWS MM—were formed to buy Zond (Attachment 5). The owners of record were Kathy Wetmore and Bill Dodson: Fastow's real estate agent and Michael Kopper's domestic partner, respectively. Where these owners got the $510,000 needed to reach the 3 percent equity requirement was unclear. Circumstances, however, continued to point to Fastow and Kopper as still being involved behind the scenes.

This history comprised the SPE trajectory that formed the backdrop to the Chewco transaction. Enron had certainly mastered the use of vehicles to attract outside capital while insulating Enron's balance sheet. Increasingly however, Enron was also using them to disguise its actual financial condition; most recently, it appeared that SPEs were employed as vehicles for the involvement of Enron executives in their own deals. If so, this involvement would contravene express advice from Enron's deal lawyers and accountants.

Chewco Investments

As he stared at the Chewco documents, Ben was aware that he had been at Enron only a short time. Glisan knew that he was a good, maybe exceptional, accountant. He had graduated from the University of Texas MBA program, earning a 4.0 grade point average in the process. His first job was something special. Glisan was hired as one of only two MBAs brought into a pilot Coopers & Lybrand program to test the concept of combining audit and consulting services for clients regarded as high risk engagements. In 1995, Glisan moved to Arthur Anderson for the chance to work on the Enron account. Late in 1996, he followed the path of other Anderson accountants and joined Enron. Glisan was then thirty years old.

Andy Fastow quickly spotted Glisan. Fastow liked Glisan's in-depth knowledge of structured-finance accounting rules and his ability to massage them to make deals work. Glisan had spent time at Bank One in between undergraduate and MBA school. Fastow noted that Glisan knew how to discuss deals with bankers and how to present aggressive accounting in the most favorable light. Glisan found himself thrilled to be working at Enron for a well-known figure like Andy Fastow.

This history now made Glisan's Chewco dilemmas more acute. Crying foul on Chewco's structure would mean turning against Fastow, his boss and mentor. Glisan knew that Fastow's immediate reaction would be surprise that Ben was abandoning "creative problem solving". Fastow was also well known for becoming intensely angry at individuals who objected to his deals. Crossing Fastow would almost certainly produce an instant reevaluation of Glisan and could convert Fastow into an enemy.

What was the problem with Chewco, anyway? Most of the deal is straightforward enough. CalPERS wants out of JEDI I before investing in JEDI II. There is nothing troublesome about that. The price for CalPERS' stake also is not an issue. Enron has agreed that CalPERS' interest is worth $383 million. That is the price Chewco is set to pay, and it is a fair market valuation. CalPERS can hardly complain; at that price it will have earned a 22 percent annual return on its original $250 million investment.

No, the problem with Chewco didn't lie with these fundamentals. Rather, it lay with what seemed to be a minor detail: the provision of the $11.4 million of independent equity needed to render Chewco independent of Enron for accounting purposes. It was the RADR issue all over again.

As outlined in Attachment 6, Chewco needed $383 million to buy CalPERS's stake in JEDI. By December 17, that step had already been taken. In order to assure CalPERS that the sale would occur in 1997, Enron had simply lent Chewco the purchase price in November. Chewco had then paid CalPERS for its share of JEDI. With that piece finalized, the rest of the deal had to be transacted by December 31; otherwise, Chewco and JEDI would be consolidated Enron subsidiaries, and all their assets and, most especially, their debts would show up on Enron's 1997 financial statements.

Completing the transaction principally meant finding the $11.4 million of independent equity. Here is where the problems began. Most of this money was supposed to come from Barclays Bank. However, Barclays was balking at putting up real equity. It was seeking a more protected return. The current discussion was focused on Barclays' purchasing fixed-return "equity certificates." Would these stand scrutiny as equity? Barclays wasn't making this issue any easier by also talking in terms of getting some form of cash collateral in reserve accounts to guarantee its investment.

The remainder of the equity money—a minuscule $125,000—was supposed to be provided by Michael Kopper. One reason that Andy Fastow was so confident about Chewco was that he had already pitched the deal to Jeff Skilling on the basis of Kopper both putting it together and being the "outside investor." Skilling apparently had been OK with that. However, no accountants or lawyers had been in the room when Fastow and Skilling had this conversation. Moreover, Fastow and Kopper had worked hard to keep the identity of the Chewco investors secret from the lawyers reviewing the deal. One lawyer had asked Kopper for details of the investor group and had been told: "Enron doesn't have a right to know more. We're negotiating for Chewco, but it's behind a black curtain. You're not supposed to know what's there. That's what all the parties have agreed to."[3]

Kopper had structured his part of the deal as follows: the bulk of his "equity," $115,000, was to be injected into Chewco from an entity, SONR 1, controlled by Kopper. The remaining $10,000 would go into another SPE, Little River Funding (LRF). This entity was to own Big River Funding (BRF). Barclays would lend most of the necessary $11.4 million to BRF, which in turn would purchase Chewco's equity certificates (Attachment 6). Making sure that Little River Funding was an independent SPE would also keep BRF independent. The document sitting in Glisan's pile transferred Kopper's equity in LRF to Dodson.

Glisan knew that having someone like Kopper put up the equity money risked invalidating the deconsolidation of Chewco. It was the same as with RADR; the accountants and lawyers had been very clear that employees of Enron were not sufficiently "independent" to meet the test, and since the invalidation of any part of the 3 percent equity would cause the structure to fail, including Kopper in the deal for any percentage could be a fatal flaw.

Would Kopper's transferring his interests to his domestic partner, change this result?

Ben again thought about the issue of crossing the line. Was it wrong to dress up Enron's financial statements? Companies did that all the time. What was so different here? Were any laws being broken?

Glisan took a deep breath and eyed the document pile anew. A Kopper/Dodson transfer only highlighted a fundamental point: Having Kopper anywhere in the deal endangered the technical integrity of the transaction. Was now the moment for Glisan to point this out?

A sinking feeling afflicted Glisan's stomach. To whom would he point it out? Fastow and Kopper undoubtedly knew and either thought that it was all right or thought these facts would never see the light of day. Pointing out the obvious to them would lead nowhere except to negative career implications. Was there anybody else to talk to, someone who could do something about the Chewco deal at this late stage and would not be inclined to "shoot the messenger?"

It is tempting just to let the transaction go forward. Fastow and Kopper are probably right. The details associated with the 3 percent independent equity will probably never come to light. So long as Arthur Anderson signs off on the deal, nobody else will ever dig that deep. After all, the only non-Enron party in the deal with interests to protect is CalPERS, and it is satisfied. Fastow and Kopper act as though they already had Anderson on board for the whole deal.

Ben Glisan seemed to make up his mind. Then he thought again: What else might be sitting in those documents?

Attachment 1—Cactus SPE Off Balance Sheet Structure

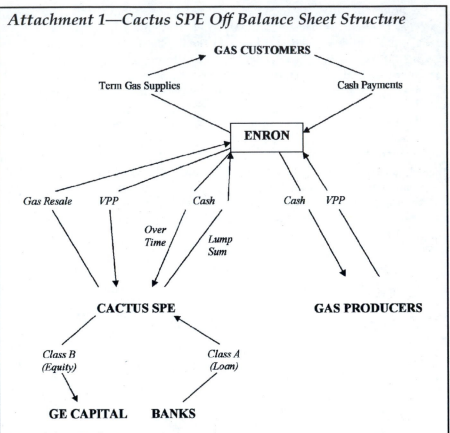

Deal in Substance

- Enron loans money to Gas Producers in return for a Volumetric Production Payment (VPP), a producer commitment to deliver specified volumes of gas in the future
- Enron sells the Producer loans and VPP to an SPE (Cactus) financed by banks and owned by GE Capital. The cash from selling the VPP allows Enron to recover the funds used to make its loan to Gas Producers
- Enron agrees to purchase the VPP gas at a fixed price over time from Cactus. Enron's payments will allow Cactus to repay its loans and pay its owner a return.
- Enron agrees to provide long-term gas supplies to industrial customers at a premium price

Accounting Results

- All financing of gas producers ultimately is on the SPE's, not Enron's balance sheet

Attachment 2—Joint Energy Development Investors (JEDI)

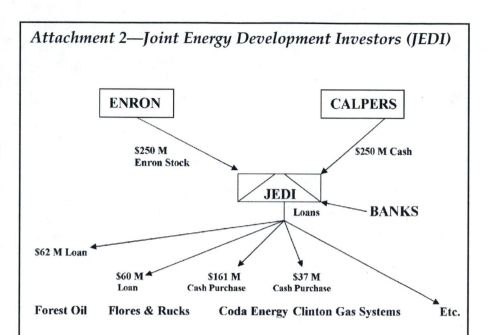

Deal in Substance

- Enron and CalPERS have a joint investment in a partnership making merchant investments and loans to energy companies.
- Enron invests stock while CalPERS invests cash in JEDI.
- Enron's stock investment helps secure borrowings from banks, which proceeds are combined with CalPERS's cash to fund loans and acquisitions.
- Enron acquires a 50 percent interest in profitable loans and merchant investments without investing any cash or borrowing any money "on balance sheet."

Accounting Results

- Enron books investment in non-consolidated entity as an asset, equity as a liability
- Enron books 50 percent of JEDI's annual profits; later, it will mark-to-market the value of its investment in JEDI, including the increased value of Enron's stock.
- JEDI investments and borrowings are not on Enron's balance sheet.

Attachment 3—MAHONIA Pre-Pay Structure

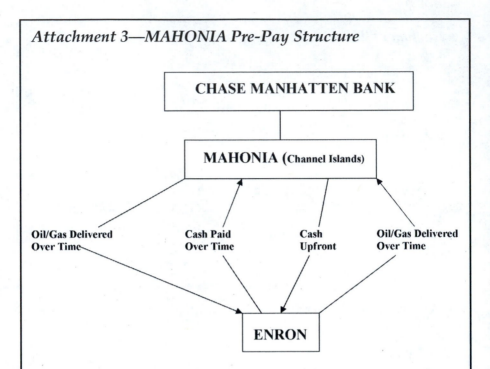

Deal in Substance
- Chase's Mahonia subsidiary pays cash in return for Enron's commitment to deliver oil/gas over time.
- Enron simultaneously agrees to repurchase the oil/gas delivered to Mahonia
- The contract price difference between what Enron receives for its delivery commitment and what it pays for the oil/gas repurchases provides Mahonia with the equivalent of payment of interest and loan principal.

Accounting Results
- Enron booked the transactions as prepaid oil/gas sales and oil/gas purchases made over time.
- Enron did not "net" the oil/gas sales/purchases, revealing the loan.
- No debt was thus reflected on Enron's balance sheet.

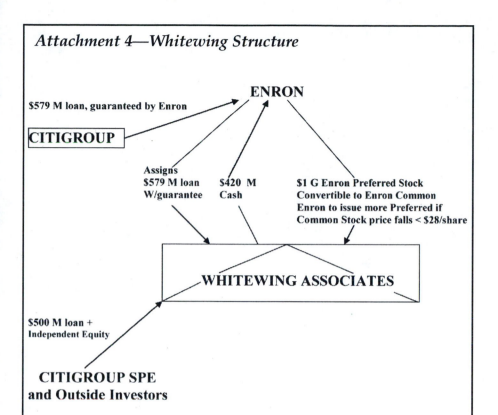

Deal in Substance

- Stage 1: Enron raises $1 billion from a bank but converts it to a minority equity interest in an SPE; $79 million pays return to Citigroup lenders. Outside investors contributes 3 percent independent equity to convert Whitewing into a deconsolidated entity.

Accounting Results

- Stage 1: Enron strengthens balance sheet via booking issuance of preferred stock, while receiving and booking $1 billion cash from Whitewing; Enron retains guarantee on $500 million loan from Citibank, which is off balance sheet (footnote).
- Stage 2: Enron books sales of assets to Whitewing as revenue and operating profits

Attachment 5—RADRs Structure

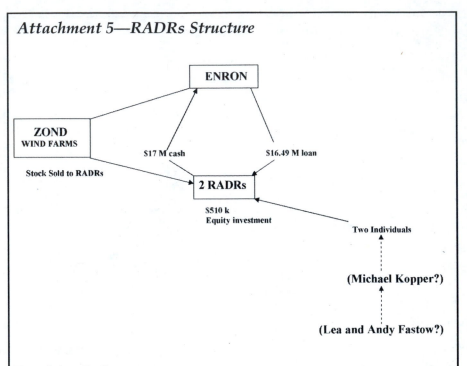

Deal in Substance

- Enron sells Zond wind farms to an "independent" entity to retain "Qualifying Facilities" (QF) benefits in wake of Enron's acquisition of Portland General Utility.
- Entity is controlled by Enron employees, including Kopper and Fastow and his wife, whose involvement is not known by Enron; the other individual is Bill Dodson, Kopper's domestic partner.
- RADRs receive a 50+ percent guaranteed return from Enron, which is ultimately realized by the Fastows.

Accounting Results

- Transaction was not treated as a sale for accounting purposes. Enron retained all economic risks and rewards of the wind farms and had an option to repurchase the Zond stock
- Enron advised the Federal Energy Regulatory Commission (FERC) that the Zond assets were now owned by the RADRs and described the structure; FERC approved continuing Zond's QF status

Attachment 6—CHEWCO

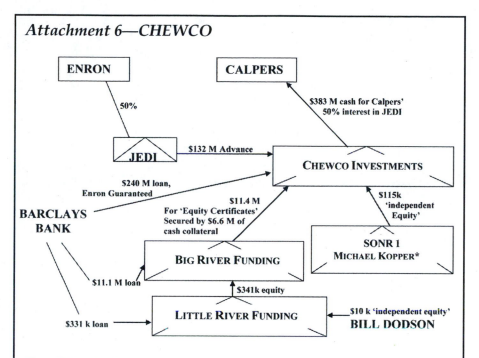

Deal in Substance

- CalPERS is persuaded to participate in JEDI II by having its demand to divest its share of JEDI I satisfied by Chewco's buying its interest for $383 million, a 22 percent annual return.
- Barclays' equity in Chewco has characteristics of a collateralized loan.
- Kopper/Dodson equity in Chewco is more than equaled by the management fee paid one week after deal closed; it could be argued that thereafter, Kopper/Dodson have no equity economically at risk.

Accounting Results

- Enron treated the equity in Chewco as independent and thus booked neither the $240 million loan nor the $132 million JEDI advance as Enron balance sheet obligations.

Author's Note

When does creativity cross the line into unethical behavior? Few companies pushed these boundaries as aggressively as did Enron. This case presents a full trajectory of this issue, tracking the progression of Enron's use of SPE finance vehicles. It then presents the predicament of one key figure, accountant Ben Glisan, who finds himself questioning whether Chewco, the "next deal," has, in fact, crossed the line. This case also illustrates how technical details bear on ethics issues. Finally, it presents a classic case in which the driving force for unethical action is less Enron's business needs, which can be satisfied in a variety of ways, than the personal agendas of certain employees.

In September 2003, Ben Glisan pleaded guilty to conspiring to commit fraud and was sentenced to five years in prison. *Conspiracy of Fools* provides an account (p. 672) of Glisan's being brought from prison in jump suit and handcuffs to the Houston federal courthouse on February 19, 2004, where he crossed paths with Jeff Skilling on the day the Enron Task Force presented its forty two count indictment against the former Enron CEO. Glisan was indicted for his work on the Raptor vehicles, a series of SPE structures that built on the RADR and Chewco transactions. Glisan's ultimate decision in the Chewco matter was to say nothing about any problems; he thereafter became a willing ally of Fastow and Kopper.

Because he was so clearly at the center of Chewco and had knowledge of the detailed terms and conditions, this case is built around Glisan. It was Glisan who had the clearest opportunity and the most detailed knowledge to spot the ethical lines being crossed with Chewco. Although he later denied that he knew about Barclays' receiving collateral or that Kopper was the other "outside investor" in Chewco, various eyewitnesses cited in *The Smartest Guys in the Room* (p. 169) say that he was present at meetings where it was discussed. An investigator cited in the same book later concluded: "It is implausible…that he [Glisan] would have concluded that Chewco met the 3% rule."[4]   Finally, the Powers Committee Report had this to say on the subject of Glisan and Chewco:

> "There is little doubt that Kopper (who signed all of the agreements with Barclays and the December 30 letter) was aware of the relevant facts. The evidence also indicates that Glisan, who had principal responsibility for Enron's account for the transaction, attended meetings at which the details of the reserve accounts and the cash collateral were discussed. If Glisan knew about the cash collateral in the reserve accounts at closing, it is implausible that he (or any other knowledgeable accountant) would have concluded that Chewco met the 3% standard."[5]

It is not clear from the published sources whether Glisan ever had a moment of doubt such as is depicted in this case. However, the Chewco deal happened early in Glisan's Enron career; indeed, it is the first deal for which Glisan attracted attention. When he first joined the company, Glisan was well liked; at that time, according to *The Smartest Guys in the Room,* Glisan was described as affable and even a "boy scout." In those early days at Enron, Glisan may indeed have had one or several moments of doubt about whether the deal would work. By 1999, however, he is described in *The Smartest Guys in the Room* as having "morphed into the swaggering arrogance that characterized so many Enron executive."[6]

The sequential description of Enron's SPE deals draws from several accounts including *Enron, The Rise and Fall* (pp. 122-127), *Power Failure* (pp. 155-164), *The Smartest Guys in the Room* (pp. 153-161,166-170) and *Conspiracy of Fools* (pp. 142-147, 152-158, 161-164). Details of Whitewing, Mahonia, and RADR appear in *The Smartest Guys in the Room* (pp. 155-156, 159, and 166-167 respectively). The various accounts were written in that order, and some details came out later that were not available or not picked up by the earlier authors. For example, *The Smartest Guys in the Room* has a detailed account of the RADR transaction, yet it is only with *Conspiracy of Fools* that the identity of the two outside investors, through whom Kopper funneled the Fastow money, becomes clear. The Kopper quote denying Chewco information to one of the deal lawyers also comes from *Conspiracy of Fools* (p. 156). The diagram of the Chewco transaction (Attachment 6) is consistent with that provided in the Powers Committee Report (p. 51).

The other aspect of Chewco that merits attention is its disproportionate impact on Enron's ultimate fate. Fundamentally, the deal involved finding a buyer for the CalPERS's stake in JEDI. The underlying assets were valuable. Multiple sources indicate that Enron could have found arms-length buyers for the position. However, Andy Fastow had other plans.

Emboldened by getting away with a "fronted investment" into the RADRs, Fastow kept his private-equity specialist, Jim Timmons, from shopping the JEDI opportunity to pension funds; Fastow and Kopper also stonewalled Jordan Mintz, an attorney working on the deal, as to the identity of the outside investors. A legitimate solution to CalPERS's requirement was preempted while information that might have enabled the deal's fatal flaws to be spotted was denied to those documenting the transaction. Other than Kopper, only Glisan was probably aware of all the pieces of the puzzle.

Chewco then became the moment when Fastow and Kopper's pursuit of private gain began to put Enron at risk. They went against the explicit advice received earlier about the necessary independence of the 3 percent outside equity. Later on, when Enron could least afford it, the lawyers and accountants would discover Fastow's deception. Near the end of October 2001, the Chewco collateral accounts and the money trail back to Kopper would come to light. Enron would have no choice but to take both Chewco and JEDI and all their debts back onto Enron's consolidated balance sheet. This would happen just as Enron was caught in a spiral of debt-rating downgrades. It would also help convince Chuck Watson and Dynegy that they could not rely on Enron's financial statements or representations to accurately portray the company's financial position. Dynegy would soon terminate its proposal to merge with Enron, ending the company's last hope of avoiding bankruptcy.

Notes

1. *Conspiracy of Fools,* p. 54.
2. Ibid., p. 54.
3. Ibid., p. 156.
4. Ibid., p. 168.
5. Powers Committee Report, pp. 52-53.
6. *The Smartest Guys in the Room,* p. 154.

Jeff Skilling and LJM (A): The "Shoot the Moon" Meeting

Maybe I need to quit being the treasurer and find something else to do.

OWN ON STAGE AT THE COMPAQ CENTER, Crosby, Stills, Nash and Young worked through their Reunion Tour repertoire. In a skybox high above, Jeff McMahon, the Enron treasurer, had just finished recounting how unhappy he was at work. Cliff Baxter, Enron's head of asset divestments, sipped his drink and turned towards McMahon.

"I'll talk to Skilling. And before you do anything, you should talk to him too." [1]

It was March 8, 2000. Over the past six months, McMahon's people had been negotiating to sell assets to LJM2, an entity which had been put together by Enron CFO Andrew Fastow. In each negotiation, Michael Kopper, still an Enron employee, would sit on the other side of the table representing LJM2. The arrangement didn't make sense to McMahon; even worse, his people were reporting that it was making a travesty of the negotiations. Kopper would wear his "Enron hat" one moment and sit in on the staff meetings where McMahon's negotiators discussed minimum prices they'd accept. Later, Kopper would represent LJM2, state that he knew what price Enron would take, and make it clear that LJM2 would pay nothing more. When McMahon's team resisted, digging in to get a better price, they'd sometimes receive a call from Fastow implying that they were being unreasonable and that the deal needed to close quickly. McMahon was beginning to sense that his team was becoming intimidated. After all, Fastow would be representing them at Enron's Performance Review Committee (PRC), whose rankings ultimately determined employee salary and bonus treatment.

Bonus treatment was a very sore subject for McMahon. On more than one occasion, he had spoken to Fastow about the problems of negotiating with Kopper/LJM2. Coincidentally, in January, McMahon found his annual bonus cut back and the reduction channeled into a larger bonus for Kopper.

All this ate at McMahon during the concert. Chatting casually, it occurred to him that Baxter was the perfect individual to consult about LJM2. Baxter was an Enron veteran who had seen it all. He was one of Jeff Skilling's close confi-

S.V. Arbogast, *Resisting Corporate Corruption* (pp. 127–140)
© 2008 by M & M Scrivener Press

dents. Moreover, Baxter was known as one of the few at Enron who could speak his mind to the COO; this included telling Skilling bad news and things he did-n't want to hear. Despite his leaving the company on more than one occasion, Skilling had always kept the door open for Baxter, and he had always come back.

McMahon began by asking Baxter what he knew about LJM2 and got a "more than you think" response. They discussed the Enron board's granting Fastow a waiver of the Conflict of Interest Policy. (A brief resume of Jeff McMahon's career with Enron to this point appears in Annex A.)

Then McMahon broached the heart of his concerns:

"You can't run a finance department this way. You have Enron people negotiating against other Enron people. And Andy is their supervisor, controls all the promotions and raises and bonuses, and he has an interest in the compa-ny Enron's negotiating against. It's just a mess."[2]

When Baxter indicated that he had similar problems with LJM, McMahon acknowledged that he felt stymied. He told Baxter that he had spoken to Fastow about the need to fix things and about how to do it. Nothing had happened. Now McMahon was thinking that his next best move was to get out of the trea-surer's role and to move somewhere else within Enron. It was this comment that had elicited Baxter's advice to speak to Skilling before doing anything else.

One week later, McMahon sat in his office, staring at a pad of lined paper. In the interim, he had given Fastow one more chance to fix the LJM conflicts and had gotten the same runaround. Now McMahon had an 11:30 meeting with Skilling. He penciled "Discussion Points" at the top his pad and began to organize his thoughts.

It had seemed so clear after talking to Baxter that going to Skilling was the way to fix the problem. Now McMahon wasn't so sure. Fastow would regard "going over his head" as a declaration of war. Fastow was not only his boss. Fastow was known within Enron as a vicious political infighter. In going to Skilling, McMahon was probably compromising his Enron career prospects and possibly betting the career itself.

Well, the die was cast. McMahon was on Skilling's calendar and had only a couple of hours left to prepare. Going to Skilling on LJM was a one-shot deal. McMahon had to set up exactly the right issues, marshal just the right argu-ments and evidence, and give Skilling his best thoughts on how to fix LJM. If McMahon got it wrong, he would pay a price, probably a big one. Skilling could easily end up seeing McMahon—the messenger—as the problem, one to be turned over to Fastow's tender mercies for disposition.

McMahon eyed his pad and began to decide how to open the discussion with Skilling. It occurred to him that getting exactly the right issue on the table upfront was essential. Skilling was lightening-quick mentally; that could be a curse as well as a blessing if he jumped on the first point McMahon trotted out and drew the wrong conclusions. No, Skilling had to be directed to the right agenda. McMahon began to reflect back over his group's encounters with LJM and to look for that best opening message.

Fastow Forms LJM

Andy Fastow had actually been recruited by Jeff Skilling. Fastow was working in structured finance at Continental Illinois Bank when Skilling hired him in 1991. Skilling's objective was to use structured-finance techniques to raise capital for funding loans to natural gas producers. Skilling would then use the Volumetric Production Payment (VPP) agreements concluded with these producers to provide the physical supplies he needed to put his Gas Bank scheme into effect.

Fastow quickly succeeded in developing innovative financing structures that impressed Skilling. Gas trading eventually expanded into electricity trading, and Enron's need for capital only grew. Fastow's organization grew with it, enhanced by his penchant for self-promotion. At company offsite meetings, Fastow would hand out dollar bills with his picture on them and the logo "Come to me; I'll fund all your deals."

Ambitious and aware that for all its creativity, finance was simply a support function at Enron, Fastow lobbied for a chance to run one of the business groups. In late 1995, he got his opportunity. Skilling was looking for a leader to jump-start Enron's entry into the retail electricity business, and decided to give Fastow the chance. Fastow jumped at the opportunity and promised a creative, out-of-the-box entry strategy. After assembling a team and devoting some months of feverish activity, he ended up producing a thin presentation that Skilling dismissed as "gobbledygook." Soon thereafter, by mutual consent, Fastow moved back to finance.

Humiliated by this failure, Fastow channeled his frustration into another plan that had been forming in his mind. Enron was always looking to sell off assets. Sometimes, this involved harvesting profits on good investments; other times, it was done to raise needed cash, move impaired assets off the balance sheet or insulate Enron's P/L statements from losses. It was not always easy to find third parties that would pay what Enron thought the assets were worth (or needed them to be worth). It was even more difficult to find them in time to close a deal before an accounting reporting date.

Fastow thought that he had a solution to this problem. He would organize an equity fund that Enron could count on as a buyer for its assets. Fastow had noticed that only 3 percent of an entity's capitalization had to be "independent" equity for that unit to be treated as independent. With Enron effectively providing 97 percent of any vehicle's capitalization and with Fastow having inside knowledge of the assets in play, he thought that it would be easy to raise slivers of independent equity from friendly sources. During the early 1990's, when Fastow first began thinking along these lines, some "independent" money raised was from "Friends of Enron" (FOEs), one of whom was Fastow's real estate agent.

Now on the heels of his retail-electricity humiliation, Fastow began thinking in bigger terms. He would build a big private-equity fund that could handle anything Enron might care to offer up, and he, Andy Fastow, would be both an "independent" investor and the operator of the fund.

It was an audacious scheme. Essentially, Fastow would offer Enron instant accounting convenience. Whenever Enron needed to produce an accounting result, Andy's fund would be there offering a ready option. In return, Fastow wanted three things: (1) high returns on equity, (2) minimal risk, and (3) the opportunity to benefit personally. Naturally, Fastow couldn't spell his terms out that baldly; corporate policies and normal commercial practice clearly stood in the way. It would take Fastow some time to dismantle these barriers. This he now set out to do.

Fastow began the dismantling with the RADR transaction. This involved the sale of Enron's wind farm assets in 1997. Fastow had originally proposed that he, his family, and certain FOEs provide the independent equity for a vehicle to purchase the assets. Arthur Anderson (AA) had balked at the participation of Fastow and his family. So, Fastow decided to use Michael Kopper, Kopper's domestic partner (Bill Dodson), and FOE Kathy Wetmore as fronts through which to invest his money. The deal closed in May 1997. On August 26, 1997, Kopper returned $481,850 to Fastow, which sum equaled 100 percent of Fastow's fronted investment plus a $63,000 profit. Further payments followed in subsequent years. Fastow was now benefiting personally from his own deals.

Fastow took another chunk out of the barriers with the Chewco transaction prior to year-end 1997. This deal didn't involve Enron assets per se. Enron's partner in Joint Energy Development Partners (JEDI) was the renowned California Public Employees Retirement System (CalPERS). Enron now wanted CalPERS to invest in a new opportunity, and CalPERS conditioned their doing so on being allowed to divest its JEDI stake. Although Enron was the obvious buyer and both parties quickly reached agreement on price, Enron balked at having JEDI's assets and debt return to its balance sheet. So, Fastow proposed that he and certain associates form an "independent" entity to purchase the CalPERS's stake. Fastow thought that because the deal would be with CalPERS and not Enron, his open participation would be allowed. However, deal lawyers from Vincent and Elkins (V&E) objected, demanding that the Enron board approve any Fastow involvement as an investor. This Fastow was not yet ready to attempt, but after thinking about the problem, he saw another route to go.

Fastow decided to insert Michael Kopper into his place as a Chewco investor and to clear this substitution with Jeff Skilling. Then, he and Kopper would come to their own private understanding as to the ultimate disposition of returns from Chewco.

The conversation with Skilling took place in September 1997. Fastow opened the discussion:

"We've got an idea for how we can really do some great stuff for CalPERS on JEDI...You know, we could get Michael [Kopper] to do this. I've talked to him, and he's willing to put together a deal. He's willing to do it at a higher price than we could get if we sold it to a third party."[3]

When Skilling questioned how this could be, Fastow gave him two reasons:

1. Kopper would not have to replicate the extensive due diligence that third

parties would conduct. He wouldn't have to pay consultants and analysts to investigate the assets and perform valuations. Kopper knew the assets well and would trust Enron's in-house valuations.

2. Because he was familiar with the assets, Kopper would see less risk in the deal; this would allow him to accept a lower return than would be demanded by a third party. Applying a lower discount rate to the JEDI pro forma cash flow would result in a higher price for CalPERS.

Skilling indicated that if such an approach would make CalPERS more money, it was OK with him. Fastow then took the plunge. He asked about the possibility of his wife's family investing in the deal. Skilling turned this down, and Fastow agreed not to do it.

It hadn't been a complete victory, but Fastow had gotten most of what he wanted. Skilling was now on board with the JEDI assets being sold to an entity formed by Michael Kopper. There hadn't been any talk about competitive bids or open auctions to make sure that Kopper offered the highest price. Skilling also laid down no rules for deal authorization or internal review. For example, he hadn't said that he wanted V&E and AA to give him their independent assessment of the deal's legal and accounting effects. Skilling accepted Fastow's arguments that the price would be better and that the legal/accounting details would be worked out. Fastow could now represent that he had cleared with Skilling a noncompetitive JEDI sale to a Kopper-led vehicle. Chewco closed on that basis at year-end 1997. Fastow now had Skilling's sanction for his guiding deals to entities run by an Enron employee.

Emboldened by this success, Fastow took his next step in 1999. In April of that year, Rhythms NetConnections (RNC), an Internet start-up, launched an IPO and saw its stock price nearly triple to $56 on the first day of trading. Enron had bought a stake in RNC thirteen months earlier. The IPO's success meant instant big profits for Enron under its mark-to-market accounting. Jeff Skilling was euphoric at the news. However, if RNC's stock price later declined, Enron would have to record subsequent losses. Skilling began to ponder how Enron might hedge this downside P/L risk.

Fastow had continued to talk to Skilling about his heading up a private-equity fund to do deals with Enron. Skilling had noted the conflict of interest issue but had not said no. Now Fastow saw his chance to make it happen. In June, Fastow went back to Skilling with a plan to form a new fund that would provide Enron with a hedge protecting against declines in RNC's stock price. Outside investors would provide the bulk of the independent capital but Fastow himself would invest and be the fund's general partner. Although noting that he wanted to talk to Rick Causey, Enron's chief account officer, Skilling was encouraging. Fastow should keep developing the idea and bring back a fully formed plan.

Within a week, Fastow had his plan. Skilling and Fastow took it to Ken Lay on June 18. Enron would contribute some $250 million of its own stock to capitalize an SPE. Fastow would ultimately name it LJM, after his wife and kids. Two banks—CSFB and Greenwich NatWest—would provide the bulk of the

independent equity. Fastow would invest $1 million and be the general part-
ner. LJM would then write Enron a put option on its RNC stock. In theory, the
put's value would increase if RNC's stock fell below the exercise price, thus
hedging Enron's investment. However, the plan amounted to Enron hedging
with itself. The only way LJM could pay for any gains Enron realized on this
put would be by monetizing its Enron stock. Economically, Enron would pay
for its own losses. In accounting terms, however, Enron could avoid reversing
the profits it had already booked on RNC stock. Skilling had thought that
incentive enough to take the plan to Lay.

Fastow justified his becoming LJM's general partner as a way for Enron to
keep better control over the "independent investor." For Fastow to act as LJM
general partner, Enron's board would have to waive the company's Conflict of
Interest Policy. Anticipating this need, Fastow told Lay that he was reluctant to
assume the general partners role, stressing the personal risk he would be taking. Then, Fastow expressed a statesmanlike willingness to accept the risk in
Enron's broader interests. Lay listened and then told Skilling and Fastow to
prepare a board presentation. Lay would support the plan at the board meeting. This duly happened on June 28, 1999. The board approved capitalizing
LJM with Enron stock and waived the Conflict of Interest Policy to allow
Fastow to be LJM's general partner. Enron's CFO was now officially cleared to
run a private equity fund negotiating with Enron.

Enter LJM2

Fastow now had all the ingredients in place to launch his ultimate scheme:
a large private-equity fund, with himself as the general partner, that would do
multiple Enron deals. Over the remainder of 1999, Fastow set about raising
capital for this fund from Enron's relationship banks. Fastow also retained
Merrill Lynch to pitch the fund to wealthy investors. The new fund would be
called LJM2; it wanted to raise an initial $200 million; a major selling point for
investing in it was Fastow's open affirmation that he would have inside knowledge of the Enron assets up for sale.

LJM2 would need to be big. Enron's profit outlook for 1999 was looking
grim. The Azurix water venture was in trouble and Enron's international assets
were performing way below forecast. All this damage was going to require a
flurry of year-end deals to repair. Fastow and Skilling took steps to make sure
that LJM2 would be ready.

On the afternoon of October 11, Fastow presented LJM2 to the Enron
Board's Finance Committee. Fastow introduced the fund as a follow-on to LJM
and laid out his rationales for why dealing with LJM2 would be in Enron's interests. Foremost among these was having a ready buyer available to purchase
Enron assets without high-cost investment banking fees. With LJM2, Fastow
asserted that Enron would also have increased financial flexibility and greater
ability to manage risk. The fund's limited partners would be the traditional pension funds. Fastow would serve as the fund's general partner, which would

require another board waiver. However, Fastow assured the directors that both Rick Causey and Rick Buy would review all Enron-LJM2 transactions. In addition, the board's Audit Committee would review all LJM transactions annually.

Director Norm Blake asked whether AA had reviewed the deal and expressed concern about Fastow's conflict of interest. Rick Causey assured him that AA was fine with the arrangement. Regarding Fastow's acting as both Enron CFO and LJM2's general partner, Causey had this to say:

"We've addressed that [in] lots of ways. We've given the limited partners enough authority to keep Andy from having too much power. The limited partners can remove the general partner without cause."[4]

Skilling then added: "No one has to do a transaction with LJM. We will only do a transaction if it's better than the alternative, which means it's no-lose for Enron."[5] Fastow then assured the committee that time spent on LJM2 would be minimal: no more than a couple of hours per week. His compensation would consist of "typical private-equity fund fees and promotes" and would be modest relative to his Enron remuneration.

With this, the Finance Committee approved Fastow's conflict of interest waiver on a voice vote; the full board followed suit on October 12. Merrill released the LJM2 placement memo the next day.

Problems with LJM2 Begin

Within a week, Jeff McMahon began feeling the repercussions of the board's decision. His subordinate responsible for bank relations was getting calls from Enron's "Tier 1" banks. The essence of the calls was that Andy Fastow had run a road show encouraging them to invest in LJM2. The banks were worried that failure to do so would result in Enron's CFO "putting them in the penalty box" as regards future Enron deals. It came as a surprise to McMahon that LJM2 was soliciting Enron's banks and not simply pension funds or wealthy individuals.

McMahon immediately went to see Fastow to advise him of this feedback. Fastow acknowledged that he was pitching LJM2 to these banks. However, he denied that this had anything to do with their relationship with Enron; when McMahon told Fastow that banks were worried that participation in future Enron deals was tied to investing in LJM2, the CFO curtly dismissed the concern. McMahon persisted, demanding that Fastow provide him with a list of banks receiving an LJM2 marketing pitch. Fastow agreed to provide the list.

Weeks went by. No list of banks solicited by Fastow reached McMahon. Running into Fastow in the hallway, McMahon asked about the list. Fastow reiterated his promise to get it to McMahon.

November turned into December, and still no bank list reached McMahon. Then he received a call from a banker at First Union. The banker wanted to know why Enron was planning a competitive auction for a prospective bond deal. When McMahon answered that auctions were the standard process, the banker responded that he was confused because Fastow had promised First

Union the next bond deal if it invested in LJM2. McMahon told the banker that he had heard nothing of the sort from Fastow and directed the banker to pursue his issue with the CFO. He then reported the call to Fastow, who denied having said anything to suggest that LJM2 and the bond deal were tied.

On December 13, 1999, McMahon presented Enron's financial outlook to the Finance Committee. The news was not positive. Enron had exceeded its investment budget by almost $4 billion. With reported earnings also tracking below target, some $2.8 billion in year-end transactions were being developed. All would involve Enron's selling assets to entities set up and funded by the company.

LJM2 was one of those entities. McMahon had tasked Bill Brown to represent Enron in negotiations with LJM2. Michael Kopper was on the other side of the table. Brown reported one of their conversations to McMahon:

"Man, Jeff, this thing with Andy and LJM really stinks. It's crazy. We walk in, and before we make our pitch, they're telling us they know what we'll take. It's like selling a house when the buyer knows your bottom line. There's not a lot of negotiating going on."[6]

McMahon told Brown that he saw the problem and would talk to Fastow immediately.

That same day, McMahon confronted Fastow in his office. The conversation resembled previous exchanges. McMahon recited feedback he was getting from various sources and the problems implied. Fastow simply denied that any real problems existed. This time however, McMahon had a focus for his objections: Michael Kopper's dual role as Enron employee and LJM2 negotiator. Citing the facts as relayed by Bill Brown, McMahon demanded that Fastow implement certain changes:

- Personnel should be either Enron or LJM employees, not both; this implied that if he wanted to work for LJM2, Kopper should separate from Enron.
- Those working for LJM2 should be in their own offices and out of the Enron building.
- Kopper should be prevented from sitting in on Enron strategy meetings.

Fastow resisted all of these suggestions: "Michael is a key player here. He needs to know what's going on...He needs to know everything."[7]

The meeting ended inconclusively. McMahon told Fastow that he didn't see how the current arrangements were workable. Fastow ambiguously replied that he would "think about it."

Things didn't get better. The flurry of year-end 1999 deals brought another confrontation with Fastow when Kopper demanded a $1 million fee on one transaction, a fee McMahon estimated to be ten times the appropriate market rate. Then, as the new year began, McMahon waited anxiously for Fastow to advise him of his annual bonus. Fastow was initially cagey about the number; although almost all other bonuses had already been communicated, Fastow said that McMahon's still needed board review. After a delay, Fastow did communicate a bonus amount that McMahon found satisfactory. However, when McMahon got the check, the amount was lower by approximately 25 percent.

Fastow sloughed off the discrepancy. Last-minute adjustments had been made by the board, but next year would be better. Shortly thereafter, McMahon came across a list revealing that the reduction in his bonus number coincided with a much-increased figure for Kopper.

At around this time, McMahon and Bill Brown decided that the Chewco transaction had outlived its usefulness. An Enron buyout was the recommended course, even though it meant negotiating again with Michael Kopper. McMahon decided to offer Kopper $1 million for his $125,000 stake in Chewco; McMahon was stunned when Kopper turned the deal down and demanded $10 million instead. Discussions were terminated, leaving McMahon with further bad feelings about dealing with Kopper but also further insight into the levels of profit Kopper and Fastow were seeking.

Now it was March 2000. The conversation with Baxter had occurred and set McMahon on a path to see Skilling. Before doing so, he had one last session with Fastow on March 15. McMahon put everything out on the table. In four months, Fastow had not taken any of the steps McMahon had recommended to rectify the unhealthy LJM2 situation. He also told Fastow that he felt his bonus had been affected for his pressing these issues. Fastow denied that was true and said that McMahon just need to be patient and to trust him.

McMahon left the meeting and got himself on Skilling's calendar for the next day.

Planning the Meeting with Skilling

McMahon's brain filled with questions and troubled recollections as the clock ticked toward 11:30.

- What exactly am I expecting Jeff Skilling to do?
- What reasons can I provide to justify his taking action against a favored, long time subordinate?
- How much is Skilling "on board" with what Fastow is doing? What does he know about the details of LJM's structure and operations? How much does he want to know the details?

Their discussion clearly had the potential to fly off in several directions. Somehow, McMahon had to get Skilling to focus on the right issue, one that would both grab his attention and cause him to look more deeply into LJM matters.

Skilling. What could he count on from Skilling? Cliff Baxter seemed to retain some belief that Skilling was dedicated to doing the right thing for Enron. Certainly, Skilling seemed intent on finding solutions to Enron's problems; he was known to be focused on shutting off the tap for the loss-generating Azurix venture and on divesting underperforming international assets. Skilling also was always looking for innovation and the next strategy that would deliver a lucrative new Enron franchise. Furthermore, it was clear that Skilling was not involved in Fastow's plans to profit personally from intra-Enron deals.

On the other hand, Skilling seemed curiously indifferent to the question of

the real financial condition of Enron. The COO had been the instigator for bringing mark-to-market accounting into Enron. He had not been interested in the
distortions that later crept in when that method mutated into mark-to-model.
Moreover, Skilling had encouraged Fastow in all the arrangements that moved
debt off Enron's balance sheet and manufactured accounting profits to meet
quarterly reporting dates. Skilling had said yes to Fastow's LJM proposals and
had sponsored Fastow's requests to the board for conflict of interest waivers.

No, Skilling was not some innocent in these matters. In sponsoring Fastow,
he implicitly and perhaps explicitly had endorsed a certain approach toward
Enron's accounting and to the profile Enron presented to the stock market. Given
this, what aspect of Fastow's conduct would engage his concern? What would
come as a sufficient surprise to provoke Skilling to discipline his own protégé?

Here, McMahon began to identify the various issues that he could raise in
the meeting:

- The tying of banks investing in LJM2 to participation in future Enron
  financings.
- Enron's true financial condition, Fastow's ignorance of same, and the need
  to repair Enron's total financial strength, on and off balance sheet.
- Fastow's intimidation of Enron employees negotiating with LJM2.
- The lack of process, including testing the third-party market, to ensure that
  LJM2 was paying prices at or better than market.
- Fastow/Kopper using inside information to negotiate down to Enron's
  minimum price.
- McMahon's experience of having his bonus whacked for defending Enron
  against LJM2.
- Fastow's true level of compensation and involvement with LJM2.
- Changes needed to fix the structural and process problems involved in
  negotiating with an "independent" entity run and partly owned by Enron
  employees.
- McMahon's acute dissatisfaction and his plans either to transfer within or
  leave Enron.

As he contemplated this mental list, several of thoughts crossed his mind.

- Personal career issues are all wrapped up in this discussion. Which issue
  is my real agenda here?
- Am I prepared to lay out a coherent plan for Skilling to take action, or am I
  just complaining here?
- How hard am I going after Andy? Do I register my complaints, hope Skilling
  does the right thing, and hope to live with Fastow in the aftermath? Or, am
  I going after Andy all-out, because that is the only way anything will happen?

Jeff McMahon turned back to his pad and wrote "WILL NOT COMPRO-
MISE MY INTEGRITY" on the bottom of the first page (Attachment 1). Then
he began to write.

Attachment 1

Discussion Points
(Exercise - Prepare own discussion points)

WILL NOT COMPROMISE MY INTEGRITY

Annex 1—Enron Career History of Jeff McMahon

Jeff McMahon joined Enron in1994 as a business unit coordinator, and served in that capacity for one year. The job involved business unit accounting and stewardship. Prior to that time, McMahon had been employed by Arthur Anderson.

In 1995, McMahon transferred to London, where he took charge of Enron's UK Treasury activities. In 1996-97, McMahon structured financing deals in support of Enron's Teesside and Sutton Bridge power projects.

The Sutton Bridge transaction earned McMahon a reputation for innovation. In this financing, McMahon used Financial Accounting Standard (FAS) 125 both to raise capital and bring future power profits forward into the current reporting year. FAS 125 was intended to allow banks to bundle and securitize financial contracts, such as home mortgages. Under a broad interpretation of the rule, McMahon, supported by AA, wrapped financial contracts around the power plant's basic commitments to deliver electricity. The contracts were then packaged in a manner that produced committed cash flows resembling loan interest and principal repayments; these packages were sold to financial institutions, with the sale being accounted for as a sale of future power. Enron then recognized the net present value of the divested payment stream as current profit. These deals received considerable notice at Enron headquarters; McMahon was identified as a high potential financial executive.

In 1998, McMahon returned to Enron in Houston. At that time, Andy Fastow was disenchanted with his treasurer, Bill Gathmann for being too forthcoming in disclosing information to the rating agencies. Fastow found another position for Gathmann (in India) and offered McMahon the treasurer's position. McMahon accepted.

During his time working for Fastow, McMahon promoted the idea that Enron Finance should develop an "in house" private-equity fund to do deals with Enron. Indeed, he sold the idea to Andy Fastow and convinced him to recruit Mike Jakubiak away from Bankers Trust London. McMahon's version of the plan would have Jakubiak raising private equity from legitimate institutional investors so that it would be ready when Enron needed independent equity for an SPE transaction. Fastow quickly cooled on the idea of having Jakubiak raising money for such a fund, preferring instead that Michael Kopper and he do the fund-raising and entity management.

At year-end 1999, McMahon crafted a deal whereby Enron's Nigerian barge power plants were sold to Merrill Lynch. According to *Conspiracy of Fools* (pp. 293-296, 302-303) Merrill earned fees, a 22 percent annual return on its $7 million investment, and received a Fastow oral indication that Enron/LJM would facilitate Merrill's exit from the transaction by June 30, 2000. With this transaction, Enron booked $12 million of earnings and $28 million of cash flow at year-end 1999.

In June 2000 Merrill sold the Nigerian barges to LJM2. The assets changed hands again three months later, when they were bought by a third-party trade buyer.

Author's Note

Going over your boss's head to the senior manager of the company is a high-risk endeavor. Yet in a company whose financial-control system has been thoroughly compromised, going to the top is one of the few internal options for working an ethics issue. This case presents the dilemma of Enron treasurer Jeff McMahon, whose direct boss is the agent of corruption. McMahon decides to go over Andy Fastow's head to oppose gross breaches of arms-length negotiating practices. McMahon knows that this will burn his bridges with Fastow. His concerns about unethical practices are thus complicated by the knowledge that he may be betting his Enron career. McMahon will have maybe thirty minutes to get his message to Jeff Skilling just right. In fact, Skilling's mind may be made up in the first two minutes of the conversation.

This account of Jeff McMahon's resistance actions on LJM is based on the events as reported in *Conspiracy of Fools* and *The Smartest Guys in the Room*. McMahon did put himself on Skilling's calendar after trying and failing to move Fastow one last time. McMahon also prepared pages of "Discussion Points" that he did refer to in his meeting with Skilling. McMahon did write "WILL NOT COMPROMISE MY INTEGRITY" on page 1 of his discussion points.

McMahon's concert conversation with Cliff Baxter appears on pp. 324-325 of *Conspiracy of Fools*; the exchanges with Fastow over banker feedback and the problems of negotiating with LJM appear on pp. 270-271, 277, 279, and 283-284. McMahon and Fastow's conversation, in which McMahon insisted that changes be made regarding Kopper's dual LJM/Enron role, is reported on pp. 291-292. The account of what happened to McMahon's bonus appears on pp. 304-305 and 307-308.

The history of Fastow's career within Enron and his persistent efforts to create a private-equity fund that he could run (and profit from) are covered in both sources. Fastow's recruitment by Skilling and his protégé status are discussed in *The Smartest Guys in the Room* (pp. 136-139). The same source covers Fastow's approach to SPEs, bank relations, and his drive to profit personally from his Enron deals (pp.150-170). Details of the first and second LJM structures and Enron's board approval of same appear on pp.191-200. *Conspiracy of Fools* covers the same ground in more detail. Fastow's conversations with Skilling and Ken Lay, in which he sold the LJM concept, are reported on pp. 227-228, 235-236 and 244-245. The Enron Finance Committee and board reviews of Fastow's conflict-of-interest waivers appear on pages 249 and 268-269.

The general history, structures, and impacts of LJM and LJM2 in the case are confirmed by the findings of the *Report of the Special Investigation Committee of the Board of Directors of Enron Corporation* (the Powers Committee Report), February 1, 2002. See especially pp. 1-28, 68-76 and 135-147.

The account of Jeff McMahon's Enron career is drawn primarily from *Power Failure* (p. 136), supplemented by the other two sources.

The questions that Jeff McMahon ponders as he considers his Discussion Points are a creation intended to sensitize students to the conflicting elements at work in his situation; he must sort out his concerns with Fastow/Kopper/LJM, the risks to his career, his resentment over recent bonus treatment, and the tactical question of how to present effectively to an executive like Jeff Skilling. Based on evidence presented in all the source materials, McMahon was well aware of all these issues.

Notes
1. *Conspiracy of Fools*, p.325.
2. Ibid.
3. Ibid., p. 155.
4. Ibid., p. 269.
5. Ibid.
6. Ibid., p. 291.
7. Ibid., p. 292.

Jeff Skilling and LJM (B): Managing the Meeting's Aftermath

Am I really doing this? Am I really trying to persuade
Jeff Skilling to discipline Andy Fastow?
I hope to God I have the ammunition to pull this off.

JEFF MCMAHON LOOKED OVER HIS DISCUSSION POINTS one more time before heading toward Jeff Skilling's office. His eyes quickly locked in on his key messages:

- Untenable situation; LJM situation where AF wears two hats and upside comp is so great creates a conflict I am right in the middle of.
- I find myself negotiating with Andy on Enron matters and am pressured to do a deal that I do not believe is in the best interests of the shareholders.
- My integrity forces me to continue to negotiate the way I believe is correct. I MUST know I have support from you and there won't be any ramifications. If can't make this promise, I must be transferred.
- Bonuses do get affected.
- Will not compromise my integrity.[1]

McMahon showed up, notes in hand, at Skilling's office right before his 11:30 appointment. Skilling waved him in, directing McMahon to the conference table. After composing himself and writing McMahon's name on a pad, Skilling asked: "Okay, what's up."

McMahon shifted in his seat, glanced at his notes, and dove into his opening topic:

> I want to talk to you about the whole LJM thing. I've got some real concerns about the conflicts of interest.

> I understand the notion and I know the board approved Andy being the general partner. I'm not questioning that. My issue is how it's being managed. It's at the point where I can no longer manage the conflicts.[2]

S.V. Arbogast, *Resisting Corporate Corruption* (pp. 141–144)
© 2008 by M & M Scrivener Press

McMahon elaborated on the consequences of how the conflicts around LJM were playing out. His peoples' behavior was being affected. They saw that LJM2 staffers were being allowed to attend Enron's strategy meetings; this was a signal of preferential treatment that they couldn't miss. Consequently, his people were feeling pressure to do deals that weren't in Enron's best interests.

As an example, McMahon cited a deal called Yosemite. This had been a small year-end 1999 deal involving the sale of some investment certificates held inside a trust controlled by Enron. McMahon didn't recite the gory details for Skilling. Rather, he recounted how LJM2 had demanded a $1 million fee to accompany its purchase of the certificates. McMahon's people had complained to him that this fee was ten times above normal commercial rates. This type of demand was becoming all too typical of dealings with LJM. That was the problem of negotiating with "related parties" who took no pains to keep dealings on a proper "arms length" basis.

McMahon had taken the issue to Fastow, only to be told that "your guys are negotiating way too hard on this deal." Now, McMahon told Skilling that Fastow had applied pressure to accept terms that were wrong for Enron and that Fastow wouldn't back down.

> Here's the CFO of the company, a few weeks before bonuses are paid, telling me to close the deal under bad terms. I didn't do it, we got it fixed and done right. But, man, that was major pressure.
>
> I think my compensation's been affected because of that. I didn't ask to be in this position. But now here I am, stuck in the middle.[3]

So far, Skilling had listened and said nothing. He took no notes.

McMahon now directed the conversation toward decisions he felt needed to be made. He was in an impossible situation. He told Skilling that there were really only two alternatives. Either all the conflicts around LJM2 needed to be fixed, or he needed to change jobs. "Those are the two options. And I need something to happen pretty quickly."[4]

After a moment, Skilling asked "Is that it?" After McMahon nodded yes, Skilling stood and led McMahon toward his office door. As they walked, Skilling spoke: "Listen, thanks for coming up. It's important for me to know that. And I'm glad you told me."[5]

At the doorway, Skilling opened the door for McMahon and then added: "I've heard you loud and clear. Trust me; I'm going to fix this. I'm going to fix this for you."[6]

Skilling quickly pondered what to do next to fix McMahon's situation. His schedule was packed that day, and he was leaving the next day for a family vacation. Skilling decided to visit with Enron vice chairman Joe Sutton and ask him to work the issue.

Ushered out and now back in his office, McMahon let out a deep breath. Well, he hadn't been fired. That, at least, was good news. His next thought was that Fastow would be furious when word reached him of McMahon's having gone to Skilling. Well, that was done and couldn't be helped now.

Then McMahon began to think back over the conversation with Skilling. How had it gone? When Skilling had promised to fix it for him, what exactly did he mean?

Was his work now finished? Had he, Jeff McMahon, done the necessary task and put these issues on the radar screen for Enron's top management? Or did he need to prepare for follow-up events?

And how would he handle his boss, Andy Fastow, when their inevitable conversation occurred?

Author's Note

Escalating ethics issues to the top is a rare occurrence. When it does happen, resisters are tempted to conclude that their job is completed. This is especially the case when the senior executive gives reassuring responses. Yet senior executives seldom take a resister's story at face value. Instead, they usually launch a follow-up investigation to ensure that they have a complete story and that all company implications are considered. In this case, Jeff McMahon has elicited a reassuring response from Skilling, perhaps the best he could have expected. Now McMahon must decide whether to sit back and wait for Skilling's "fix" to materialize or to be proactive in influencing whatever follow-up Skilling is likely to launch.

The depiction of McMahon's notes going into his meeting with Skilling is drawn from the account in *The Smartest Guys in the Room*. All of the points cited in the case are recounted in that source. The account of McMahon and Skilling's conversation is as found in *Conspiracy of Fools*. Major passages have been footnoted, while the minor conversational exchanges are not.

The two sources have consistent accounts of what McMahon said at the meeting. *The Smartest Guys in the Room* provides interesting information on how Skilling viewed the meeting. According to this source, Skilling later provided his version of the meeting; apparently, Skilling felt that McMahon's primary concern was not ethics but the awkwardness of negotiating with his own boss and how that might impact his compensation package. *Conspiracy of Fools* confirms that this was Skilling's conclusion, an interpretation also consistent with this book's account of Skilling's subsequent actions in the matter.

Whether Skilling's interpretation more accurately reflects what McMahon was saying or what Skilling was hearing is for the reader to ponder.

McMahon's post-meeting reflections are a creation intended to focus the case study on evaluating the meeting and determining whether McMahon should engage in follow-up actions. Having taken the step of raising ethics concerns at the highest level and having been assured that the problem would be fixed, McMahon must now consider what kind of "fix" Skilling may initiate. How much will this concern the merits of McMahon's complaint versus other considerations Skilling may have in mind? If there is a risk that Skilling's follow-up process may recast the issues, how exactly can McMahon keep his concerns on the table and influence that process's ultimate determinations?

Endnotes

1. *The Smartest Guys in the Room,* p. 210.
2. *Conspiracy of Fools,* p. 328.
3. Ibid.
4. Ibid.
5. Ibid.
6. Ibid.

Case Study 12

New Counsel for
Andy Fastow (A)

My God, this place is a shambles.
What have I gotten myself into here?

NOTHING IN HIS PREVIOUS LIFE had prepared Jordan Mintz for
what he found in his first week at Global Finance. Mintz had been
at Enron for four years. He was a lawyer in the Tax Department.
Then, in October 2000, Andy Fastow summoned him and asked him to
become general counsel for Global Finance. The opportunity to move from
tax to general corporate and securities law was enticing. Global Finance was
controversial but was also known as a "creative shop". In fact, Global
Finance was now one of the "places to be" at Enron. Andy Fastow had
become Enron's chief financial officer in 1998. He immediately set about
making Global Finance a major player within the organization. Fastow ran
a secretive shop; it was known mostly for fiendishly complex financial transactions that seemed to coincide with Enron's hitting its quarterly earnings
guidance to Wall Street analysts. For this, Fastow and Global Finance had
been rewarded with handsome compensation and powerful influence with
Jeff Skilling, Enron's COO.

Mintz accepted Fastow's offer and reported for work late in 2000. One
of the first things he found in his Global Finance files concerned a deal
between Enron and a special-purpose company called LJM.

Mintz had known something about LJM before he transferred offices.
He knew that it was a special-purpose vehicle set up for the express purpose
of purchasing assets from Enron. He had heard that LJM was one of the
ways Enron pursued its "asset lite" business strategy and that Andy Fastow
was the creative force behind the vehicle. There had also been more disturbing rumors. One hinted that Andy Fastow was part owner of LJM and was
thus engaging in a blatant conflict of interest. However, Mintz had also
heard that Fastow had reviewed LJM with the Enron board. In all likelihood, whatever relationship Fastow had with LJM had been vetted and
approved.

S.V. Arbogast, *Resisting Corporate Corruption* (pp. 145–157)
© 2008 by M & M Scrivener Press

As part of learning his new job, Mintz sought more information about LJM. He came across a draft Global Finance memo that contained considerable background on the origins, purpose, and structure of LJM1 (Attachment 1). The memo was also of interest because it was addressed to the board and sought to justify a Fastow exemption from the Enron Ethics Policy.

In reviewing the draft memo, Mintz noticed a number of disturbing points. First, the paper was crafted in such a way as to make Fastow's exception request seem a sacrifice for the benefit of Enron. Yet Fastow would not only profit from the transaction but also make the most money if the option proved worthless to Enron. Moreover, the Enron shareholders seemed to be taking most of the risk. Should the option be "put" and LJM1 forced to absorb a loss, the partnership would have to sell off Enron shares to cover the deficit. Doing some quick sums in his head, Mintz estimated that at the current stock price, the 3.4 million shares Enron contributed were worth about $276 million. After deducting the $64 million in notes given back to Enron, LJM1's net capital would consist of $212 million in Enron stock and $16 million in cash. Enron stock thus constituted about 93 percent of LJM1's net worth and would fund essentially that percentage of any partnership loss. Enron's stockholders would feel any partnership loss directly via "dilution effects," i.e. an increase in the total number of shares outstanding and trading, if LJM1 ended up having to sell shares.

Mintz also noticed a scarcity of detail in the memo regarding the LJM partners' compensation. Clearly, Andy Fastow, in addition to receiving one-half million dollars in management fees, was to benefit along with the limited partners, but what was the "high return" that partners would earn if the option was never exercised? Were there any special partnership provisions that shifted even more of the risk to the Enron partner and away from Fastow and the private investors? Indeed, how substantive would the proposed transaction appear if all the facts were known?

So, Jordan Mintz had more than a few questions about LJM1. However, the file contained little in the way of further detail. Normally, a transaction of this size and complexity would be evaluated by Rick Buy's Risk Assessment and Control department (RAC). However, no RAC assessment resided in the file. Mintz had heard that RAC had brought in Vince Kaminski to do an assessment of LJM1. However, Kaminski and his research group had shortly thereafter been transferred to Enron North America, where it reported to the VP of Trading, Greg Whalley. Whatever analysis Kaminski had provided was no longer available. There also was nothing in the way of analysis or opinion from Enron's auditor, Arthur Anderson (AA). What the file did contain was a memo from Enron's board secretary, documenting that on June 28, 1999, the directors reviewed and approved Fastow's request for an exception to the corporate Ethics Policy. Additional papers confirmed that the Enron-LJM1 transaction closed on June 30. So, it was a "done deal" approved at the highest level. Mintz put the file in his drawer and turned to other matters.

Over the subsequent weeks, more disturbing questions surfaced for Mintz's regarding Global Finance in general and LJM in particular. Other LJM-Enron deals had followed the swap transaction. Uniformly, they were poorly documented. Files were unorganized, and key documents were missing. Approval forms were lacking required signatures. Corporate separateness was not being respected; indeed, LJM people and Enron employees were working side by side without evidencing particular care or scruples about who was doing what. The cumulative effect added up to an extremely negative message. Either Global Finance was hugely disorganized as regards its many, highly complex, transactions and/or it had an interest in hiding matters pertaining to LJM.

Mintz decided to find out which was the case. He resolved to begin by testing Fastow directly. On January 16, 2001, Mintz met with Fastow and mentioned his concerns on LJM. Year-end Enron financials would soon need to be prepared. Mintz told Fastow that in his view, Enron should disclose more details about the LJM transactions and in particular report how much money Fastow was making from LJM. Fastow disputed the point. Instead, he asserted, Enron should use the same argument that had been applied to its 1999 financial filings, namely, that a sufficient number of transactions were still open that it wasn't practical to estimate Fastow's remuneration. After then commenting that he probably shouldn't discuss his compensation before talking to his lawyer at Kirkland & Ellis, Fastow told Mintz: "Let's figure out a way not to disclose it [Fastow's compensation]. Hell, if Skilling knew how much I made, he'd have no choice but to shut LJM down."[1]

Jordan Mintz had his answer. Global Finance, it was certain, was hiding things. Put together with the documentation and approval shambles, this amounted to a monumental set of risks for Enron. Should an investigation ever uncover these facts, SEC and shareholder suits were a likelihood, if not a certainty.

The damage might not stop there. Things could get personal in a hurry. If Mintz was convinced that Fastow's compensation needed to be disclosed but then acquiesced to Enron's publishing year-2000 accounts without such disclosure, was Mintz himself liable for abetting an accounting fraud? Where did Mintz's responsibilities to his client, Enron, stop and his responsibilities to the law start? Even if Mintz convinced himself that he was making the correct decision about his responsibilities as an Enron attorney, would the SEC, in the "cold light of day," see it the same way? Mintz became deeply concerned and a bit panicked.

Determining a Course of Action

What to do? It occurred to Mintz that his immediate problem was internal to Enron. Matters involving the SEC would come to a head only if he failed to persuade Enron to disclose Fastow's compensation. Therefore, Mintz must remain focused on persuading Enron to discover Fastow's compensation and make the appropriate disclosures.

Mintz closed the door of his office one evening at 6.00 pm, turned out the lights, and sat in the dying light, pad and pencil in hand. Sipping on a Diet Coke, he began to list the practical options available for action. The immediate objectives were twofold: (1) prevent Enron from incurring new legal violations while limiting the damage of those that might already have occurred, and (2) make sure that Jordan Mintz was himself not complicit in any legal violations. To pursue these objectives, Mintz would have to chart a course up the Enron management chain, escalating matters if initial reviews failed to produce results.

Mintz quickly determined that he first needed to decide what objection to raise as the most effective means of galvanizing concern at high levels in Enron. Where should he start the discussion if the objective was for it to end up addressing the extent and disclosure of Fastow's compensation?

There were several candidates:

- **Internal procedure and documentation.** Necessary signatures and documents were not in condition to withstand audit or a more serious investigation.
- **Failure to disclose material facts to the Board.** By failing to disclose the extent of his compensation relative to his capital at risk or to lay out clearly the economic consequences for shareholders if the option were exercised, Fastow failed to provide the board with a reasonable basis for deciding on the exemption request.
- **Failure to conduct risk analysis and advise on the consequences of a downside case.** By not being provided with a RAC analysis or audit report, management lacked the basis for assessing the consequences of adverse developments affecting LJM. Thus, management lacked a basis for deciding whether to continue doing business with the LJM partnership.
- **The absence of controls and monitoring of Andy Fastow's ethics exception.** Global Finance had failed to propose means by which Fastow's conflict of interest would be monitored and reported on to the Board.
- **The failure to provide adequate disclosure about LJM in Enron's public filings.** A detailed outline of the parties to and the substance of the transactions should be provided so as to evidence that Enron management and its board had carried out their fiduciary duties, that no "sweetheart deal" existed, that transactions were substantive, and that the com-

pensation paid to LJM's investors, including Andy Fastow, was appropriate.

Next, Mintz considered whom to approach with his chosen concern(s). There were several possibilities:

- Andy Fastow, his boss.
- Rick Buy, chief risk officer.
- Rich Causey, chief accounting officer.
- Jeff Skilling, COO and Fastow's boss.
- Kenneth Lay, Enron chairman.
- Greg Whalley, head of Trading.
- Arthur Anderson (relationship manager David Duncan), Enron's auditor.
- Someone on the Enron board, perhaps the Audit Committee chairman Janiche.
- Jim Derrick, Enron's chief legal counsel.

Mintz also had to consider the potential consequences for him personally. He could not know in advance the reaction of the person to whom he would first voice his misgivings. It was likely that he could expect resistance and/or be told that his concerns were exaggerated. How hard was he prepared to press his case? That would certainly be influenced by what consequences Mintz was prepared to accept. If he chose to go above his boss's head, Mintz knew that Andy Fastow would react angrily. Fastow had gotten his previous counsel and an earlier treasurer reassigned for lesser offenses. Potentially, Mintz was risking transfer, demotion, and possible termination.

So, Jordan listed his potential personal "end-game" options. He could:

- Threaten to resign and be prepared to follow through.
- Ask for a transfer back to Tax.
- Back off for the moment and look for further opportunities to press the issue.
- Document fully that he had raised all matters with appropriate superiors, create secure files with backups, and be prepared to produce them if trouble arose down the road.

The tactical choices were obviously many and complicated. Mintz organized them into rough matrices and jotted down some pros/cons. Next, he converted the matrices to Word Documents (Attachments 2 and 3), secured them into an encrypted file, shut down his computer, and went home for the weekend to mull over the options.

Attachment 1—Historical Recreation (HRC)

DRAFT MEMORANDUM

May 15, 1999

To: The Board of Directors

From: Andrew Fastow

Subject: Special Exemption from Ethics Policy

This memo is intended to request a special exemption from the Enron Corporate Ethics Policy to allow the author, Andrew Fastow, to participate as general manager and minority owner of a private-equity fund, LJM. By granting this exemption, the Board will enable LJM to complete its organization, fund-raising, and the actions necessary for it to enter into a derivatives transaction with Enron that is decidedly in Enron's interest. This transaction must be completed during the second quarter if it is to meet Enron's objectives. Therefore, an immediate decision of the board is requested.

The transaction in question will allow Enron to hedge a large gain that has accrued on an investment made during the last year. In March 1998, Enron Broadband made a $10 million investment in a high-speed Internet start-up, Rhythms NetConnections (RNC). This investment was one element of the implementation of Broadband's strategy: that of identifying and investing in emerging technologies in the broadband sector. RNC has since gone public and the stock has appreciated dramatically (last close at $69/share). Enron's original $10 million investment is now worth upward of $300 million.

Management has reviewed RNC's business plan and outlook. Although the future for the company remains bright, Enron has already captured all the technology and know-how that it is entitled to receive from RNC. In addition, Global Finance's valuation indicates that RNC's stock is now trading at a substantial premium to long-term fundamental valuation. Not only is there little further technology upside for Enron should it retain its RNC shares, but it is also more likely than not that the current investment valuation may erode, perhaps substantially. Therefore, Global Finance has recommended and management has endorsed a course of Enron's divesting its position in RNC as soon as practicable.

When it made its pre-IPO investment in RNC, Enron agreed to a "lockup" provision. This lockup expires in November of this year. Enron therefore remains exposed to the erosion of its investment's value until that time. Management believes that the prudent course would be to hedge the value of RNC shares with a derivative security for the period June to expiry of the lockup in November.

Normally this would be accomplished by Enron's purchasing a "put" option on RNC's shares. However, technical factors make this impossible. Enron owns approximately 50 percent of all RNC shares that trade. Trading volume in the stock is very thin. This condition is not atypical for start-up companies. Unfortunately, the combination of thin trading volume and the large size of Enron's block of shares renders it virtually impossible to find counterparties willing to sell a RNC "put" option. Global Finance is thus of the view that no market hedge option is available to Enron.

RNC's illiquid trading also implies that Enron is exposed to dramatic price declines at any time. Therefore, time is of the essence as regards development of an alternative hedging strategy. Accordingly, Global Finance has developed a near-term hedging alternative that involves the immediate raising of funds from outside investors.

Under this strategy, a private-equity fund, LJM1 will be formed. Third-party investors contacted personally by me are prepared to contribute $15 million to the fund. However, they will invest only if I am both general partner and an investor. Therefore, I have agreed in principle to serve and to invest $1 million of my personal funds. Enron must also invest in the fund to ensure that it is adequately capitalized to bear the risks of the hedge transaction. However, it may do so by contributing stock, a total of 3.4 million shares. LJM1 will then use a portion of the cash and stock to form a subsidiary (Swap Sub) for purposes of providing Enron with the RNC hedge it seeks.

Once LJM1 and Swap Sub are formed and capitalized, Enron will receive the following:

- A "put" option on its entire position in RNC stock at a strike price of $56 per share

- $64 million in LJM1 notes

Essentially, this transaction provides Enron with the hedge it seeks at no cost to the company. If RNC stock never falls below the $56 strike price, the option will expire, and Enron may sell its stock in the market at a higher price. Should RNC shares decline below $56 per share, Enron may "put" its entire block of shares to LJM1 Swap Sub and realize $56 per share. Should the "put" option be triggered, Swap Sub will use its cash and/or the sale of Enron stock to cover its losses when it disposes of any "put" RNC stock in the open market. Enron has no obligation to contribute cash to cover any LJM losses. Once the RNC shares are disposed of in the market, either by Enron directly or by Swap Sub, the fund will liquidate itself at an appropriate time and deliver all proceeds to the respective partners.

In this fashion, Enron is hedged on some 80 percent of its RNC gain. It also benefits from being able to recognize the receipt of LJM1 notes as operating cash flow in this reporting quarter.

As regards LJM1, the general partner (GP) will receive a $500,000 annual management fee. In addition, the GP and the limited partners will each earn fees and/or premium on their risked capital in the event the "put" option is never exercised. Should the option be exercised, the partners' return will depend on the relationship between the strike price and the market price at which LJM1 disposes of the RNC shares. It is possible that the partners may lose a material portion or even all of their risked capital; it is to compensate for this risk that the partners' return is high in the scenario in which the option is never exercised by Enron. The accounting firm of PricewaterhouseCoopers will be issuing a fairness opinion confirming that the transaction as described is fair to Enron.

For this transaction to be put in place promptly, it is necessary to work with the external investors who have indicated a willingness to commit sizable cash funds. Their participation is essential to establish LJM1 as a legitimate external counterparty for Enron and to secure hedge accounting treatment. These investors have made it clear that they desire that I be involved in the fund in the manner noted. This involvement will also be in Enron's interest, as it will enable the transaction to be concluded in a timely manner and will provide Enron with more control over its subsequent operations.

Under normal circumstances, an Enron officer who was also a principal of another party transacting with Enron would be engaged in a conflict of interest prohibited by our Ethics policy. Under the special circumstances described, management has deemed it appropriate to disclose the facts and circumstances to the board and request that an exception to the Ethics Policy be granted. Such exceptions may be granted by the CEO when they do not adversely affect the best interests of the company. In this instance, both CEO Ken Lay and COO Jeff Skilling have reviewed and endorsed the granting of such an exception. However, the matter was felt to be of sufficient importance that it was deemed appropriate to inform the board and seek its endorsement as well.

Accordingly, an exception to the Enron Corporate Ethics Policy is requested to allow Andrew Fastow to engage in the aforementioned transaction in the manner as described.

Andrew Fastow
Chief Financial Officer
Global Finance

Attachment 2—Historical Recreation (HRC)

Potential Objections to Raise	Pros/Cons
Internal procedure and documentation	Pros: Proper concern for legal counsel; Low-key way to highlight bigger issues Cons: Lacks impact; could be remedied w/o addressing bigger issue
Risk analysis and sensitivities	Pros: Highlights legitimate issue; new information would come out; can be used to spotlight other issues; lower risk personally Cons: Assumes that management wants to know; Not analysis a legal counsel would do; Management can say "thanks" and move on
No controls/monitoring of Fastow ethics exception	Pros: Valid issue; appropriate for legal counsel; correction could, in turn, identify other issues that might lead to general reform; technical/ procedural objection lowers personal risk Cons: Impact issue? Board's responsibility; puts Board in bad light; management may use 'protecting the Board as reason for no action; or could adopt control procedure w/o teeth
Inadequate disclosure in Enron Public filings	Pros: Impact issue; appropriate for legal counsel; Leaves 'tracks' for external regulatory body; Provides management with new facts to act against Fastow and 'excuse' for prior approvals Cons: Assumes management wants to know; Fastow will say it invites an investigation & law suits; high personal risk; be prepared to resign or be fired if push it

Full disclosure to the Board

Pros: Way to reopen big issues at highest level; Gives Board new facts to prompt fuller review/ basis for reversing earlier decision

Cons: How to get to the Board? If bypassed, management will object and work to block/discredit the move; high risk personally; expect to be fired

Attachment 3—Historical Recreation (HRC)

Potential Objection to Raise	Target Contact	Approach
Internal procedure and documentation	Andy Fastow first, then Chief Legal Counsel Derrick	Cleanup needed or we'll get into trouble; if no response, transfer back to Tax
Risk analysis & sensitivities	Andy Fastow and Trading VP Whalley then COO Skilling	First meeting is analytical, i.e. what if "this" happened? With Skilling, tie into housekeeping first, and personal disclosure risks for him; could become high risk if pushed, so consider job alternatives after first conversation
No controls/monitoring of Fastow ethics exception	COO Skilling, then Chairman Ken Lay; test Counsel Derrick's appetite first	Management should do itself and board a favor and ensure that controls process exists; make it a "process" issue but hint that management will want a rigorous process and want to use it going forward to protect itself; if no appetite, document and request transfer back to Tax
Inadequate disclosure in Enron public filings	Andy Fastow first, then Causey/Buy, then Skilling, then Lay; worst case: consider leaking outside	Progressive escalation on grounds legal risks are too great; focus disclosure on Fastow's compensation, which he is keen to hide; if Derrick and Skilling don't support, prepare for resignation scenario
Full disclosure to the Board	CEO Skilling first, Audit Committee chair	Andy withheld key information; board then should request further data and reconsider; start looking for new job now and be prepared to resign

Author's Note

Jordan Mintz's dilemma is similar to that of Jeff McMahon in that it involves going up the management chain with a complaint. Enron's legal and accounting gatekeepers have already signed off on the LJM transaction Mintz finds questionable. There is no internal financial-control organization to which he can appeal with much expectation of success. Thus, Mintz is left with the internal option of escalating to senior management.

Unlike McMahon's case, however, Mintz has not yet decided where to take his message. Mintz's situation also differs in other ways. Mintz is an attorney. This gives him certain knowledge about the public company legal framework surrounding Enron; it also makes him aware of the personal risks if he ends up complicit in a securities law violation. Finally, it affords him tactical options not available to non-attorneys. Students must consider his options and craft the best tactical plan for doing so.

Key facts in this case draw on the *Conspiracy of Fools* account of Mintz's campaign to force Fastow's LJM compensation out into the open. This account is consistent with that provided in *The Smartest Guys in the Room* but provides more details about Mintz's reactions to LJM, his conversations with Fastow, and his subsequent efforts to force disclosure. The account of what Mintz originally discovered in the LJM files is consistent with the published reports of incomplete documentation but is not intended to be historically accurate about the specific documents missing or found. The account of Mintz's January 16, 2001, conversation with Fastow is found in *Conspiracy of Fools* (pp. 412-413). The reference to Kirkland & Ellis appears in *The Smartest Guys in the Room* (p. 328). This case has also been read by Jordan Mintz for accuracy as regards the key historical events.

In fact, Mintz did not create planning lists like those outlined in Attachments 2 and 3. These are historical recreations designed to focus attention on Mintz's tactical choices. Mintz advises that he did go through a process of considering many of these same points; however, it took place over time and in pieces as opposed to being focused into a single planning document.

Attachment 1 also is a historical recreation (HRC). It is designed to depict the type of restricted disclosure Fastow provided to the board in his PowerPoint presentation requesting the Conflict of Interest waiver. **It is important to acknowledge and recognize that this Attachment is not a historical document from the Enron archives.** For that reason, it is crafted as a DRAFT, i.e. something like a first Fastow attempt at a board communication that Mintz might have found in the files on moving into Global Finance. The real purposes of including this attachment are twofold. First, it provides a succinct summary of the LJM1 transaction. Second, it displays the type of care Fastow did take in communicating with the board. It is carefully economical with the truth. It serves up those facts that display the transaction to best advantage, avoiding or deemphasizing others that might have been "red flags" to board members, such as any sort of numerical projection of compensation for the LJM partners if the "put" was never triggered.

Although this document is a creation, it does accurately reflect the public accounts of the LJM 1 transaction and the rationales Fastow provided to the board, including the assertion that the outside investors wanted him to be the general partner for the deal. *Conspiracy of Fools* contains a detailed account (p. 244-45) of the June 18, 1999, meeting at which Lay and Skilling gave Fastow their consent to take LJM1 to the Enron board. According to this account, Fastow told Lay that he would be LJM's general partner in order to give Enron more control over it and that his investing in LJM would be the best way to get the deal done quickly and was the right thing for Enron. Fastow also asserted that Enron would continue to be a far more important source of income for him.

The Smartest Guys in the Room details Fastow's presentation to the Enron Board on June 28. According to this account, Fastow "spun" his proposed activity as follows: " ...his personal involvement in the new partnership was an act of altruism, an unfortunate but necessary ingredient to attract outside investors to LJM and essential to Enron's goal of hedging the Rhythms investment."[2]

In *Conspiracy of Fools*' account of the Board review, Fastow is quoted as saying: "I do have serious concerns about me being general partner. But if the board and the company want me to do this, I'll be happy to do it."[3]

Attachment 1 thus attempts to capture Fastow's "spin", namely, that he didn't really want to be LJM's general partner but that it was necessary for various reasons-outside investor demands, time pressure, Enron control-in a document that also explains the workings of the Rhythms NetConnections hedge.

This case contains one other element touched on in other cases but never systematically developed. This element concerns the possible implications of resistance for Mintz's career. These risks Mintz enumerates near the end of the case narrative. Students should incorporate plans to mitigate Mintz's career risks into their final tactical plan.

Endnotes

1. *Conspiracy of Fools*, p. 413.
2. *The Smartest Guys in the Room*, p. 193.
3. *Conspiracy of Fools*, p. 249.

Case Study 13

New Counsel for Andy Fastow (B): Attorney Responsibility to Report Fraud

They just don't want to deal with what Fastow's doing.
Are they blind, in on the deal, or do they just not want to know?
Where do I go from here?

JORDAN MINTZ HAD GOTTEN NOWHERE. In fact, maybe he had gotten to someplace worse than nowhere. Mintz was increasingly worried that he was becoming liable for Enron's misleading financial reports.

After meeting with Fastow, Mintz had consulted with an attorney at Enron's outside counsel. The recommendation was to continue the previous year's limited disclosure: that Fastow's compensation could not be calculated and thus didn't need to be disclosed.

Mintz's next effort was made on February 2. He visited with chief accounting officer Rick Causey and let on that Fastow's compensation struck Mintz as a big number. Mintz opined that Enron's directors seemed to want to know what Fastow was making. He then told Causey: "So I think it's important for you to make sure it gets before the board how much Andy is making from LJM."[1]

Causey answered that he understood that it was important. There the matter rested. On February 12, Causey made a presentation on LJM's financial controls to the Enron board's Audit Committee. No mention of Fastow's compensation was made.

Mintz's next effort was a memo summarizing his LJM concerns. These included the disclosure issue on Fastow's compensation and such matters as the conflicts of interest McMahon had protested earlier. Mintz also wanted to implement a more rigorous, documented approval process for transactions. Making sure that Jeff Skilling reviewed deals and signed off was one of the recommendations.

158

S.V. Arbogast, *Resisting Corporate Corruption* (pp. 158–167)
© 2008 by M & M Scrivener Press

The memo went to Causey and Rick Buy on March 8. A week passed with no response. Mintz set up a meeting. Arriving at the meeting, he asked Causey and Buy for their reactions. They hadn't read it.

Late in March, Enron filed its proxy statement for the year 2000. The statement contained no disclosure regarding the amount of Fastow's compensation. Mintz chose to rely on the advice of outside counsel and to continue nondisclosure on the basis of open transactions/inability to calculate. However, he immediately followed this action by sending Fastow a memo which stated: "The decision not to disclose in this instance was a close call; arguably, the more conservative approach would have been to disclose the amount of your interest."[2]

Despite having a reason to justify nondisclosure and the support of outside counsel for that position, Mintz was more than frustrated. He was increasingly worried that he was becoming personally liable for the questionable financial-disclosure approach Enron was taking. Enron's financials for 2000 were now officially filed. Mintz had let them go out despite his view that the more conservative and better course would have been to disclose Fastow's compensation. Mintz was feeling torn. He felt conflicted by his understanding that his role as an attorney was primarily to serve the best interests of his client, Enron, and his apprehension that the Securities Exchange Commission might question his acquiescing to nondisclosure of Fastow's compensation.

Attorney Ethics and Legal Obligations

Before considering what to do next, Mintz decided to clarify his conflicting responsibilities as an Enron attorney. First he revisited the Texas Bar Association Canon of Ethics, which all attorneys practicing in the state are required to observe. Relevant sections of the code are in Attachment 1.

After reviewing the canon, Mintz concluded that he was on solid ground as far as the Texas Bar Association was concerned. The canon made clear that Mintz's primary responsibility was to his client, and does not oblige attorneys to act as "whistleblowers." In this, the position of attorneys differs from what public accountants are legally obligated to do. Assuming they discover a fraud, auditors are legally required to so advise management and, if necessary, bring it to the board attention. If neither management nor the board takes proper action, public accountants must take further steps. The Private Securities Litigation Reform Act of 1995 states the requirements as follows:

> "Whenever an 'independent public accountant' discovers 'information indicating that an illegal act...has or may have occurred,' she must inform the Audit Committee or the Board of Directors of the illegality. If the legal violation is material and management fails to 'take timely and appropriate remedial actions,' the accountant shall notify the board of her conclusion

that remedial action was not undertaken. Any issue who receives such a notification from an accountant must inform the SEC and copy its SEC report to the accountant. If the accountant does not receive that copy, she must either resign or report her original complaint to the Commission (SEC). Her resignation also triggers an obligation to send a report to the SEC."[3]

No comparable responsibilities have been legislated for the legal profession. As is clear from the canon, attorneys' primary responsibility is to serve the "best interests" of the organization employing them. This same language is embedded in the American Bar Association's (ABA) Model Rule of Professional Conduct 1.13 (see Attachment 2). Neither the canon nor the ABA's Model Rule contains an affirmative requirement for attorneys to report their employers to outside authorities. Protection of attorneys' obligation to advise their clients and of attorney/client privilege lies at the heart of the ABA's ethical posture. The ABA's Model Rule does, however, clarify that attorneys who suspect their firms of illegal activities may request a "separate legal opinion" on the matter.

To Mintz's dismay, regulatory agencies, such as the SEC, had begun taking a broader view of the attorney's role. They were now pressing attorneys to act in a manner similar to public accountants. The SEC had the ability to put pressure on attorneys by asserting that their obligations as lawful citizens trumped their responsibility to protect clients. From this point of view, an attorney who became aware of fraud would have an affirmative obligation to report it to appropriate authorities even if this amounted to informing on a client. In parallel, Congress was beginning to talk about legislating "up-the-ladder reporting" by attorneys to the SEC in cases where there is evidence of a breach in fiduciary responsibility or a material violation of securities laws.

To date, no such legislation had been enacted. Still, Mintz had to wonder whether the SEC was about to begin pursuing attorneys who had failed to act as whistleblowers on their clients. The legal issue was tricky. Just because bar association codes of ethics held the client's interests to be paramount did not mean that government regulators couldn't treat attorneys like citizens, i.e. hold them accountable if they failed to report evidence of fraud. In fact, the SEC might be looking for an opportunity to make an example out of a major company lawyer.

Pressing the Internal Fight, Addressing the External Risk

Mintz pushed aside his personal concerns for the moment and tried to concentrate on the internal battle over Fastow and LJM. Once he sorted out plans on that front, he would come back and see whether his plans could be squared with the risk of becoming an SEC target.

The battle really was over LJM. Mintz was uncomfortable about many things, all of which he had listed in his memo to Causey and Buy. Focusing on disclosing Fastow's compensation was only one point at issue. It was, however, a powerful point because of the potential legal implications: SEC investigation, shareholder suits, and so on. But forcing Fastow's disclosure was not the only, and maybe not even the most, important objective Mintz had. He wanted Enron management to revisit what it was doing with LJM, realize the risks, and reconsider whether the benefits were worth the risks.

Mintz surveyed his options for pushing the effort to undo LJM. He had fired more than a few arrows at the target in recent months. None had scored a direct hit. Several, however, had made Fastow and his sidekick, Kopper, very nervous. Perhaps another push on the right front would finally achieve results. Mintz listed four possibilities:

1. Follow up his warning note to Fastow by forcing the issue of compensation disclosure at the next opportunity. Perhaps Mintz could find some way to strengthen his case, such that the excuse "too uncertain to compute" would no longer be sustainable. He had been considering the option of asking for an opinion on the disclosure question from a firm other than Enron's long-standing outside counsel. Would that really help?

2. Force a report to the board, disclosing and documenting Fastow's compensation. As indicated to Rick Causey, the board had documented its desire to know Fastow's LJM remuneration.

3. Ask for a meeting with Jeff Skilling on his need to sign off on all the LJM deals to complete the necessary documentation. Use the meeting to acquaint Skilling with Mintz's disclosure concerns and their implied message about the size of Fastow's compensation.

4. Take the issue of disclosing Fastow's compensation to the SEC.

In reviewing this list, Mintz recognized that he still did not know the actual amount of Fastow's compensation. Fastow was not going to provide this. Mintz would have to go through the documents for all the LJM deals and make his own estimate.

Mintz studied his list again. The various approaches might well have different outcomes. What would constitute a "success" that would make continuing the internal struggle worthwhile? Were the prospects good enough to justify the potential career consequences: an almost certain confrontation with Fastow and a possible exit from Enron for Mintz?

And last but not least, would that success get Mintz "off the hook" regarding difficulties with the SEC?

Attachment 1—Excerpts from Texas State Bar Association Canon of Ethics

Rule 1.02 Scope and Objectives of Representation

...a lawyer shall abide by a client's decisions:

> (1) concerning the objectives and general methods of representation...

(c) A lawyer shall not assist or counsel a client to engage in conduct that the lawyer knows is criminal or fraudulent. A lawyer may discuss the legal consequences of any proposed course of conduct with a client and may counsel and represent a client in connection with the making of a good faith effort to determine the validity, scope, meaning or application of the law.

(d) When a lawyer has confidential information clearly establishing that a client is likely to commit a criminal or fraudulent act that is likely to result in substantial injury to the financial interests or property of another, the lawyer shall promptly make reasonable efforts under the circumstances to dissuade the client from committing the crime or fraud.

Rule 1.03 Communication

(a) A lawyer shall keep a client reasonably informed about the status of a matter and promptly comply with reasonable requests for information.

(b) A lawyer shall explain a matter to the extent reasonably necessary to permit the client to make informed decisions regarding the representation.

Rule 1.05 Confidentiality of Information

A lawyer shall not knowingly: ...

> (2) Use confidential information of a client to the disadvantage of the client unless the client consents after consultation.

(c) A lawyer may reveal confidential information: ...

> (4) When the lawyer has reason to believe it is necessary to do so in order to comply with a court order, a Texas Disciplinary Rule of Professional Conduct, or other law...

> (7) When the lawyer has reason to believe it is necessary to do so in order to prevent the client from committing a criminal or fraudulent act...

Rule 1.12 Organization as a Client

(a) A lawyer employed or retained by an organization represents the entity.

(b) A lawyer representing an organization must take reasonable remedial actions whenever the lawyer learns or knows that:

(1) an officer, employee, or other person associated with the organization has committed or intends to commit a violation of a legal obligation to the organization or a violation of law which reasonably might be imputed to the organization;

(2) the violation is likely to result in substantial injury to the organization;

(c) Except where prior disclosure to persons outside the organization is required by law or other Rules, a lawyer shall first attempt to resolve a violation by taking measures within the organization. ....

In determining the internal procedures, actions or measures that are reasonably necessary in order to comply with paragraphs (a) and (b), a lawyer shall give due consideration to the seriousness of the violation and its consequences, the scope and nature of the lawyer's representation, the responsibility in the organization and the apparent motivation of the person involved, the policies of the organization concerning such matters, and any other relevant considerations. Such procedures, actions and measures may include, but are not limited to, the following:

(1) asking reconsideration of the matter

(2) advising that a separate legal opinion on the matter be sought for presentation to appropriate authority in the organization; and

(3) referring the matter to higher authority in the organization, including, if warranted by the seriousness of the matter, referral to the highest authority that can act in behalf of the organization as determined by applicable law...

Rule 1.15 Declining or Terminating Representation

(a) A lawyer shall decline to represent a client or, where representation has commenced, shall withdraw, except as stated in paragraph (c), from the representation of a client, if:

(1) the representation will result in violation of Rule 3.08, other applicable rules of professional conduct or other law; ...

(4) a client insists upon pursuing an objective that the lawyer considers repugnant or imprudent or with which the lawyer has fundamental disagreement;

Rule 4.01 Truthfulness in Statements to Others

In the course of representing a client a lawyer shall not knowingly: ...

(b) fail to disclose a material fact to a third person when disclosure is necessary to avoid making the lawyer a party to a criminal act or knowingly assisting a fraudulent act perpetrated by a client.

Rule 8.04 Misconduct

(a) A lawyer shall not: ...

(3) engage in conduct involving dishonesty, fraud, deceit or misrepresentation;

(4) engage in conduct constituting obstruction of justice;

Attachment 2—Excerpts from American Bar Association Code of Ethics

Rule 1.13 Organization as Client

(a) A lawyer employed or retained by an organization represents the organization acting through its duly authorized constituents.

(b) If a lawyer for an organization knows that an officer, employee or other person associated with the organization is engaged in action, intends to act or refuses to act in a matter related to the representation that is a violation of a legal obligation to the organization, or a violation of law that reasonably might be imputed to the organization, and that is likely to result in substantial injury to the organization, then the lawyer shall proceed as is reasonably necessary in the best interest of the organization. Unless the lawyer reasonably believes that it is not necessary in the best interest of the organization to do so, the lawyer shall refer the matter to higher authority in the organization, including, if warranted by the circumstances to the highest authority that can act on behalf of the organization as determined by applicable law.

(c) Except as provided in paragraph (d), if

(1) despite the lawyer's efforts in accordance with paragraph (b) the highest authority that can act on behalf of the organization insists upon or fails to address in a timely and appropriate manner an action, or a refusal to act, that is clearly a violation of law, and

(2) the lawyer reasonably believes that the violation is reasonably certain to result in substantial injury to the organization, then the lawyer may reveal information relating to the representation whether or not Rule 1.6 permits such disclosure, but only if and to the extent the lawyer reasonably believes necessary to prevent substantial injury to the organization.

(d) Paragraph (c) shall not apply with respect to information relating to a lawyer's representation of an organization to investigate an alleged violation of law, or to defend the organization or an officer, employee or other constituent associated with the organization against a claim arising out of an alleged violation of law.

(e) A lawyer who reasonably believes that he or she has been discharged because of the lawyer's actions taken pursuant to paragraphs (b) or (c), or who withdraws under circumstances that require or permit the lawyer to take action under either of those paragraphs, shall proceed as the lawyer reasonably believes necessary to assure that the organization's highest authority is informed of the lawyer's discharge or withdrawal.

(f) In dealing with an organization's directors, officers, employees, members, shareholders or other constituents, a lawyer shall explain the identity of the client when the lawyer knows or reasonably should know that the organization's interests are adverse to those of the constituents with whom the lawyer is dealing.

(g) A lawyer representing an organization may also represent any of its directors, officers, employees, members, shareholders or other constituents, subject to the provisions of Rule 1.7. If the organization's consent to the dual representation is required by Rule 1.7, the consent shall be given by an appropriate official of the organization other than the individual who is to be represented, or by the shareholders.

Author's Note

When a potential legal violation is at issue, does an attorney owe ultimate allegiance to the client or to the regulatory body charged with enforcing the law? This case depicts Jordan Mintz's dilemma on this score as the LJM disclosure issue unfolded. Internal initiatives have not borne fruit. Mintz may already be legally vulnerable given Enron's filing of its year-2000 financials. Is he still free to consider ways to force a change on Fastow/LJM within Enron? Or has the time come to take matters outside the company?

This description of Jordan Mintz's ongoing efforts to force disclosure of Andy Fastow's LJM compensation is based on the accounts documented in *Conspiracy of Fools* and *The Smartest Guys in the Room*. The former provides the quote wherein Mintz urged Rick Causey to disclose Fastow's earnings to the Enron board. The account of Mintz's meeting with Causey and Rick Buy is on pp. 434-435. The quoted "close call" warning to Fastow appears in *The Smartest Guys in the Room*.

Jordan Mintz reports that during these events, he was not as concerned about SEC actions as the case depicts. Mintz knew that the potential for difficulties with the SEC existed, but felt that his internal efforts to force disclosure of the material information about Fastow and LJM would ultimately be understood by the commission. This did not occur. The commission has filed a formal complaint against Mintz, which matter is presently under adjudication.

The case study presents Mintz as concerned about his SEC risk in order to highlight the dilemmas that attorneys face even today. An attorney's conflicting responsibilities to client and to the law have in fact spawned an argument between the SEC and various bar associations. Background on this dispute is drawn from Leslie Griffin's article "Whistleblowing in the Business World," published in *Enron, Corporate Fiascos and Their Implications*. This article's discussion of the legal responsibilities of accountants versus attorneys appears on pp. 229-235. In conversations with Dr. Griffin, she has confirmed that controversy has persisted between bar associations and the SEC over whether attorneys are required to report evidence of fraud to the commission.

The excerpts from the Texas State Bar Association's Canon of Ethics were provided by Brock Akers, a Houston attorney. Akers presented this material with an earlier version of this Mintz case study to a continuing legal education (CLE) course in 2004. The American Bar Association material was provided courtesy of Dr. Griffin.

Notes

1. *Conspiracy of Fools*, p. 419.
2. *The Smartest Guys in the Room*, p. 328.
3. "Whistleblowing in the Business World," p. 229.

Case Study 14

Nowhere to Go with "The Probability of Ruin"

This is unbelievable, even worse than I thought. Even with only partial information, it's unarguable that Enron sits under a huge overhang of debts. Many of these debts are not quantified and unacknowledged. We need to get this study in front of a manager who will listen before something sets off the avalanche.

O N MARCH 7, 2001, VINCE KAMINSKI, Enron's top risk analyst, received confirmation that the nightmare hovering over Enron was real. One year earlier, Kaminski had set in motion a comprehensive study of Enron's financial risks. Because of their complexity, any study of Enron's financial operations had to cover more than debt levels and fixed charges. Trading exposures, customer credit risks, derivative positions, corporate guarantees, and Enron's ties to off-balance sheet vehicles also had to be tracked down and analyzed. Compiling this assessment had taken Kaminski's team a full year to complete. Even so, the information contained big gaps.

Still, the overall picture was clear. Enron had a staggering amount of debt, near-debt, and assorted financial commitments, much of which was lodged in structures that obscured their existence. Perhaps most disturbing, Enron's top financial managers, the very architects of this liability mountain, didn't possess any sense of its cumulative size or risks; in fact, they not only didn't know the situation, they apparently didn't want to know it.

Kaminski's plan was to confront this state of denial with an unassailable fact case, one that would force management to take the hard corrective measures it had avoided until now.

The Enron Companywide Risk Management Report

Kaminski's team leaders, Kevin Kindall and Li Sun, handed around their report. It laid out in cold, hard facts that Enron was flirting with disaster. Enron's year-2000 financial statements were telling investors and rating agencies that the company's non-trade debts totaled some $10 billion.

S.V. Arbogast, *Resisting Corporate Corruption* (pp. 168–184)
© 2008 by M & M Scrivener Press

(Attachment 1 summarizes Enron's 2000 balance sheet and provides a sample of Enron's disclosure about its related-party transactions.) Kaminski's team did not yet have all the information to compute the real figure, but what it had discovered suggested that Enron owed a much higher amount.

Getting to a comprehensive measure of Enron's risk required both detective work and financial know-how. For example, Enron Global Finance made profligate use of corporate guarantees. Kaminski's team had tracked down 2,700 such guarantees and had no confidence that they all had been found. Global Finance kept no central record of guarantees. Arriving at a companywide risk assessment required that such guarantees not only be tabulated but also quantified as "debt equivalents."

A similar situation existed regarding Enron's huge, ever-changing derivatives positions. Trading was the beating heart of Enron; the firm constantly bought and sold gas, electricity, and other commodities on a forward basis and then bought and sold futures and options to hedge these positions or profit from spreads. All these positions might then be traded, using other derivative products and creating new ones. At any given point, the result for Enron might be a huge net obligation to deliver physical goods or their financial equivalent to third parties. These liabilities were volatile and could add massively to the trading obligations that the company did acknowledge on its year-end balance sheet.

Most disturbing of all was Enron's connections to the off-balance sheet Special Purpose Entities (SPEs) concocted by Enron Global Finance. These entities warehoused huge amounts of suspect merchant assets and their associated debts. Global Finance deliberately designed the SPEs to avoid their inclusion in Enron's consolidated financial reports. Yet the details of many deals contained provisions that required Enron to support the SPEs financially should adverse events materialize. Kaminski thought these "contingent obligations" to be especially dangerous, as they would likely be activated only when Enron's financial condition was already deteriorating.

One exceptional example of Enron's disguised connections with the SPEs was the "Total Return Swap" (TRS). Global Finance used this arrangement to provide guaranteed returns to "independent" SPE investors while drawing the underlying economic risks of "sold assets" back into Enron. The company had encountered increasing resistance from investors to whom Enron wanted to divest troubled assets; this was especially so when Enron, up against a financial reporting deadline, sought to sell assets for a certain price-either to book needed profits or to avoid losses on values previously "marked to market". So, Enron had turned to the related-party SPEs put together by Enron CFO Andy Fastow. These vehicles provided the appearance of "independent equity" doing deals that allowed Enron to achieve its desired accounting results; they also were willing to pay asset prices consistent with Enron's accounting targets. The quid pro quo for the SPE's owners, however, was a high and almost riskless financial return. Enron would use the TRS tool to provide that return without disturbing the accounting result it sought to achieve.

Total Return Swaps worked as follows. Enron might sell a set of merchant assets and associated liabilities to an SPE. Normally, such an asset sale would transfer full upside and downside economic risk to the SPE buyer. Under the TRS, however, Enron and the SPE would swap returns immediately after the asset sale. Enron would contract with the SPE to receive the more risky and volatile return on the merchant assets. In return, Enron would agree to pay the SPE a specified formula return, such as London Inter-bank Offer Rate (LIBOR) + 3%. This return would be calibrated at a sufficient spread over the SPE's own debt costs such that it generated a high return on the vehicle's small equity capital.

The result of the TRS was to reverse the normal effects of an asset sale. Enron effectively took back all economic upside potential and downside risk associated with the underlying assets. It simultaneously paid the SPEs investors a high return on their small "capital at risk." This effectively amounted to paying a service fee to the SPE for its helping to produce needed accounting results. Enron's own board minutes acknowledged this relationship by noting that these SPEs "did not transfer economic risk" but served to hedge accounting volatility.[1]   Attachment 2 illustrates the structure of a TRS.

Even more frightening to Kaminski and his team was the embedding of "trigger events" into these SPE deals. Triggers had come into widespread use during the 1990s as a financial engineering tool. Typically, they were used by lenders when a financially stronger parent wanted lenders to fund a weaker subsidiary without receiving a parent guarantee. In such circumstances, lenders might demand the comfort of a covenant specifying that the parent must inject certain funds into the subsidiary if some trigger event occurred. Usually, the trigger events occurred when: (1) the parent's debt rating was downgraded or (2) the parent's stock price fell below a threshold price. The effect of the trigger was to assure lenders that their SPE borrower would immediately be strengthened before other calls on the now weaker parent came into play. In agreeing to deals with triggers, Enron remained obligated to support supposedly "independent" parties if/when specified adverse circumstances materialized.

Enron Global Finance used this technique to persuade "independent" investors to enter into transactions that otherwise involved unacceptable prices or risks. One example of how Enron used triggers was the Whitewing transaction. There Enron induced Citibank to lend $500 million on a non-guaranteed basis to the Whitewing SPE. Whitewing used this money to purchase an Enron preferred stock that was also convertible into Enron common stock. Whitewing's source of cash flow to pay loan debt service would be the preferred stock dividends from Enron.

Citibank, however, had a reasonable concern: How was Whitewing to repay loan principal? Ultimately, the vehicle's ability to do so would depend upon converting the preferred stock itself into cash. However, no ready market existed for what was, in effect, a privately placed preferred. Hence, the preferred stock had been made convertible to Enron common stock, for which there was a ready market. So far, so good, but Citibank had one more question: What if Enron's common stock fell below the price level needed to generate the cash to repay the Citibank loan? Citibank refused to accept the argument that such a scenario was too improbable to consider. So, Enron agreed that if such an event occurred, it would trigger a change in the preferred's conversion ratio. Said differently, if Enron common stock fell below $28/share, Enron stood ready to issue to Whitewing whatever additional common stock was needed to ensure loan repayment.

What seemed a brilliant technical solution to the Whitewing financial architects was positively frightening to Vince Kaminski. He understood that within a broader scenario of troubles for Enron, Whitewing's financial architecture could produce a cascade of additional repayment obligations. Focusing for the moment on Whitewing, Kaminski and his team pondered this hypothetical train of events: 1) suppose something really bad happened, such that Enron's stock is under severe pressure, and falls below $28/share; (2) Whitewing's trigger is pulled, and Enron must issue more convertible preferred; (3) Citibank gets nervous and forces Whitewing to convert to common and sell stock into the open market; (4) Enron's stock is blindsided by a surge of selling from a new source and falls further; (5) other triggers in other deals come into play, feeding the spiral.

And there were other triggers embedded in Enron's other deals with LJM. The effect of seeing one trigger after another pulled was almost beyond imagining. Kaminski and his team knew that they had to get Enron's senior management to look at a full picture of what they would face if worst came to worst. There might still be time to undo the worst of the deals and perhaps store up financial reserves to handle others. But Kaminski knew that the task would not be easy. He would not simply be bringing bad news to management; he would be presenting a possible disaster scenario that was the product of management's own proud creation. Kaminski also knew that he had something of a reputation as a Cassandra; in fact, he had already paid a price for this. As he pondered how best to bring his findings to management's attention, Kaminski found himself thinking back over a previous experience when he had questioned some dubious Enron practices.

Kaminski and LJM

The case in point occurred in June 2000. At that time, Jeff Skilling was seeking to hedge a large capital gain Enron had accrued on its investment in a small Internet company: Rhythms NetConnections (Rhythms). Using mark-to-market accounting, Enron had already booked several hundred million dollars of this paper gain into net income. Skilling was concerned that a reverse in the Rhythms stock price would force Enron to realize large losses and was therefore interested in hedging this exposure. The Rhythms stock was thinly traded. This made it difficult, if not impossible, to hedge over the six-month time period of concern to Enron. So, CFO Andy Fastow had proposed that Enron capitalize a new partnership, called LJM, with Enron stock. Fastow, two banks, and some other individuals would provide a small sum of "independent" equity. Fastow would run the partnership. LJM would then provide Enron with a "put" option on Rhythms stock, thereby hedging the exposure that worried Skilling.

At the time, Vince Kaminski was working in Enron's Risk Assessment and Control (RAC) Department. His boss, Rick Buy, had asked Kaminski to price the LJM put option on Rhythms' stock. Kaminski's initial reaction was that the hedge could not be priced; any put option price would depend upon the put writer's ability to hedge by shorting Rhythms stock; that hedge, Kaminski argued, would be almost impossible to accomplish, because Rhythms stock was so thinly traded.

Upon learning further details, Kaminski quickly concluded that the LJM transaction itself was a sham. It amounted to Enron's hedging with itself. LJM's only means to cover major losses on the hedge resided in the stock Enron had contributed. Economically, Enron would be covering losses from a Rhythms stock price decline by issuing new common shares and diluting its shareholders.

When he learned that CFO Fastow had not only conceived of the idea but was going to run LJM, Kaminski was outraged. He had told Buy: "I am very uncomfortable with this whole thing. This is a cockamamie idea. This idea is so stupid, only Andy Fastow could have come up with it…Enron should never go forward with such a thing. It's a terrible conflict of interest."[2]

Buy asked Kaminski not to jump to conclusions. However, three days and detailed analysis by his top experts did not alter Kaminski's view. When they met again on June 21, Kaminski told Buy that the conflict of interest involved in Fastow's running the partnership was a disaster in the making. He showed Buy how this conflict of interest had already influenced Fastow's structuring of LJM: "You can already see why, the way the partnership is structured. The payout of the structure is completely skewed against Enron shareholders. It's heads, the partnership wins, tails Enron loses…the structure is simply unstable. It's a partnership funded with Enron stock, and if Enron stock drops at the same time Rhythms stock drops, the partnership will be unable to meet its obligations."[3]

Buy professed to see the light and told Kaminski that he would stop the deal. Four days later, however, Buy admitted that he had been unable to do so: "I couldn't stop it. The momentum was too strong...It will be fine. It's just temporary."[4]

Kaminski had walked away enraged but also thinking that this was the end of it as far has he was concerned. He was wrong. Late on a Friday afternoon shortly thereafter, Kaminski received a phone call from Jeff Skilling. Kaminski's group was to be transferred out of RAC and into Wholesale Trading. No longer would Kaminski and his team evaluate firm-wide transactions. Kaminski asked the reason for the change; Skilling replied: "There have been some complaints, Vince, that you're not helping people to do transactions. Instead you're spending all your time acting like cops. We don't need cops, Vince."[5]

This history weighed on Kaminski. Obviously, taking the risk study to Andy Fastow would be a waste of time, and given his previous reaction, Jeff Skilling did not look like a good bet, either. Still, he had to start somewhere in the financial management. After all, they were the architects of the deals and entities responsible for these frightening risks.

It occurred to Kaminski that Ben Glisan, the new treasurer, might be a good place to start. Clearly Glisan was one of Fastow's protégés. On the other hand, he had been around for only a couple of years and had taken the treasurer's role only a year ago. Kaminski decided to start with Glisan and see where that led.

Meeting with Ben Glisan

Kaminski and his team met Glisan in his office on March 9, 2001. Kaminski introduced the companywide risk assessment and its rationale and then asked Kevin Kindall to cover it in detail.

Kindall went through a series of findings that amounted to a powerful indictment of how Global Finance was conducting business. Kindall started with the structured deals that used total return swaps with triggers. These, he argued, involved unleashing massive potential liabilities under certain downside scenarios. The danger was that Global Finance was neither tracking these liabilities and their triggers nor weighing the probabilities of multiple trigger thresholds being crossed.

Next, Kindall noted that Global Finance was not keeping track of Enron's swap book. Neither the swap amounts nor the specific deal terms were being monitored. Kindall mentioned that his team had also identified 2,700 corporate guarantees. Again, Global Finance was not aware of their implied liability amounts because it possessed no central database for tracking these obligations.

Perhaps most damning, Kindall noted the absence of any system for determining Enron's daily cash position. Data came in from different business units in an uncoordinated and untimely fashion; as a result, Enron needed to borrow extra money to make sure that it didn't run out of cash.

Kindall saved certain off-balance sheet transactions for last. Specific vehicles, such as the Raptors, were known for combining large debts and stock price triggers with poorly performing assets. Kindall's team could not, however, quantify the implied risks for Enron, because transaction details had not been made available.

> We weren't able to gain access to a lot of information. But what we could review pointed to the existence of huge risk exposures that Enron simply hasn't fully analyzed and does not understand. We've assessed the likelihood of hitting one of those triggers. For example, we have a five-percent chance of a credit downgrade in the next twelve months. But you have to understand, these are just the triggers we have located. There appear to be other triggers embedded in other vehicles as well. It's likely the occurrence of one trigger will push down the share price so far that we hit another one embedded in some other vehicle...
>
> In truth, it's conceivable we could hit a cascading series of triggers, setting off a domino effect, where each trigger pushes down our stock price even more. That would result in a massive decrease in the share price and lower our bonds to a junk rating.[6]

Kaminski followed up Kindall's remarks by emphasizing the need for more budget funds and more information to finish the project. A complete list of off-balance sheet SPEs was needed, so that all their assets and obligations could be examined. Only then could the potential for interrelated negative trigger events be assessed. Adding that piece of the puzzle to the information already compiled would allow Kindall and his team to estimate Enron's "probability of ruin."

So far, Ben Glisan had listened without comment. Casually, he perused the written report while Kindall and Kaminski spoke. It was dense with data and analysis. Near the end, however, the report referenced a recent Fortune article that had shed unflattering light on Enron's financial results. Clearly, bringing to light the type of information Kindall and Kaminski were compiling would result in a further journalistic feeding frenzy. That could not be good for Enron.

Glisan then closed the report and spoke: "Well, I appreciate all the work that went into this. But there really isn't anything to worry about. Vince, I've been involved in designing almost all of these vehicles. We know what the risks are. It's not an issue."[7]

Kaminski pressed Glisan to consider authorizing more study. Glisan responded by saying that he'd take another look at the report and get back to Kaminski.

Weeks passed. Kaminski never heard another word on the matter from Glisan.

What now? Without Glisan's say-so, Kaminski and his team could not get details on the transactions that constituted the holes in their report. Global Finance held all the files on the off-balance sheet vehicles. Above treasurer Glisan there was only CFO Fastow. Kaminski was not optimistic that Fastow's reaction would be more favorable; potentially, it could be a lot worse, such as seizing and destroying all work done to date.

Was there an audience outside of Global Finance? Remembering his "cops" conversation with Jeff Skilling, Kaminski quickly discarded him as a possibility. Ken Lay was too detached from the business details and anyway tended to take Skilling's word on structured transactions.

There was one other possibility, however. Greg Whalley, head of Wholesale Trading, was a rising star within Enron. Whalley was now also Kaminski's ultimate boss. If Enron's credit rating was to slip because of the sudden revelation of disguised debts in poorly structured vehicles, it was Whalley's lucrative trading franchise that would be most severely impacted. Perhaps Kaminski could interest Whalley in his companywide risk assessment.

How then, should Kaminski present this material to Enron's head trader?

Elsewhere in Enron

In July 2001, Margaret Ceconi, a sales executive in Enron Electricity Services (EES) was disturbed about how her division was faring. EES had reported a $40 million profit for the first quarter. Yet the business was widely known to have suffered serious business reverses and trading losses. Informal estimates within the group put the losses at a minimum of $500 million. Enron had responded by merging EES into the larger Wholesale Trading business and calling the merger an overdue efficiency move. Still, Ceconi could not understand how EES was reporting profits or how its losses could be submerged into Wholesale Trading and not reported separately.

Ceconi decided to contact the SEC anonymously. Filling out a form on the agency Web site, Ceconi posed a hypothetical question about merging a loss-making unit into a profitable larger unit. Did the losses still have to be broken out and reported?

Ceconi had given the SEC her phone number and got a call back. An SEC officer advised that both the size of the losses and their separate origin had to be disclosed to avoid a distortion of reporting for both segments. No follow-up discussion occurred, however.

Ceconi soon found herself laid off as part of the EES/Wholesale Trading merger. Before departing, Ceconi addressed a signed, ten-page letter to the Enron board, alleging SEC violations regarding the non-reporting of EES's $500 million in losses. The letter, which went to board secretary Rebecca Carter, was never shown to Ken Lay or the board. Ceconi began also e-mailing information to Prudential Securities analyst Carol Coale; these e-mails included tough questions for her to use on analyst conference calls.

Elsewhere, a former Enron executive noted how the press had begun to circle around Enron's off-balance sheet transactions. This executive still possessed copies of the offering documents for LJM2. Fastow had used these documents when trying to raise capital for his fund from Wall Street investment bankers. Among other revelations, the documents made statements that the Powers Committee Report later described as follows:

> ... LJM2 solicited prospective investors...using a confidential Private Placement Memorandum (PPM) detailing ... the 'unusually attractive investment opportunity' resulting from the partnership's connection to Enron. The PPM emphasized Fastow's position as Enron's CFO, and that LJM2's day-to-day activities would be managed by Fastow, Kopper, and Glisan...It explained that '[t]he Partnership expects that Enron will be the Partnership's primary source of investment opportunities' and that it 'expects to benefit from having the opportunity to invest in Enron-generated investment opportunities that would not be available otherwise to outside investors.' The PPM specifically noted that Fastow's 'access to Enron's information pertaining to potential investments will contribute to superior returns.[8]

The former executive decided to send the documents to John Emshwiller and Rebecca Smith at the *Wall Street Journal.*[9]

Attachment 1

Enron and Subsidiaries

Summary Income Statement

in $ millions	Year ended December 31	
	2000	**1999**
Revenues	$100,789	$40,112
Less:		
Cost of inputs	94,517	34,761
Operating expenses	3,184	3,045
Depreciation and Amortization	855	870
Taxes and other expenses	280	634
Total Costs & Expenses	9,8836	39,310
Operating Income	1,953	802
Other Income:		
Equity in earnings of non-consolidated subs	87	309
Gains on sale of non-merchant assets	146	541
Gain on stock issuance by TNPC, Inc.	121	
Interest income and other, net	175	343
Income before Interest, Minority Interest & Income Taxes	2,482	1,995
Less:		
Interest and related charges, net	838	656
Dividends on preferred to subsidiaries	77	76
Minority interests	154	135
Income taxes	434	104
Accounting changes		131
Net Income	979	893
Preferred Stock dividends	83	66
Earnings on Common Stock	896	827

Source: Company annual report

Enron and Subsidiaries

Summary Consolidated Balance Sheet

$ millions	Year ended December 31	
	2000	**1999**
Cash and equivalents	1374	288
Trade Receivables	10396	3030
Assets from Price risk mgt. activities	12018	2205
Inventories	953	598
Deposits	2433	81
Other Current Assets	3207	1053
Total Current Assets	30381	7255
Investments and Other Assets	23379	15445
Net Property Plant and Equipment	11743	10681
Total Assets	65503	33381
Accounts Payable	9777	2154
Liabilities from Price risk mgt. activities	10495	1836
Customer deposits	4277	44
Other current liabilities	2187	1724
Short term debt	1670	1001
Total Current Liabilities	28406	6759
Deferred Credits & Other Liabilities:		
Deferred income taxes	1644	1894
Liabilities from Price risk mgt. activities	9423	2990
Other	2629	1587
Total Deferred Credits, etc.	13759	6471
Long Term Debt	8550	7151
Commitments/Contingencies Minority Interests	2414	2430
Company-Obligated Preferred Securities to Subsidiary	904	1000
Total Shareholders Equity	11470	9570
Total Liabilities and Shareholders Equity	65503	33381

Enron and Subsidiaries

Summary Consolidated Statement of Cash Flows

$ millions	Year ended December 31	
	2000	**1999**
Net Income	979	893
Depreciation and amortization	855	870
Deferred income taxes	207	21
Subtotal	2041	1784
Proceeds from sales	1838	2217
Changes in working capital	1769	(1000)
Additions and unrealized gains	(1295)	(827)
Net assets from price risk management activities	(763)	(395)
Impairment of long lived assets	326	441
Gains on sales of non-merchant assets	(146)	(541)
Realized gains on sales	(104)	(756)
Cumulative effect of accounting change		131
Other operating activities	1113	174
Subtotal	2738	(556)
Net Cash Provided by Operating activities	4779	1228
Cash Flows from Investing activities:		
Capital Expenditures	(2381)	(2363)
Equity investments & business acquisitions	(1710)	(1033)
Proceeds from sales on non-merchant assets	494	294
Other	(667)	(405)
Subtotal	(4264)	(3507)
Cash Flows from Financing activities:		
Issuance of long term debt, net	1657	(61)
Net (decrease) in short term debt	(1595)	1565
Issuance of common stock	307	852
Net issuance of subsidiary stock	404	568
Other	321	(1)
Dividends paid	(523)	(467)
Subtotal	571	2456
Increase (Decrease) in cash	1086	177
Cash at beginning of year	288	111
Cash at End of year	1374	288

Source: Company annual report

Excerpts from Notes to Financial Statements filed April 2, 2001, for Enron's 2000 Fiscal Year

15. COMMITMENTS

Firm Transportation Obligations. Enron has firm transportation agreements with various joint venture and other pipelines. Under these agreements, Enron must make specified minimum payments each month. At December 31, 2000, the estimated aggregate amounts of such required future payments were $91 million, $88 million, $89 million, $85 million and $77 million for 2001 through 2005, respectively, and $447 million for later years...

Other Commitments. Enron leases property, operating facilities and equipment under various operating leases, certain of which contain renewal and purchase options and residual value guarantees. Future commitments related to these items at December 31, 2000, were $123 million, $98 million, $69 million, $66 million and $49 million for 2001 through 2005, respectively, and $359 million for later years. Guarantees under the leases total $556 million at December 31, 2000...

Enron guarantees the performance of certain of its unconsolidated equity affiliates in connection with letters of credit issued on behalf of those entities. At December 31, 2000, a total of $264 million of such guarantees were outstanding, including $103 million on behalf of EOTT Energy Partners, L.P. (EOTT). In addition, Enron is a guarantor on certain liabilities of unconsolidated equity affiliates and other companies totaling approximately $1,863 million at December 31, 2000, including $538 million related to EOTT trade obligations.

The EOTT letters of credit and guarantees of trade obligations are secured by the assets of EOTT. Enron has also guaranteed $386 million in lease obligations for which it has been indemnified by an "Investment Grade" company. Management does not consider it likely that Enron would be required to perform or otherwise incur any losses associated with the above guarantees...

16. RELATED PARTY TRANSACTIONS

In 2000 and 1999, Enron entered into transactions with limited partnerships (the Related Party) whose general partner's managing member is a senior officer of Enron. The limited partners of the Related Party are unrelated to Enron. Management believes that the terms of the transactions with the Related Party were reasonable compared to those which could have been negotiated with unrelated third parties.

In 2000, Enron entered into transactions with the Related Party to hedge certain merchant investments and other assets. As part of the transactions, Enron (i) contributed to newly formed entities (the Entities) assets valued at approximately $1.2 billion, including $150 million in Enron notes payable, 3.7 million restricted shares of outstanding Enron common stock and the right to receive up to 18.0 million shares of outstanding Enron common stock in March 2003 (subject to certain conditions) and (ii) transferred to the Entities assets valued at approximately $309 million, including a $50 million note payable and an investment in an entity that indirectly holds warrants convertible into common stock of an Enron equity method investee. In return, Enron received economic interests in the Entities, $309 million in notes receivable, of which $259 million is recorded at Enron's carryover basis of zero and a special distribution from the Entities in the form of $1.2 billion in notes receivable, subject to changes in the principal for amounts payable by Enron in connection with the execution of additional derivative instruments. Cash in these Entities of $172.6 million is invested in Enron demand notes. In addition, Enron paid $123 million to purchase share-settled options from the Entities on 21.7 million shares of Enron common stock. The Entities paid Enron $10.7 million to terminate the share-settled options on 14.6 million shares of Enron common stock outstanding. In late 2000, Enron entered into share-settled collar arrangements with the Entities on 15.4 million shares of Enron common stock. Such arrangements will be accounted for as equity transactions when settled.

In 2000, Enron entered into derivative transactions with the Entities with a combined notional amount of approximately $2.1 billion to hedge certain merchant investments and other assets. Enron's notes receivable balance was reduced by $36 million as a results of premiums owed on derivative transactions. Enron recognized revenues of approximately $500 million related to the subsequent change in the market value of these derivatives, which offset market value changes of certain merchant investments and price risk management activities. In addition, Enron recognized $44.5 million and $14.1 million of interest income and interest expense, respectively, on the notes receivable from and payable to the Entities.

In 1999, Enron entered into a series of transactions involving a third party and the Related Party. The effect of the transactions was (i) Enron and the third party amended certain forward contracts to purchase shares of Enron common stock, resulting in Enron having forward contracts to purchase Enron common shares at the market price on that day, (ii) the Related Party received 6.8 million shares of Enron common stock subject to certain restrictions and (iii) Enron received a note receivable, which was repaid in December 1999, and certain financial instruments hedging an investment held by Enron. Enron recorded the assets received and equity issued at estimated fair value. In connection with the transactions, the Related Party agreed that the senior officer of Enron would have no pecuniary interest in such Enron common shares and would be restricted from voting on matters related to such shares. In 2000, Enron and the Related Party entered into an agreement to terminate certain financial instruments that had been entered into during 1999. In connection with this agreement, Enron received approximately 3.1 million shares of Enron common stock held by the Related Party. A put option, which was originally entered into in the first quarter of 2000 and gave the Related Party the right to sell shares of Enron common stock to Enron at a strike price of $71.31 per share, was terminated under this agreement. In return, Enron paid approximately $26.8 million to the Related Party.

In 2000, Enron sold a portion of its dark fiber inventory to the Related Party in exchange for $30 million cash and a $70 million note receivable that was subsequently repaid. Enron recognized gross margin of $67 million on the sale.

In 2000, the Related Party acquired, through securitizations, approximately $35 million of merchant investments from Enron. In addition, Enron and the Related Party formed partnerships in which Enron contributed cash and assets and the Related Party contributed $17.5 million in cash. Subsequently, Enron sold a portion of its interests in the partnerships through securitizations...Also, Enron contributed a put option to a trust in which the Related Party and Whitewing hold equity and debt interests. At December 31, 2000, the fair value of the put option was a $36 million loss to Enron.

In 1999, the Related Party acquired approximately $371 million, merchant assets and investments and other assets from Enron. Enron recognized pre-tax gains of approximately $16 million related to these transactions. The Related Party also entered into an agreement to acquire Enron's interests in an unconsolidated equity affiliate for approximately $34 million.

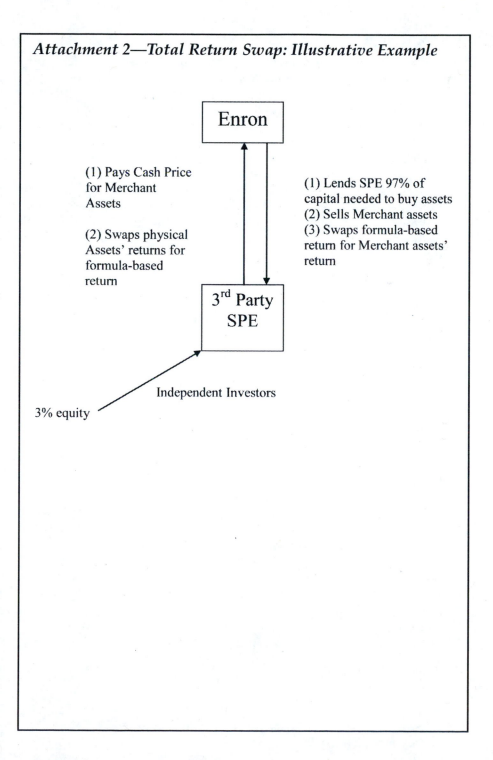

Attachment 2—Total Return Swap: Illustrative Example

Author's Note

Vince Kaminski's dilemmas are symptomatic of those that resisters face inside a company whose ethical decomposition is well advanced. The internal financial control system and its gatekeepers are compromised, and some senior managers are by now complicit in unethical dealings. Potentially, Kaminski has nowhere to go with his well-researched warnings.

At this stage, being the bearer of potentially bad news is a lonely, unwelcome business. This Kaminski had already discovered via his encounter with Jeff Skilling on LJM. Now, he may have one remaining inside option in Greg Whalley. How must he approach Whalley? What message will engage Whalley's interest at a time when senior executives are beginning to sense the ground moving under their feet? Or, does Kaminski really have no viable internal options? If so, is this the time to take matters to outside parties, as other former Enron employees have begun to do?

Details of Vince Kaminski's thinking on the need for an Enron companywide risk management study and the content of that study are as recounted in *Conspiracy of Fools* (pp. 309-310). The account of the meeting with Ben Glisan, which includes the study's initial findings and Glisan's unresponsiveness, is found in the same text (pp. 429-432). Kaminski's decision to approach Greg Whalley is found on pp. 471-472.

The accuracy of this account has been affirmed by multiple interviews with Vince Kaminski. These discussions have also provided additional insights into the tactical choices Kaminski felt he had, the risks associated with each course of action, and Enron's usage of the Total Return Swap.

The account of Margaret Ceconi's actions is found in *The Smartest Guys in the Room* (303-304, 358-359). The action of an ex-Enron executive to disclose LJM's offering circular to the *Wall Street Journal* is as reported in *Conspiracy of Fools* (p. 503).

Summarized financial statements and excerpts from footnotes are drawn from Enron's SEC filing dated April 2, 2001. Their inclusion is intended to give a sense of the picture Enron was presenting of its financial condition and the nature of its disclosure on such matters as related-party transactions.

Notes

1. *Conspiracy of Fools*, p. 345.
2. Ibid., p. 244.
3. Ibid., p. 246.
4. Ibid., p. 248.
5. Ibid., p. 250.
6. Ibid., pp. 430-431.
7. Ibid., pg. 432.
8. The Powers Committee Report, p. 72
9. *Conspiracy of Fools*, p. 503.

Lay Back ... and Say What?

What a day! Things sure haven't work out as planned. All that positioning so that I could make a graceful exit is now down the drain. Well, I'm back again as CEO. What do I tell the analysts and employees tomorrow? How do I explain Jeff Skilling's jumping ship after only six months as CEO?

KEN LAY WAS DRAINED. August 13, 2001, had been an emotionally wrenching day. The Enron board had convened during the day and then continued with a working dinner at the Four Seasons Hotel. Shortly after 8:00 pm, Lay had called the board into executive session. All who were not directors filed out. It was then that Ken Lay announced that Jeff Skilling was resigning as CEO. Lay would be taking his place, stepping back into the position he had relinquished the prior February.

Some of the Enron directors gasped in astonishment. Others had known for a month that this was coming. Lay commented that he and several others had tried to talk Skilling out of leaving but had failed. He gave Skilling the chance to explain his reasons for resigning. Skilling began to speak, then broke down in tears. He talked about not being there for his family; he apologized for disappointing the board. It was an emotional and awkward moment.

Two of the directors "in the know", John Duncan and Norman Blake, probed Skilling's explanation.

Were there problems that Skilling knew about but the board did not—was something in Enron's business causing Skilling to leave?

Skilling had responded:

"Not causing this. But I've made no secret about my feelings about the international assets. We've wasted billions of dollars, and that still upsets me. And, I'm not interested in being the one to fix that problem. Of course, there was California where we are still owed north of $600 million...and Broadband."[1]

Duncan followed up: But is there anything else? Skilling made it clear that there was nothing more—the only issues were the things he had already told them about. The questioning continued but Skilling's answer didn't change. Lay finally brought the discussion to a close, signaling that Skilling could leave the room. Skilling wiped his hand across his eyes, thanked the

S.V. Arbogast, *Resisting Corporate Corruption* (pp. 185–202)
© 2008 by M & M Scrivener Press

board, and said: "I'm sorry I disappointed you. But I think it's the right thing
to do, and I hope it doesn't have serious consequences on the company."[2]

And then he was gone.

Back inside the room, Norm Blake looked at Lay and said: "I'm sorry
this happened. But Ken, I'm delighted that you're here to pick up the
pieces."[3] Before closing down for the night, the board decided not to
announce Skilling's departure until after the financial markets closed the
next day.

The meeting ended, leaving Lay to ponder what picking up those pieces
would involve. Once word got out that Skilling was leaving, there would be
a firestorm of questions to answer. Enron would have to talk to the analysts,
most of whom still had "buy" recommendations on Enron's stock. Enron's
employees would be shocked at Skilling's departure. They too would need
an explanation. Moreover, it wouldn't be long before the employees, the
markets and everybody who did business with Enron would be asking what
Ken Lay would do now that he's back as CEO.

Lay realized that he had a lot of explaining to do: He would need
answers to many tough questions posed by various audiences over the next
several days.

Problems Deciding What to Say

Thinking back over the day's events, Lay's attention was grabbed by the
dialogue between Skilling and the directors. Blake and Duncan had seemed
convinced that Skilling was leaving to escape Enron's problems, possibly
ones the board didn't know about. Could that be the case?

The whole scenario made Lay nervous. He wasn't sure that he was on
top of all the necessary details. In recent years, Lay had left more and more
of the operating work to Skilling. Assuming a "senior statesman" role, Lay
had concentrated on building relationships with key politicians, lobbying for
more market deregulation and, not coincidentally, planning for his departure
from Enron. Was it possible that he hadn't paid enough attention to the
details of what Skilling was doing? Was it also possible that on some level,
he had decided that was the best thing to do?

Lay realized that he didn't have much time to get this right. The risks,
for Enron and for him personally, were quite substantial. The markets
would be unnerved by Skilling's departure. If Lay said the wrong things,
he could scare the analysts and bankers; they could pummel Enron's stock
price, undermine its credit rating, and constrict its financial liquidity. On
the other hand, if he painted what later proved to be too rosy a picture, Lay
risked destroying his credibility at the outset of his return.

Lay also knew that both he and Enron faced serious legal consequences
if he made incorrect statements or omitted matters that would be material to
investors. As Enron's CEO, Lay had repeatedly been briefed on legal guide-

lines for discussing company results. Consequently, Lay was aware that if he made misleading statements, he and/or Enron could be liable under the Securities Exchange Act of 1934. During Lay's tenure as CEO, this law and related federal and state regulations had been interpreted more and more broadly by regulators, plaintiff's lawyers, and judges. Attachment 1 provides more details on the legal framework surrounding communications by the executives of publicly listed companies.

There was also the matter of his personal financial situation. Ken Lay was hugely invested in Enron's stock. His family had advised him to diversify, and he had done so; however, Lay had diversified in a curious, risky fashion. He had borrowed a lot of money, about $95 million and secured the loan with his Enron stock holdings. Lay had then invested the proceeds in "alternative investments," many of them speculative, almost all of them illiquid. He had not counted on Enron's stock falling. Each time it fell appreciably, Lay received margin calls from his bankers. Enron's stock, which had been over $80 per share early in the year, was now down to just under $43 a share. The level of Enron's stock price was thus important to Lay for reasons over and above the company's welfare.

If he were to convey a sense of confidence about Enron's prospects without misleading the markets or employees, Lay needed to assess where the company stood. Lay decided to think back over his conversations with Skilling since he first mentioned resignation. Maybe those discussions held clues to any "submerged logs" Skilling was leaving behind. Lay also decided to revisit the company's major issues and decisions over the past two years.

Before deciding what to say to employees, analysts, and bankers, he would need to know whether something was about to blow up.

Skilling Decides to Call it Quits

Ken Lay had had premonitions that Skilling was struggling emotionally with the CEO job. Early in June 2001, Lay and John Duncan, chairman of the board's Executive Committee, took an overseas trip. Lay used the opportunity to share his concerns about Skilling: "Jeff Skilling really isn't a happy camper. There's a lot of frustration and stress...I just wanted you to know that he's not enjoying his job. I'm trying to help, but he's just having a rough time right now...When somebody gets unhappy, sometimes they do weird things."[4]

The conversation was only a mention item, a note of caution to a key director. Lay subsequently made similar comments to Herb Winokur, chairman of the Finance Committee.

There the matter rested until Friday, July 13. Lay had just returned from another trip and another unsuccessful effort to resolve the troubled Dabhol power project. Skilling showed up for a scheduled afternoon meeting. He went through a checklist of current items. This took about ten minutes. Then he mentioned another item. "I've come to a decision that I need to share with you. I've decided I want to resign."[5]

Even knowing that Skilling had been struggling, Lay was not prepared for this bombshell. He probed Skilling's reasons and heard about family and health concerns. Lay voiced concern about damaging investor confidence. He asked Skilling to reconsider, to take the weekend and reflect further on what he was saying. Skilling agreed but indicated that his decision was "pretty firm."

The first thing the following Monday, Lay wandered over to Skilling's office. After pleasantries, Lay commented: "So, maybe you've decided to change your mind?"[6] Skilling hadn't. Lay tested this decision several ways, repeatedly finding Skilling's mind made up. Then the conversation took a different turn. Yes, Skilling still cited family reasons and leaving being the right thing for him. But then he added: "And probably, this is the best thing for the company too...Given all the problems and everything going on, I think people might be reassured by you coming back in...certainly the stock price hasn't performed well. Maybe by you stepping back in, it will restore confidence that obviously we've lost."[7]

This was a very different rationale. Lay knew that Skilling was attuned to, even obsessed with, the progress of Enron's stock price. Its continuous negative trend since Skilling had assumed the CEO role had obviously gnawed at him. (Attachment 2 charts the trajectory of Enron's stock price in 2001.) Still, Skilling typically was characterized by a brusque, almost arrogant confidence. It was not like him to imply that someone else, let alone his predecessor, could do a better job.

Lay decided to press Skilling on what lay behind what amounted to an admission of job failure: "I think there's a very large risk here that it [your resignation] will further shake confidence. You haven't been CEO very long and for you to step down like this may not be perceived well. The directors have a question, Jeff. Do you know something we don't know?"[8]

Skilling was obviously surprised by the question. After replying that he didn't think so, Skilling had cycled quickly through Enron's major business units. Wholesale was tearing it up, Retail was fine, Broadband was troubled but that was now submerged into Wholesale. India was India, as Lay, who was heading the Dabhol troubleshooting, clearly knew. No, things were pretty good. Skilling then promised that just to make sure, he would review matters with Rick Causey and get right back to Lay.

That same morning, Skilling dropped in to Causey's office. "Rick, I need to ask you. Is everything okay? Anything on the horizon that worries you?"[9] Causey thought and then responded: "No...Well, the Raptors. We've got some that are in the money, some that are out of the money...That's just a wash, though. No, I think things are about as good as they have ever been."[10] Lay got this feedback shortly thereafter.

Later that month, Enron's management committee began reviewing the company's second-quarter 2001 results (see Attachment 3 for highlights).

Earnings were on track Cash flow, however, had been a negative $1.3 billion for the first six months of 2001.

Preparations went forward for Skilling's resignation. It would be announced to the board at its August meeting. The Board reconvened on August 14. Prominent on the agenda was a report from CFO Andy Fastow on Enron's financial condition. His report was not reassuring. Enron's total debt, both on and off-balance sheet, had climbed to $34.3 billion, an increase of over $14 billion from the prior year. Cash flow for the first half of 2001 was down $2.3 billion versus the same period in 2000.

Lay tried to connect these facts with the "everything's fine" picture Skilling had painted. The facts didn't seem to fit neatly together. Lay decided to stretch his memory farther, casting it back over all the major reviews and events of the last twenty-four months. (Attachment 4 provides a summary of Ken Lay's major business involvements, 1999-2001.)

What was the condition of Enron as Jeff Skilling was leaving the bridge?

Assessing the Broader State of Enron

Lay thought back over the presentations he'd received over the last two years. His mind focused first on the most recent briefings.

The most concerning issue seems to be near-term pressure on Enron's financial position. Cash flow has turned negative, and debt levels are way up. Wall Street's analysts are starting to notice and complain. How much is this influencing stock price performance?

On the other side, earnings are on track. I'm not really sure what's going on in Retail, but its weight in earnings is small. Although Broadband and International are troubled, Wholesale is turning in a stellar performance. Its performance has been so good that a large reserve ($1+ billion) was tucked away at year-end 2000; this could be used to help meet earnings targets in 2001. The pipelines continue to make money, as does Portland General. So, earnings are not going to be a problem. Sooner or later, this Wholesale performance will reverse the negative cash flow trend, right?

It is worrisome that events in California seem to suggest fewer trading profits going forward. There also seem to be problems collecting monies owed us and some potential for nasty litigation. We've faced that before, however; we are well connected politically, especially with George Bush now in the White House.

We've been doing a lot of deals with Andy Fastow's partnerships. Now we're up to LJM3. Many of those deals were fixes for short-term problems. The truth is, I don't remember much about the details of the transactions.

Skilling did have Enron's risk managers look closely at our ability to withstand a major external-event crisis in the financial markets. The advice seems to be that Enron would need to have several billion dollars of reserve liquidity. Fastow and Glisan have indicated that Enron has reserve bank lines that more than total that amount.

There was also that Enron-specific scenario, whereby a combination of a falling stock price and a debt downgrade whipsaws the company. But what were the chances of such adverse events piling one atop the other? Surely, a company with Enron's reputation could always count on support from its lenders. Our management team is also bright and capable of reacting to crises.

That management team has changed a lot, however. Rebecca Mark, Ken Rice, Cliff Baxter, and Lou Pai are all gone; now, Jeff is gone, too. I am going to have to find a new chief operating officer. The Wholesale Traders probably think they now run the place and that Greg Whalley has to be the choice. We'll see. Rebuilding the management team could be one of my major challenges.

Lay found it difficult to draw hard-and-fast conclusions. He had Skilling and apparently Rick Causey's word that things were generally OK. Sure, there were problems, but Enron always faced problems. What distinguished the company was the sheer ability of its creative management to fashion solutions or to create new opportunities to overcome its problems. Was now any different?

Still, there was a worrying confluence of issues: financial pressures combined with fewer trading opportunities and seemingly intractable problems in Broadband and International. Moreover, Lay sensed that he didn't know enough of the details to know whether this set of problems was harder than those faced before; if Jeff Skilling did know something critical, it would be in the details.

Focusing on The Task at Hand

Lay turned to his immediate challenges. What should he say to the financial analysts about Skilling's departure and his return? What should he say to Enron's employees? Was there to be any difference in the two messages?

Both groups will want to know why Skilling is leaving. Frankly, we're not entirely sure we understand his reasons. Do we stand by Skilling's rationale and affirm that his reasons also represent our assessment? Or, do we imply that we too are surprised and cautiously looking to see whether there's more here to understand?

Both groups, but especially the analysts, will want to test if Skilling is leaving because of problems within Enron. What do we say here? The markets and rating agencies want to be reassured.

This is the tricky part. It is easy to make reassuring statements. However, you don't want them immediately undermined by new developments or discoveries. On the other hand, appearing scared or confused will only feed doubts in the markets and among our employees.

That does bring up the question of what I signal about Enron's outlook. Is it to be the same outlook, that is, the same business model with the same expectations for dynamic revenue and earnings growth? Or, do I signal that my plans include some sort of reassessment or restructuring to address any of the business issues that have developed?

Part of that signal will involve what I communicate about the future management team. Will I really be running the show? If so, for how long? Or, is my primary task to hold the fort and rebuild the management team? If so, do I signal that now?

At last, Lay glanced down at a set of notes developed by Investor Relations. The notes contained recommendations for handling the analyst conference call that would follow Enron's issuing the announcement of Skilling's resignation. Lay noted its key points:

- Both Lay and Skilling need to affirm that Jeff's reasons for leaving are purely personal and that everything at the company is fine.
- Skilling should anticipate being pressed to explain his reasons for resigning. He should stick to the explanation that it is personal and as such, he can gracefully decline to provide details. General references to family are fine. Skilling should be prepared to refute specific questions as to whether he has health problems or internal political reasons for leaving.
- Lay, as the returning CEO, should especially affirm his confidence in the company's future.
- It is also recommended that Lay preempt any concerns as to whether Skilling's resignation relates to unknown problems in trading, accounting, reserves, or other similar issues.

As for the employee meeting, Enron staff had already drafted an invitation whose message was consistent with the Investor Relations' notes (Attachment 5). Lay's brief called for him to express his enthusiasm for being back and to treat the company's known problems as similar to issues successfully resolved in the past. If Lay wanted to signal any change in direction, he should express this in terms of reaffirming the values that had made Enron great. Finally, it was recommended that all employees be given a one-time stock option grant. This would both signal confidence in the future and help cement employee loyalty for the ride back up.

Attachment 1

Legal Guidelines for Public Communications by Senior Executives

This note provides background regarding pertinent laws governing public statements made by executives of companies whose securities are listed on public exchange markets.

The principal governing laws are the Securities Act of 1933 and the Securities Exchange Act of 1934. Both are federal laws passed in the wake of the 1929 stock market crash. The former act specifies requirements for companies that issue securities to the investing public and lays out the process for private placements. The latter regulates securities markets and broker dealers, and establishes the reporting requirements for public companies.

Section 10 of the 1934 Act requires companies to file quarterly and annual reports (10-K, 10-Q, 8-K) and establishes both civil and criminal penalties for making "materially misleading" statements in these reports. This statutory provision forms the basis for SEC Rule 10b-5, which prohibits not only misleading statements but also omissions of material information. This rule applies to the purchase or sale of any securities. Typically, public companies find themselves technically in the mode of continuously offering or purchasing their securities; this happens not only as a function of the occasional share or bond offering but also as a result of employee stock option issuance/redemption, pension/benefit plan activities, or share-repurchase programs. When public companies find themselves in such mode, the public statements of virtually any officer or director can be considered relevant to an offering and subject to scrutiny for materially misleading statements or omissions.

Section 20 of the 1934 Act defines a special category of "controlling person." A company CEO clearly fits into this category. These individuals bear potential personal liability if any of the required company reports are materially in error. Their only defense is for the controlling person to prove that there was no reason for them to know that the report was erroneous or misleading.

Controlling persons attempting such a 'lack of knowledge' defense against an SEC allegation should bear in mind that they may be inviting charges of violating fiduciary responsibilities under state law. Senior executives will need to explain how they were discharging their fiduciary responsibilities to know what was happening at their firm but did not have reason to know that public reports of their results contained materially misleading information or omissions.

More recently, senior executives have had to consider their exposure under ERISA, a law governing employee benefit plans. In some cases, executives have been charged with breach of fiduciary responsibilities for not disclosing adverse information about their company while still allowing employees to continue investing benefit- plan holdings in the company's stock.

Executives charged with breaches under the two referenced laws have used the defense that they had no intent to defraud. If they can establish that they had no such intent, it is then argued that any misstatements or omissions were errors, not deliberately misleading acts. It should be noted, however, that the burden of establishing the lack of intent to defraud falls on the accused.

Attachment 2

Performance of Enron Stock During Skilling's Tenure as CEO

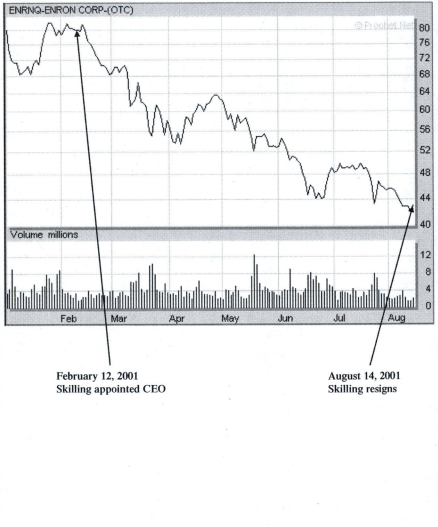

February 12, 2001
Skilling appointed CEO

August 14, 2001
Skilling resigns

Attachment 3

Enron Summarized Financials: 1ˢᵗ H 2001

$ millions (except per share amounts)

	Six Months Ended June 30	
	2001	**2000**
Revenues	100,189	30,030
Operating Income	1,218	690
Earnings on Common Stock	788	580
Earnings per share (Diluted)	$0.94	$0.73
Short-term Debt	1,820	4,277
Long-term Debt	9,355	8,550
Shareholders Equity	11,740	11,470
Net Cash Used in Operating Activities	(1, 337)	(547)
Net Cash Used in Investing Activities	(1,161)	(2,254)
Net Cash Provided by Financing Activities	1,971	3,231
Increase (Decrease) in Cash	(527)	430

Segment Earnings
(Income before interest, minority interest, taxes)

Wholesale Services	1,557	844
Retail Energy Services	100	52
Broadband Services	(137)	(8)
Transportation and Distribution	335	372
Corporate and Other*	(267)	(27)

*   This category includes Enron's investment in Azurix, results from Enron Renewable Energy, the operations of Enron's methanol and MTBE plants, certain non-core international assets, and overall corporate activities of Enron.

Attachment 4

Ken Lay's Major Enron Involvements, 1999-2001

Despite the fact that during this period, Lay was trying to arrange his departure from Enron, he remained involved in many major issues. The items below are listed chronologically and are highlighted for their importance. In addition, Lay attended normal Management Committee and board reviews. These meetings certainly would have included periodic presentations of Enron's earnings reports, business segment performance, and overall financial condition.

Lay's Major Involvements:

- On June 18, 1999, Lay reviewed and approved Andy Fastow's plan to set up and run a fund, LJM, to do deals with Enron. Lay told Fastow to take his request for a conflict-of-interest waiver to the board, where he (Lay) would be supportive.

- On October 11, Lay participated in a board meeting at which Fastow was authorized to form and run LJM2; again Fastow was exempted from Enron's code of conduct regarding conflicts-of-interest.

- In November 1999, Lay participated with Skilling, Joe Sutton, and Rebecca Mark in reviews of the International energy business and the Azurix water venture. These reviews were triggered by International's 2000 earnings forecast of $100 million on $7 billion invested capital and Azurix announcement that it expected to miss its 4Q 1999 earnings projection by 45 percent.

- On November 18, Lay recommended to the Board that Enron launch an expansion of Enron Communications (ECI, or Broadband), with Jeff Skilling to spend more time developing this business. Skilling remained Enron's COO but was also named chairman of ECI.

- On February 6, 2000, Lay chaired a review of Azurix's revised business strategy. He advised Rebecca Mark that her proposed approach was not accepted, and that severe retrenchment was needed instead.

- In late April, Lay chaired the board meeting that approved the Raptor hedge transactions with Fastow's LJM vehicles. Presenter Ben Glisan advised that the Raptor deals did not transfer economic risk but served to hedge "accounting volatility."

- In the second half of July 2000, Lay met the principal prospective buyer for a large package of international Enron assets. Dubbed Project Summer, Enron was looking to sell an 80 percent interest in the package to Middle East interests for upwards of $7 billion. That figure approximated the assets' book value before deal expenses. The following month, Lay attended a board meeting at which Skilling confronted Rebecca Mark on the performance of her International Division. Skilling estimated that International was earning a 3-6% return on net assets; even if Project Summer was concluded at the $7 billion price, Enron would record a $300 million hit to earnings. Project Summer failed to close. By spring 2001, Skilling was telling Lay and the board that International's assets were worth far less than book value.

- Early in August 2000, Lay participated in further reviews of Project Summer's asset portfolio and of a revised strategy for Azurix. Based on these meetings, Lay personally asked for Rebecca Mark's resignation; she agreed to resign at an Azurix Board meeting on August 24.

- In August 2000, an anonymous letter alleged that the Maharashtra State Electricity Board couldn't pay for electricity purchased from Enron's Dabhol plant. In September, Lay attended a meeting arranged by Skilling at which Sanjay Bhatnagar and Wade Cline, the two top executives of Enron India, explained the situation. Dabhol Phase 1 was billing the Electricity Board $30 million per month, but the board had only $20 million to pay. Enron India thus had a big and growing receivable from the State Board. Consequently, the power plant was running part time, limiting output to what the Electricity Board could afford to fund. When Dabhol Phase 2 started up, the monthly billings would grow to $110 million; there was no assurance that the Electricity Board would have any more money to pay. The local executives were sent back with instructions to step up collection efforts. Enron slowed, then stopped, Phase 2 construction. Ken Lay assumed the lead on negotiations with the Indian state and federal authorities. No progress was made, and Enron made plans to take the dispute to arbitration.

- In October 2000, Lay participated in an Enron board meeting at which Andy Fastow was granted another conflict-of-interest waiver to form a new private-equity fund, LJM3. Approval was given, conditioned on two new stipulations: (1) that new Enron deals with LJM be reviewed quarterly, not annually and (2) that Fastow review full details, also on a quarterly basis, of his compensation from LJM with the board's Compensation Committee.

- On December 28, 2000, Lay met with California Governor Gray Davis to discuss rectifying the state's electric power crisis. Enron's traders had made huge profits on California's highly volatile electricity supply/demand balance; a $1+ billion profit reserve had been set aside to contain the appearance of windfall profits. Lay advised Davis to adopt fundamental remedies: more market decontrol, raising retail electricity prices, and promoting power plant construction with relaxed environmental rules. Davis rejected the advice on raising prices and relaxing regulations; he spoke instead of state takeover of power facilities and wholesale price caps.

- Lay participated in further meetings on California in January. The meetings included Treasury Secretary Summers and Governor Davis. The meetings resolved nothing. Governor Davis reaffirmed his support for wholesale price caps. Secretary Summers warned Lay about the risk of an all-out investigation of the activities of power suppliers like Enron.

- In March 2001, Lay was briefed on the status of Enron Broadband's deal with Blockbuster Video. The twenty-year deal, under which Blockbuster provided video content to move over Enron's fiber-optic network, was canceled eight months after signing. Lay was told that Blockbuster failed to deliver quality on-demand content; Enron would now pursue that content directly with Hollywood studios. As part of quarterly earnings reviews, Lay would have seen that Broadband had booked $100 million in revenues from a partial sale of its interests in the Blockbuster contract to a set of "independent" partnerships that included Enron's own Whitewing and the Canadian Imperial Bank of Commerce (CIBC). How CIBC was persuaded to invest in such a speculative venture is unclear.

- In April and May, Lay continued to meet with policymakers in Washington and California on the problems in Dabhol and the fallout of California's power crisis. Lay took note of a research report by the blog, OffWallStreet, attacking Enron's declining profitability and rising debt levels. He also began meeting with Kohlberg Kravis Roberts & Company (KKR) about joining that firm after stepping down as Enron's CEO.

- In June 2001, federal energy regulators agreed to extend electricity price caps to all Western states. The measure, in conjunction with rising supplies, cooled California's electricity prices and dampened trading opportunities. On June 20, however, Pacific Gas and Electric,, a major California utility that owed Enron hundreds of millions of dollars, filed for bankruptcy.

Attachment 5

(DRAFT)
MEMORANDUM

From: Ken Lay@ENRON
To be Sent: Tue 8/14/2001 at ~ 4:00pm
To: All Enron Worldwide@ENRON
Subject: Organizational Announcement

It is with regret that I have to announce that Jeff Skilling is leaving Enron. Today, the Board of Directors accepted his resignation as President and CEO of Enron. Jeff is resigning for personal reasons and his decision is voluntary. I regret his decision, but I accept and understand it. I have worked closely with Jeff for more than 15 years, including 11 here at Enron, and have had few, if any, professional relationships that I value more. I am pleased to say that he has agreed to enter into a consulting arrangement with the company to advise me and the Board of Directors.

Now it's time to look forward.

With Jeff leaving, the Board has asked me to resume the responsibilities of President and CEO in addition to my role as Chairman of the Board. I have agreed. I want to assure you that I have never felt better about the prospects for the company. All of you know that our stock price has suffered substantially over the last few months. One of my top priorities will be to restore a significant amount of the stock value we have lost as soon as possible. Our performance has never been stronger; our business model has never been more robust; our growth has never been more certain; and most importantly, we have never had a better nor deeper pool of talent throughout the company. We have the finest organization in American business today. Together, we will make Enron the world's leading company.

On Thursday at 10:00 am Houston time, we will hold an all employee meeting at the Hyatt.

We will broadcast the meeting to our employees around the world where technically available, and look forward to seeing many of you there.

Author's Note

After a series of cases focused on executives within the Enron hierarchy, this case returns to the view from the top. Ken Lay has found himself thrust back into the CEO position. He has twenty-four hours after Jeff Skilling's resignation to prepare for briefings to Wall Street analysts and Enron's employees. What does he tell them?

The case depicts Ken Lay struggling with the dilemma of managing outside perceptions of Enron within a legal framework that requires accurate disclosure, including the avoidance of material omissions or misleading statements. Because of its deteriorating financial state, Enron is more dependent than ever on outside perceptions of its health. Mismanaging the disclosure of Skilling's resignation could result in a crash in the stock price, the drying up of outside credit or both. Yet Lay can't just tell the analysts, bankers, and employees reassuring sentiments. He will have to answer probing questions against a backdrop of mounting suspicion that all is not well at Enron. Can Lay do this in an accurate, not misleading way? Said differently, can Ken Lay respect the law and still say what he needs to say as regards issues the wrong discussion of which could destabilize his company?

This case draws heavily on the account of Jeff Skilling's resignation presented in *Conspiracy of Fools* (pp. 470-487). That work charts the course of Enron's increasing set of intractable problems, Skilling's gradual disenchantment, Ken Lay's notice of Skilling's condition, and the specific conversations which Skilling and Lay held on the matter during July and August 2001. Accounts of Enron directors' concerns over whether Skilling was "aware of something we're not", Skilling's responses and the content of his consultation with Rick Causey are as reported in the same source.

This material is consistent with the account provided in *The Smartest Guys in the Room* (pp. 337-351). As a second source, this book adds valuable details about Ken Lay's personal financial situation and his reaction to Skilling's decision. It also provides an account of the August 13 financial and risk-management reviews, where Rick Buy presented the "meltdown" scenario (p. 346). Skilling and Fastow reportedly dismissed this scenario as remote, especially given Enron's access to emergency bank lines. The account of Enron's board learning that the company owed $34+ billion is found in *Conspiracy of Fools* (p. 481).

This case positions readers in Ken Lay's shoes the night before Skilling's resignation is to be announced. As such, the case imagines what Lay might have been thinking about as he considered what to say to analysts and employees. There is no historical record of what

Lay considered prior to his conversations with these key audiences. The reflections near the end of the case are an imagined version of what he may have considered, developed by taking into account the issues he faced and what it is reasonable to assume he did and did not know at that point (see discussion of Attachment 4 below). The Investor Relations suggestions at the end of the case reflect the content of what Skilling and Lay actually told analysts and employees in their subsequent meetings.

While Sarbanes-Oxley has reinforced the legal liability facing CEOs who talk publicly about their firms, it is important to recall that a considerable body of law and liability risk was already present when Lay pondered what to say in the wake of Skilling's resignation. Attachment 1, which summarizes the legal context at that time, was developed in consultation with a leading securities lawyer. This attorney has advised major corporate executives for more than a decade on their meetings with the press and with financial analysts. It is highly likely that, over the course of his long tenure as Enron's CEO, a tenure that included many meetings and conversations with analysts and investors, Ken Lay would have been briefed by similar attorneys on the laws governing public company disclosure. These legal groundrules should have made it clear that Lay needed to know if Skilling was leaving hidden problems behind.

Imagining what Lay knew and considered at this pivotal moment is essential to the exercise of "standing in his shoes." Typically, Lay is described as having been disengaged and "in exit mode." These broad statements gloss the issue of what he was actually doing at Enron and what knowledge these activities would unavoidably have imparted. Consequently, Attachment 4 was developed to provide a historical record of Lay's major activities during his last Enron years. This account catalogs all major Lay activities as reported in the two sources cited above. Without question, this is only a partial record; it doesn't do justice to what Lay would have heard just by being present at routine management committee and board reviews. Still, it provides some basis for making presumptions about what Lay likely knew and therefore should have taken into account as he prepared to meet these critical audiences.

Attachment 5 is the text of the message Lay sent to employees announcing Skilling's departure and inviting them to the all-employee meeting. This text is found in Brian Cruver's *Anatomy of Greed, the Unshredded Truth from an Enron Insider* (p.91). It is positioned here as a Draft so that readers can stand in Lay's shoes and consider whether these are the correct messages to share with employees the next day.

This case raises one supremely difficult issue: Was an approach available to Lay at this point that would have saved Enron? Presumably, if Lay had concluded that the company was in mortal danger unless he took a certain path, the requirements of this path would have shaped his subsequent statements. In light of what actually happened, it is clear that simply expressing confidence in the company was not an adequate approach.

This question of "how to save Enron" will gain even more urgency shortly when Sherron Watkins, who was part of Lay's employee audience, brings forward her own concerns.

Notes

1. *Conspiracy of Fools*, p. 482.
2. Ibid.
3. Ibid., p. 483.
4. Ibid., p. 461.
5. Ibid., p. 473.
6. Ibid., p. 476.
7. Ibid., pp. 475-476.
8. Ibid., p. 476.
9. Ibid.
10. Ibid.

Case Study 16

"Whistleblowing" before imploding in Accounting Scandals

*Is this going to have any impact? Will it even make it to Ken Lay?
Should I be sending it somewhere else, perhaps to someone outside?
Or, should I just leave Enron and hand this letter
to Lay on my way out the door?*

T HE ANONYMOUS LETTER'S TEXT WAS FINISHED. Sherron Watkins stared at the words and debated her course of action yet again. In front of her sat an unsigned letter and an envelope. The letter was addressed to Ken Lay, Enron's chairman now returning as CEO. Unless Sherron came up with a better idea, her letter was headed for the mailbox where Enron collected employee feedback.

Watkins reread the draft (see Attachment 1), trying to gauge its likely impact. If her letter made it to Ken Lay, it should get his attention. Sherron was telling him in no uncertain terms that ruin was stalking Enron. During the last few months, working again in Andy Fastow's Global Finance, she had come across what she termed the worst accounting fraud she'd ever seen. Bits and pieces of this story were starting to leak to the press. Sherron was convinced that if the full story ever got out, it could quickly lead to Enron's demise.

Until today, August 15, 2001, Watkins had regarded this outcome as a matter of time. So long as Jeff Skilling was Enron's CEO, she felt there was little chance that Enron would take the radical steps necessary to reconstitute its finances. Skilling had been the senior enabler of Enron's aggressive accounting and Special Purpose Entity (SPE) deals. Andy Fastow was Skilling's protégé. Watkins doubted that Skilling would openly repudiate Fastow or his self-dealing structures. So, she had resolved to leave Enron. Her resume was out circulating. Once she had a job, the plan was to hand Skilling a letter of protest on her way out the door.

Only Skilling had beaten her to the punch. In a stunning development, Skilling had just resigned as CEO only six months after assuming the post he had coveted for years.

S.V. Arbogast, *Resisting Corporate Corruption* (pp. 203–221)
© 2008 by M & M Scrivener Press

Skilling's departure changed Watkins's calculus. Ken Lay was stepping back in as CEO. Watkins regarded Lay with mixed feelings. His most dynamic years were behind him. Lay was not a detail man, and as his staff commented, he "gravitates toward good news."[1] Lay had also been present during all the developments of the past several years. He had signed off on Fastow's deals. Still, it was clear that Lay felt responsible for Enron. He had led the firm for more than fifteen years and had seen it rise from obscurity to global prominence. His decision to return as CEO conveyed commitment. Lay would be motivated to save Enron. He also had not been the actual architect of recent business strategies. Conceivably, he might be able to change course and save the ship.

So Watkins had revised her plan, deciding to approach Lay with both a warning and a recovery proposal. Because she was unsure what to expect from Lay, the warning would be delivered anonymously. If Lay responded, she was prepared to come forward with specific fix-it suggestions. Lay had scheduled an all-employee meeting for August 16. A mailbox had been set up to receive employee questions. Watkins had tapped out her draft with the intention of dropping it in the box before the meeting.

Now that the letter was written, something approaching panic had seized her. She hadn't slept well in days. Some of the anxiety involved the risks she would be taking. Sherron was both primary breadwinner in her family and mother of a young child. If she came forward or was otherwise identified and then was fired, she might well enter an employment nether-world, being both unemployed and "damaged goods."

The rest of the panic involved the correctness of her course of action. Watkins was now plagued with doubts. These did not involve her assess-ment that Enron was in trouble. She was convinced the SPE accounting was fraudulent, that sooner or later it would come out, and that when it did the news could crush Enron's fragile financial structure. Rather, her doubts cen-tered on two other questions: (1) was she taking the information to the right audience? (2) Would her suggestions improve Enron's chances to survive, or was she merely hastening its demise?

Watkins ripped through her options one more time. In addition to Ken Lay, she had the option to take her concerns to the Enron board; the Finance Committee, chaired by Herbert S. Winoker, would be the proper entry point. Alternatively, Watkins could take her disclosures outside the company.

One external road led to the SEC. Enron was a publicly listed company. The SEC had jurisdiction over public-company financial disclosure. Presumably, the SEC would be interested in fraudulent reporting by a com-pany as prominent as Enron. This path could ultimately lead to a formal SEC investigation. Another road led to the media, especially the financial press. *Fortune,* the *Wall Street Journal,* and others were already circling Enron, sens-ing hidden issues and hungry for inside information. Watkins could feed them such information, could calibrate the pace and extent of disclosure, and could insist on anonymity.

Somehow, Sherron had to choose a course of action, knowing that by doing so, she herself would be accepting no small responsibility for Enron's fate. She also had to choose a course that gave her a reasonable chance to survive professionally. "Whistleblowers" did not always enjoy a long professional life expectancy.

Welcome Back; Now Meet the Raptors

Sherron Watkins was no Enron newcomer. After working for Arthur Anderson (AA) and then Metalgessellshaft AG, she joined Enron in 1993. Sherron's initial assignment involved working for Andy Fastow. She worked for him for almost three years, managing the JEDI joint venture with CalPERS; in the process, Watkins became wary of both his finance deals and his approach to internal politics. Then, a good opportunity opened up. Enron International (EI) was expanding from "greenfield" pipeline and power plant development into the finance and acquisition arena. Sherron jumped at the chance to join this group and leave Fastow's world. After closing a significant acquisition in 1998, Watkins was promoted to vice president.

By the start of 2000, Skilling was effectively shutting down the international focus. EI's employees were strongly encouraged to join one of two shiny new business ventures: Enron Energy Services and Enron Broadband Services (EBS). Watkins chose EBS. By 2001, circumstances had changed again. For one thing, EBS was imploding. Watkins had been told to look for another job elsewhere within Enron. For another, Watkins now had a young child. Suddenly being on the road and putting in deal hours didn't work so well. So, Sherron went looking for a less taxing position. She needed to find something quickly if she had any hope for a decent placement in the annual employee rankings. Actually finding another slot that fit her personal situation proved difficult, however; with some reluctance, she accepted an offer from Fastow to return to his shop.

Watkins reported to Global Finance M&A in late June 2001. Her immediate assignment was to review a list of potential asset sales, prioritizing them for cash flow and earnings impacts. She quickly discovered that several assets on the list had been hedged with certain SPEs called "Raptors."

The Raptors turned out to be a family of SPEs owned by LJM2, the investor partnership run by Andy Fastow. The Raptors had been conceived for the express purpose of hedging the value of certain merchant assets, which Enron defined as assets or operations that could be sold; consequently, they were treated as marketable commodities suitable for mark-to-market' accounting. In several cases, this meant that Enron had already booked operating profits derived from supposed appreciating asset values. These profits were vulnerable to being reversed should the asset values later decline. In such a case, Enron would have to record mark-to-market losses. The Raptors had been conceived as a means to insulate Enron's financial reports from such occurrences.

Upon closer inspection, the Raptors turned out to be exotic creatures. For one thing, they were operated by an Enron insider. CFO Andy Fastow acted as their general partner, operating under an express conflict-of-interest waiver granted by Enron's board. For another, although the structure of a Raptor deal was mind-numbingly complex, what Watkins saw when she peered through the boxes and lines was a phony hedge. At bottom, Enron had capitalized the Raptors with Enron shares or rights to shares; these formed the principal, if not sole, basis by which a Raptor could make good on any hedge payments owed to Enron. Fundamentally, this meant that Enron was hedging with itself.

The Raptor 1 deal illustrated this point. Attachment 2 provides a schematic depiction and a description of this LJM transaction.

It didn't take long for Watkins to realize the essence of what was happening. Sherron remembered her reaction as follows:

> In completing my work, it became obvious that certain hedged losses incurred by the Raptors were actually coming back to Enron. The general explanation was that the Enron stock that had been used to capitalize the Raptor entities had declined in value such that the Raptors would have a shortfall and would be unable to pay back what they owed to Enron. When I asked about third-party money or outside equity at risk, I never heard reassuring answers; basically the answer was that it just wasn't there. I was highly alarmed by this fact. *My understanding as an accountant is that a company could never use its own stock to directly generate a gain or, as in Enron's case, avoid a loss on its income statement.* [emphasis added][2]

By this point, four Raptor entities existed. Collectively they had lost over $700 million on the hedges provided to Enron. Specific assets on Watkins's list, Avici, New Power, and Hanover Compressor, were responsible for hundreds of millions in Raptor losses. Avici alone was down 90 percent versus the value at which it had been hedged.

With Enron's stock in decline, the Raptors could not cover these losses out of their capitalization. With its stock and credit rating already under pressure, Enron was reluctant to fix the Raptors by infusing even more stock. The alternative was to accept the credit impairment of the Raptors and recognize a loss in Enron's reported P/L. Since Enron had been less than clear when reporting the nature and condition of the related-party SPEs, recognizing losses would provoke a firestorm of questions and demands for further disclosure. Enron had boxed itself in.

Watkins recalled her assessment of Enron's predicament: "...it didn't take me long to discover the flaw in the Raptor transactions. The Raptor deals expired sometime in 2003 and 2004. It was like staring at a time bomb. When I discovered the problems with the Raptors, my first reaction was to leave Enron as fast as I could. This was some of the worst accounting fraud I had ever seen."[3]

Skilling, however, had beaten Sherron Watkins out the door. Skilling left on August 14, 2001, citing "personal reasons." Enron's board asked Ken Lay to step back in as CEO, and he agreed.

Pondering an Approach to Ken Lay

Watkins recalled her first reaction to the news of Skilling's departure: Enron's condition must be even worse than she had thought. At first, she couldn't make sense out of why Skilling would surrender the job he had fought for many years to obtain. "Personal reasons" didn't cut it as a justification. No, Skilling must have decided that Enron was in deep trouble. As Watkins noted, she had written in her draft letter: "Skilling looked down the road and knew this stuff was unfixable and would rather abandon ship now than resign in shame in two years."[4] (See Attachment 1.)

She had also concluded that Ken Lay didn't fully appreciate what he was stepping back into and that she had to warn him. Thus, she had almost decided to send Lay a warning letter now, rather than passing him a protest note later as she left for another job.

Watkins pondered for a moment what she hoped her letter might accomplish. Taking stock, she found that she hoped Lay would launch a thorough investigation of the related-party transactions. She also expected that Lay would establish a crisis-management team to address the dangers Enron would face should its accounting liberties be exposed, which Watkins believed would happen sooner or later.

Watkins knew that the company was more vulnerable than was commonly understood. Enron's core trading business was hugely dependent on having an investment-grade credit rating. Watkins saw the company's Baa rating as endangered. Enron had many skeletons in its closet. The company owed far more in financial obligations than it reported, and many of its new businesses were failing miserably. (See Attachment 3 for a summary of business-line issues.) It wouldn't take much to puncture the aura of invincibility that sustained the markets' willingness to feed Enron's appetite for capital. Once investors discovered that their cash was going down drains, financing would rapidly dry up, the company's debt rating would be downgraded to junk, trading would be severely impacted, and Enron's stock price would tank. This would trigger a need to recapitalize shaky SPEs with new Enron stock. Credit rating and stock price would decline further. The company could face a death spiral.

This was the deadly scenario that lay behind Watkins' warning that the company could "implode in a wave of accounting scandals."

Clearly, Enron needed time to get on top of problems and reverse questionable deals. That argued for working inside the company. Once warned, however, would Ken Lay take necessary corrective measures? Watkins had her doubts. What was Ken Lay capable of doing at this moment? Watkins determined that three questions held the answer to the CEO's probable course of action:

1. How much did Ken Lay know about Enron's perilous condition? Did he understand that much of the accounting was fraudulent and that the financial structure was fragile?
2. Was Lay coming back with a repair plan or just filling an unexpected opening? What first moves would he make, indicative of what new direction?
3. Who would Lay rely on for advice? In the past, he had relied upon strong number twos: Rich Kinder and then Skilling. Who would play that role now and to what effect?

Attachment 4 outlines Lay's leading internal choices to replace Skilling.

As she pondered these questions, Watkins considered her other options. Foremost among these was going straight to Enron's board. Watkins reflected that the possibilities there were intriguing:

1. The board likely had not been given full disclosure regarding the questionable related-party transactions. Giving the board new, disturbing information would invite it to demand both full disclosure and corrective measures.
2. Second, the board had the power to insist on a change of course. By doing so, it could take the matter of defending the past out of management's hands; this would remove a major barrier to needed reforms.
3. Perhaps most important, the board could, if necessary, change Enron's management. At a minimum, the board could ensure that Ken Lay selected a team dedicated to confronting Enron's problems; this would be critical given the complicity of various Enron executives in questionable deals.

But would Watkins's letter ever reach the board and if so would it act? These same directors had approved Fastow's conflict-of-interest waiver and every major related-party transaction from Whitewing and Chewco to the LJM deals. Was the board not just as complicit as Skilling and Fastow?

Bypassing management to go directly to the board would also turn Watkins into an internal whistleblower. By this, Watkins meant someone who regards the established management to be so compromised that warnings must be delivered outside of normal channels. Watkins knew what attaining whistleblower status meant: "What you hear about all the whistleblower stereotypes is true. You really get treated like a pariah...given no responsibilities, nothing to do...[until you've] seen the handwriting on the wall and found another job."[5]

At this time, neither federal nor Texas law afforded protection to private-sector whistleblowers. Watkins could be fired by Enron and would have no cause for action for wrongful dismissal. However, the full legal context was somewhat more complicated. Attachment 5 provides a more detailed description of the legal framework surrounding whistleblowers in 2001.

Watkins certainly felt at risk of being fired for taking her disclosures outside the company. Going openly to the SEC would run precisely this risk. Enron would do everything in its power to discredit her and her information. The company would point to the board's review of each transaction, its approval of Fastow's conflict-of-interest waiver, and the safeguards initiated to monitor these arrangements. Arthur Anderson's signoff of every deal and Enron's footnotes in its public filings would be cited as proof of the accounting's probity. Enron would circle the wagons, declare that no accounting rules had been broken, and label Sherron Watkins as simply a disgruntled employee. None of this would make it easy for Watkins to find new employment. It would take outside investigators years to get to the bottom of any allegations, by which time Watkins's career could be in shambles.

That did leave the option of disclosing information anonymously to the financial press. Several reporters were on the scent of Enron's accounting problems. In March 2001, Bethany McLean had published an article, "Is Enron Overpriced" in *Fortune* magazine. McLean and her colleague Peter Elkind continued to follow the Enron accounting story, paying particular attention to the related-party transactions. The *Wall Street Journal* was also showing more interest in Enron's story. WSJ's recent articles were increasingly asserting that all was not what it seemed at Enron.

However, Watkins knew that leaking information posed serious risks. If Enron discovered or even guessed that she was doing the leaking, Watkins could be gone in a heartbeat; who then would hire an obviously untrustworthy employee? From a company-oriented perspective, what would leaking information accomplish? Possibly, it might force Enron's management and board to get serious about corrective measures. Lenders and rating agencies might demand more information and then proper action. On the other hand, leaking involved partial disclosure and possible misinterpretation. The markets might overreact, dumping Enron's stock and refusing to roll over its commercial paper. Watkins might precipitate the very death spiral she was seeking to avoid.

A Decision to go Forward

The draft letter still lay on the desk. What should Watkins do with it?

Watkins reflected that the answer to this question might depend upon defining what she was trying to achieve. Was her priority to:

- End abusive practices;
- Save Enron from financial melt-down; or
- Ensure that the integrity of the broader financial markets was pro
  tected and Enron punished for wrongdoing?

Ideally, Watkins wanted to see all these goals achieved. Practically, she knew that her course of action might have to target one at some expense to the others.

There also was the question of tactically managing whatever path she chose. Could Watkins make her allegations stick when they were challenged? Which allegation and what support would she use to overcome the complexity and veil of propriety that Enron had draped over its finances? Who would stand with her when the corrupted elements within Enron closed ranks and fired back?

Within a couple of days, Ken Lay would start appointing new leadership and charting Enron's path forward. Should she send her letter to Lay or choose another route? Now was the moment of choice if Sherron Watkins wanted to influence those decisions.

Attachment 1

Draft of Anonymous Memo to Enron CEO Ken Lay

Dear Mr. Lay,

Has Enron become a risky place to work? For those of us who didn't get rich over the last few years, can we afford to stay?

Skilling's abrupt departure will raise suspicions of accounting improprieties and valuation issues. Enron has been very aggressive in its accounting—most notably the Raptor transactions and the Condor vehicle. We do have valuation issues with our international assets and possibly some of our EES MTM positions.

The spotlight will be on us, the market just can't accept that Skilling is leaving his dream job. I think that the valuation issues can be fixed and reported with other goodwill write-downs to occur in 2002. How do we fix the Raptor and Condor deals? They unwind in 2002 and 2003, we will have to pony up Enron stock and that won't go unnoticed.

To the layman on the street, it will look like we recognized funds flow of $800 mm from merchant asset sales in 1999 by selling to a vehicle (Condor) that we capitalized with a promise of Enron stock in later years. Is that really funds flow or is it cash from equity issuance?

We have recognized over $550 million of fair value gains on stocks via our swaps with Raptor, much of that stock has declined significantly—Avici by 98%, from $178 mm to $5 mm, The New Power Co by 70%, from $20/ share to $6/ share. The value in the swaps won't be there for Raptor, so once again Enron will issue stock to offset these losses. Raptor is an LJM entity. It sure looks to the layman on the street that we are hiding losses in a related company and will compensate that company with Enron stock in the future.

I am incredibly nervous that we will implode in a wave of accounting scandals. My 8 years of Enron work history will be worth nothing on my resume, the business world will consider the past successes as nothing but an elaborate accounting hoax. Skilling is resigning now for "personal reasons" but I think he wasn't having fun, looked down the road and knew this stuff was unfixable and would rather abandon ship now than resign in shame in 2 years.

Is there a way our accounting guru's can unwind these deals now? I have thought and thought about how to do this, but I keep bumping into one big problem—we booked the Condor and Raptor deals in 1999 and 2000, we enjoyed a wonderfully high stock price, many executives sold stock, we then try and reverse or fix the deals in 2001 and it's a bit like robbing the bank in one year and trying to pay it back 2 years later. Nice try, but investors were hurt, they bought at $70 and $80/share looking for $120/share and now they're at $38 or worse. We are under too much scrutiny and there are probably one or two disgruntled "redeployed" employees who know enough about the "funny" accounting to get us in trouble.

What do we do? I know this question cannot be addressed in the all employee meeting, but can you give some assurances that you and Causey will sit down and take a good hard objective look at what is going to happen to Condor and Raptor in 2002 and 2003?

Attachment 2

Raptor 1 Transaction

The transaction schematic provided below shows a simplified version of the deal. The rest of the attachment describes the transaction in more detail.

Initial Capitalization
Fastow's vehicle, LJM2, initially injected some cash into an SPE called Talon (the Raptor vehicle in this case). Enron formed its own entity, called Harrier. Enron capitalized Harrier with its common stock and contracts to deliver stock. Harrier then used these in an exchange transaction with Talon: An exchange of promissory notes between Talon and Harrier allowed Enron to report "operating cash generation" for accounting purposes (Talon's was far bigger). Harrier also contributed the stock and stock contracts to Talon, balancing the exchange. These arrangements effectively completed Talon's capitalization.

Hedge Instruments
Talon then wrote a "share settled put" in favor of Enron. This derivative gave Enron the right to "put" designated merchant assets to Talon at a specified value, one set to protect Enron's accounting values for the assets. The structure worked in the sense that if the merchant assets' value declined, the value of Enron's put from Talon should increase by a similar amount. Thus, Enron's accounting results would be hedged. Talon's ability to pay Enron cash for the value of the put would in the final analysis depend upon its ability to liquidate Enron stock.

Cash Distributions/Investors' Net Position
As a last piece of the puzzle, Enron paid Talon $41 million cash as the premium for the purchase of another "put" option, this one on Enron's stock. This cash inflow allowed Talon to make a distribution to LJM of fees and profits; in reality, this distribution amounted to a complete return of LJM's invested capital in Talon plus an $11 million profit. Fastow and his investor group thus had no net funds left at risk in the deal.

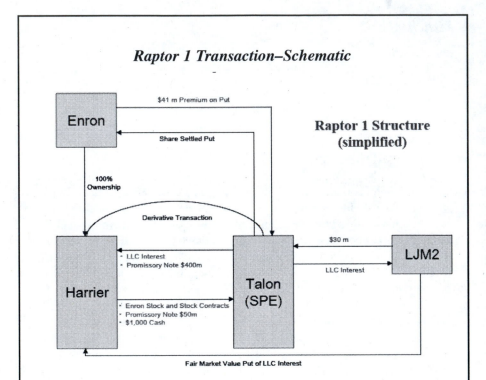

Raptor 1 Transaction–Schematic

Source: Powers committee report

Attachment 3

Summary of Enron's Troubled Business Lines
(mid-2001)

By mid-2001, Enron had organized itself into five reporting segments:

1.Transportation and Distribution: Includes regulated industries, interstate transmission of natural gas, management and operation of pipelines, and electric utility operations, such as the Portland General utility

2.Wholesale Services: Trading operations, commodity sales and services, risk management products and financial services to wholesale customers, as well as development, acquisition, and operation of power plants, natural gas pipelines, and other energy-related assets, including both international assets and merchant asset investments

3.Retail Energy Services: Sales of natural gas and electricity directly to end-use customers, particularly in the commercial and industrial sectors, and the outsourcing of energy-related activities, such as the management of energy requirements for fixed facilities

4.Broadband Services: Construction and management of a nationwide fiber-optic network, the marketing and management of bandwidth, and the delivery of high-bandwidth content

5.Corporate and Other: Includes operation of water, renewable energy businesses, and clean- fuels plants, as well as overall corporate activities

Historical performance of these segments prior to 2001 had been as follows:

$ Million Earnings Before Interest and Taxes (EBIT)

	1998	1999	2000
Transportation and Distribution			
Transportation Services	351	380	391
Portland General	286	305	341
Wholesale Services	968	1317	2260
Retail Energy Services	(119)	(68)	165
Broadband Services			(60)
Corporate and Other	(32)	(4)	(615)
EBIT ex-Minority interest	1582	1995	2482

By the end of the first half of 2001, the following situations characterized these Enron segments:

$ Million EBIT

	1Q '01	2Q '01
Transportation and Distribution		
Transportation Services	133	77
Portland General	60	65
Wholesale Services	755	802
Retail Energy Services	40	60
Broadband Services	(35)	(102)
Corporate and Other	(158)	(109)
EBIT ex-Minority interest	795	793

Earnings reported for Retail Energy Services do not include more than $500 million of trading and mark-to-market contract losses, which are either unrecognized to date or have been incorporated into Wholesale Services' results

Broadband Services' (EBS) business model has failed to progress. A joint venture with Blockbuster to provide network transmission for their video content has been terminated. EBS fiber-optic network has a large amount of spare capacity in an industry suffering from spare capacity. Downsizing and restructuring EBS will require a charge against equity of at least $180 million.

The Corporate and Other segment includes non-core businesses. The troubled Dabhol power project in India and the Azurix water venture results are reflected in this segment. Developments at Azurix are such that the value of that venture will have to be impaired by at least $287 million. This segment also contains various merchant investments, whose value has been hedged by the Raptor related-party transactions.

Cash flow deteriorated sharply in the first half of 2001:

$ million Cash Flow	Six Months ended	
	June '01	June '00
Net Cash from Operations	(1337)	(547)
Net Cash from Investment Activities	(1161)	(2254)
Net Cash from Financing	1971	3231
Change in Cash	(527)	430

Consequently, corporate indebtedness of all types, on and off-balance sheet, has reached $34 billion, an increase of $14 billion over the last twelve months.

Attachment 4

Candidates to replace Jeff Skilling as Enron's President & COO

Internal Candidates

Mark Frevert, 46: Chairman and CEO of Enron Wholesale Services since June 2000; CEO Enron Europe from March 1997 to June 2000; held various positions in Enron Capital and Trade Resources Corp. (ECT) from 1993 until March 1997

Greg Whalley, 39: Head of Wholesale Trading; set up Enron Europe's trading operations in 1996; generally regarded as having the loyalty of Enron's traders; joined Enron in 1993 after getting an MBA from Stanford Business School; served in the U.S. Army after graduating from West Point in 1984

Stanley C. Horton, 51: Chairman and CEO of Enron Transportation Services since January 1997; senior positions in Enron Operations Corp. since 1993; representative of Enron's old-guard pipeline organization

Andrew S. Fastow, 39: Executive VP and CFO, Enron Corp. since July 1999; CFO since March 1998; Managing Director, Retail and Treasury, ECT from May 1995 to January 1997; widely regarded as expert in off-balance sheet and structured finance

Richard A. Causey, 41: Chief Accounting Officer, Enron Corp., since March 1998; Held various positions in ECT from 1993-1997; CPA formerly employed by Arthur Anderson and regarded as expert in managing relations with that auditing firm

External Candidates

J. Clifford Baxter, 42: Enron's former Chief Strategy Officer, CEO of Enron North America, and Senior VP Corporate Development; resigned May 2001; close personal relationship with Skilling but one of the few who could openly disagree with him; regarded as an expert deal maker but considered emotionally volatile

Kenneth D. Rice, 42: former CEO of Enron Broadband Services and before that CEO of ECT-North America from March 1997 to June 1999; regarded as top marketer/sales executive; resigned from Enron in June 2001

Richard Kinder, 58: former Enron COO who resigned in 1996 after not being offered the CEO position; regarded as an effective executive, he made Enron's operations more efficient and profitable; after resigning, Kinder became cofounder of Kinder Morgan Energy Partners, a highly successful master limited partnership specializing in midstream assets; it is likely that he would not accept an Enron position under Ken Lay

Attachment 5

Legal Position of Whistleblowers in Texas, circa 2001

"Whistleblower" is a somewhat imprecise term, generally describing an individual who reports incidents of fraud, waste, abuse, or criminal activity to persons perceived as having the ability to take corrective action. Whistleblowers are often categorized by certain distinctions: (1) those who make disclosures to external authorities or the media or (2) those who make reports to financial control staff or higher executives within the firm. People who suffer retaliation by their employer after making their disclosure, whether internal or external in nature, are also often treated as a separate category.

In 2001, the only legal protection offered to whistleblowers in Texas was found in the Texas Whistleblowers Act. This law protects public employees who in good faith report violations to law enforcement authorities. Public employees are here defined as those who work for a state, local, or governmental agency. Corporate employees are not covered. Moreover, Texas case law (*Austin v. Health Trust, Inc.-The Hosp. Co., 1998*) makes clear that the state does not recognize a cause for action for corporate employees who are discharged after acting as a whistleblower. Thus, an employee so discharged may not sue for restoration of position and/or damages.

Texas corporate whistleblowers can have recourse to filing a Sabine Pilot claim. Such a claim relates to a 1985 case, *Sabine Pilot Service, Inc. v. Hauck,* and establishes that all Texas employees, public or private, may bring lawsuits alleging "discharge of an employee for the sole reason that the employee refused to perform an illegal act." A legal analysis prepared for Enron management during the events of this case illustrated the "Sabine Pilot doctrine:"

> ...an employee's duties involve recording accounting data that she knows to
> be misleading onto records that are eventually relied on by others in preparing
> reports to be submitted to a federal agency (e.g., SEC, IRS, etc.)...If the
> employee alleges that she was discharged for refusing to record (or continuing
> the practice of recording) the allegedly misleading data, then she has stated a
> claim under the Sabine Pilot doctrine.[6]

The same analysis indicated that Sabine Pilot cases, even meritless ones, are risky, expensive and time consuming to litigate. The principal risks are: a) the company's books and activities will be subjected to the legal discovery process; and b) sympathetic juries may award damages or compensation even when the employee in question was discharged for reasons other than those alleged in the lawsuit.

Federal law also did not offer meaningful protection to corporate employees in 2001, a fact corrected by the subsequent Sarbanes-Oxley Act.

Author's Note

Like Jordan Mintz and Vince Kaminski, Sherron Watkins finds herself deliberating tactics for resisting activities she considers dangerous to Enron's well-being. Like her two colleagues, Watkins must also decide among internal options within a management structure she now regards as corrupted; alternatively, she can take her concerns over the heads of management or to outside agents/authorities.

However, Watkins's case also exhibits real differences. For one thing, Watkins has concluded that Enron's accounting IS fraudulent. This raises the stakes in terms of her choice to work within the company, go to the Audit Committee or turn to the SEC. Second, Watkins is a CPA, not a lawyer. Expectations and even the law apply differently to accountants versus attorneys. Third, Watkins has ideas about an alternative business plan. If she gets a reasonable reception to her anonymous letter, she is prepared to weigh in with specific recommendations. Finally, Watkins has almost decided to put accusations of fraud in writing and communicate them at the highest level. This, she realizes, will invoke for her the unique status of whistleblower. Such status could have important career consequences for this family breadwinner and recent mother; in 2001, it also had a certain legal status.

This case thus serves as something of a capstone exercise. Students will need to deliberate whether they agree with Watkins's severe judgment of Enron's accounting. From there, a tactical course of action must be developed. Depending on one's perception of the seriousness of Enron's offense, this tactical plan must anticipate the potential to damage Enron. It must anticipate the possibility of intense, defensive reactions from individual executives and/or Enron as a whole. Finally, it should consider what alternative business plan to offer and when/how to offer it up: all in the hope that such recommendations may mitigate the various risks, including those to one's personal career.

The facts of this case are drawn from Sherron Watkins's account in *Power Failure, the Inside Story of the Collapse of Enron,* by Mimi Swartz with Sherron Watkins. These facts are confirmed and supplemented by the accounts in *The Smartest Guys in the Room* and *Conspiracy of Fools.* Insight into Sherron Watkins's motives and state of mind is found in her article "Ethical Conflicts and Enron: Moral Responsibility in Corporate Capitalism," published in the *California Management Review* (2003). This article documents Watkins's initial reaction to the Raptor vehicles and includes her thinking on why she went to Ken Lay and what she'd do differently in retrospect. Watkins's direct quotes are drawn from this article.

Attachment 1 reflects the text of Watkins's final letter as provided in Appendix A of Power Failure. The schematic in Attachment 2 is as provided in the Powers Committee Report (p. 101). Attachment 3's annual and quarterly financial results are as presented in Enron's SEC reports as filed on April 2, May 15, and August 14, 2001, respectively. The discussion of distressed business-line results and Enron's cash flow/indebtedness at the end of Attachment 3 reflects the account given in Conspiracy of Fools. According to this source, CFO Fastow provided the $34 billion debt figure to both COO Greg Whalley and to the Enron board during 3Q '01. The impairments indicated for EBS and Azurix reflect amounts incorporated into Enron's 3Q net worth reduction, announced in October 2001.

There is no evidence from the extensive record on Sherron Watkins that she deliberated courses of action ex ante other than submitting her letter to Ken Lay. Her article in the California Management Review mentions that in retrospect, she wishes she had taken her issues directly to the Enron board. This case is written from the perspective of "what if" Watkins had systematically considered all her options. Reports of Watkins feeling anxiety about her decision to go to Ken Lay, the reactions of colleagues, and about the consequences of her actions for Enron are historically grounded. In personal conversations with the author, Watkins reported that she felt a strong sense of urgency because of concern that Lay might appoint either Causey or Fastow to replace Skilling.

The discussion of Sherron Watkins's legal situation as a whistleblower is based upon Leslie Griffin's article "Whistleblowing in the Business World," published in Enron, Corporate Fiascos and Their Implications, edited by Nancy B. Rapoport and Bala G. Dharan. Griffin discusses Texas statute and case law, as well as the various definitions of "whistleblower." She also quotes from Vincent and Elkins attorney Carl Jordan's e-mail discussing Enron's legal situation regarding Sherron Watkins. The quote from a "legal analysis" prepared during the events of this case is drawn from this source.

There is no indication from the historical record that Watkins was aware of her legal situation when writing her anonymous letter. Material on whistleblowers' legal status circa 2001 is included in recognition of the fact that legal protection for whistleblowers would be an important consideration for anyone debating whether to work an ethics issue internally or take concerns to external authorities.

Reportedly, Watkins was shocked to discover that Enron had explored the legalities of firing her. Watkins's quote on whistle-blowers' status is drawn from her *California Management Review* article.

Subsequent to this episode, Congress passed the Sarbanes-Oxley Act of 2002. This law offers unprecedented protection for whistleblowers, described by Leslie Griffin as follows in her article:

"It expands both criminal sanctions and civil liability against retaliat-ing employers, including any companies that file reports under the Securities and exchange Act. The statute's reach is broad. 'Unlike most other federal statutes that protect employees...the Sarbanes-Oxley Act holds individual executives, agents and supervisors **personally liable** for unlawful retaliation, and it makes retaliation a felony offense under federal criminal law."[7]

Griffin goes on to quote Houston labor and employment lawyers Laurence Stuart, who observed: "We call this the **'Sherron Watkins provision"** (emphasis added).

Notes

1. *Conspiracy of Fools*, p. 489.
2. "Ethical Conflicts and Enron: Moral Responsibility in Corporate Capitalism," *California Management Review*, p. 8.
3. Ibid.
4. Ibid.
5. Ibid., p. 15.
6. "Whistleblowing in the Business World", pp. 225-226
7. Ibid., p. 225.

Investigating Accounting Improprieties at Jayen Corporation

So Karl is back as CEO. He must have very mixed feelings about returning. After all, he's been positioning to leave for two years. Well, something must be up. First McKinley blindsides everyone by resigning, and now Stands wants to talk to his lawyers.

JON ROPER AND TED BILLINGS WERE USHERED into Karl Stands's magnificent office and advised that Karl would be joining them momentarily. Jon and Ted were attorneys and partners at the Beauton, Texas, law firm of Koller and Pithias (K&P). K&P frequently served Jayen Corporation (JC) as outside counsel for all manner of legal and tax matters. JC in turn had become K&P's largest and most lucrative client. Recently, however, JC had been beset by a series of business reversals and unfavorable publicity, all of which had sharply impacted JC's high-flying stock price. Karl Stands, JC's chairman, had been called back to his old job as chief executive officer following the surprise resignation of Ben McKinley. Back in the saddle for less than a week, Karl had suddenly summoned Jon, K&P's lead attorney on the JC account, and Ted, the firm's chief securities lawyer, to a private conference. No specific topic had accompanied the summons.

Jon and Ted had two minutes to view the Beauton skyline from Stands's sixty-first floor vantage point when Karl entered through the board room door.

Sit down, gentlemen. Thank you for coming on short notice. I'm sorry to have been a bit mysterious about the agenda. I'm afraid it's a bit of a delicate matter, one with serious potential to embarrass and even hurt Jayen Corporation. It's amazing how things happen sometimes. I'm back in this job less than one week, and this lands on my desk.

Karl pointed to a multi-page letter lying on his desk. He did not pass the letter across to Jon and Ted's side of the table.

This letter originally came from an anonymous source. As you can judge from its contents, its author is a mid-upper-level executive with an accounting background. The letter makes some serious-sounding allegations

S.V. Arbogast, *Resisting Corporate Corruption* (pp. 222–238)
© 2008 by M & M Scrivener Press

against chief financial officer Richard Landsdowne. Specifically, it warns that several transactions between Jayen and certain Special Purpose Entities (SPEs) are questionable from an accounting standpoint and as such pose serious legal and business risks for the corporation. It goes on to accuse Landsdowne of unacceptable conflicts of interest due to his involvement as part owner of these same SPEs.

Jon asked which transactions were specifically mentioned. He was aware that K&P had worked on several such JC deals. Jon himself had advised on two, code named Carnival and OPM.

The letter specifically mentions Carnival and OPM, but implies that the alleged conflicts extend to other unnamed SPE's

So what is it you would like us at K&P to do? Ted was beginning to see a host of issues affecting any K&P assignment concerning JC's corporate 'whistleblower'.

What frosts me is that all these transactions were carefully vetted prior to being put in place. The accounting was all reviewed and signed off by Aaron and Barkley (A&B), our public accountant. Richard requested and received a special board dispensation to be involved as part owner of the SPEs. As you know, complex financial engineering has been important to funding JC's rapid growth. The transactions in question were not dissimilar to others we had done. In these cases, the outside investors in the SPEs wanted Richard to join them as a minority investor-I guess to make sure that the complex structure worked for both sides. In any event, the board was informed of all this and gave its consent for Richard to participate in the SPEs. It's all in the board minutes.

Ted spoke up again:

It seems pretty straightforward. Why not just address this anonymous whistleblower indirectly: Publish these facts and make clear that the company's comfortable with its actions. In the process, make clear that Jayen is not going to go off on some wild goose chase.

Karl replied:

It's not that simple. First of all, the person in question has come forward. In fact, I met with her just yesterday. She seems straightforward and sincere. She knows a lot about some of the details of these transactions. And she has recommended that an independent law firm, not K&P, be brought in to conduct an investigation, assisted by an independent accounting firm.

Second, I'm just back as CEO. My predecessor's departure was not well received by our creditors and investors. Wild rumors about improprieties and financial problems have been sloshing around on Wall Street. The stock is down 50 percent from its peak. The markets are expecting my return to be the event that sorts out the problems and rights the ship. If I stiff the author of this letter and she resigns or somehow leaks its contents, the effects on our situation could be most serious, even devastating. JC has always required large infusions of capital to fuel its rapid growth. If investors and creditors get spooked, we could face a liquidity crisis. In a worst-case scenario, things could spiral downward. So, first off, I need to ensure that these accusations don't career off into the financial markets. Then, I need to act in a manner befitting my new role, which means acting as a concerned CEO should act. This means conducting an investigation of the allegations.

Jon was quick to see where Karl was heading:

And you want K&P's help to conduct the investigation.

Karl continued:

Precisely. As the new CEO, it would be appropriate for me to seek help from independent advisers outside the company. K&P has impeccable credentials, plus it has some knowledge of the transactions; it would not be starting from scratch. Put together a team. Talk to the woman who made the allegations—she has been to see me and she's willing to discuss the matter with an outside party investigating the issues. Talk to the other parties who were involved in setting up and reviewing the transactions in question. Obviously, if you find a new "smoking gun," let me know, and we'll deal with it. If, as I expect, you find that all the i's were dotted and t's crossed, I'll need a thorough and well-drafted report to that effect. Then, it will be my job to inform the board and deal with the accuser.

Ted spoke again: Can we see the letter in question? Karl replied:

Of course you can as you conduct the investigation. For now, though, I'm holding the only copy close at hand, for obvious reasons. I've taken the liberty of creating a summary of key passages [Attachment 1]. In giving this to you, I assume that we are already operating under attorney / client privilege. The summary should give you a feel for the matter. What I'd like you to think about is how you would conduct the investigation and who would be on your team. Then come back and meet with me and chief counsel Harry Rimmer. We'd like to help you get started in a manner that ensures confidentiality and minimizes business disruption.

Ted Billings saw that the moment had come to speak on behalf of his firm:

K&P would of course like to help Jayen out on this delicate matter. There is, however, one potential complication: K&P's prior involvement in the subject transactions. We'll have to consult the senior partners and make sure that we are not conflicted in this matter. Making that determination should only take two to three days. If it turns out that we can't do it, I'm sure that you can find another firm to give you what you need.

Karl's face took on a look of deep concern along with a hint of annoyance.

I hope that K&P is not going to stand on some legal technicality here. We are in a delicate situation. Who else would we turn to but our lead outside adviser? How long have you been in that role for Jayen? At least a decade,

I'd say. As our lead counsel, we look to you for help in times of difficulty. K&P is more than a law firm to Jayen; it is a trusted friend. If we can't count on you to step up and help in time of need—well, that will be a serious message from K&P to Jayen. Yes, I'm sure that we can find another firm in town to do this work. Most of them have worked on Jayen's financial transactions at one time or another. But we'd prefer to work with you. If there are technical "conflict" issues, we'd ask that you work them so that K&P can undertake the mission.

Ted promised to convey all that sense to his partners and to respond by week's end. With that, the meeting adjourned.

On the ride back to K&P, Ted asked Jon for his thoughts:

Well, reading between the lines, I'd say that Karl thinks that this couldn't have happened at a worse time. He's just come back to the top operating job. There must be serious problems, or Ben McKinley wouldn't have resigned. You heard Karl mention the potential for a liquidity crisis. He probably doesn't even know the full extent of the problems yet. Now, these allegations have surfaced. Based upon what Karl does know, there is nothing to them. But he can't afford to just brush them aside. He needs a way to deal with the matter so as to avoid a new public crisis and give him time to get a handle on the rest of Jayen's issues. And he's turned to K&P as trusted advisers for help.

Ted responded:

You make it sound as though Karl's an outsider coming in. Don't you think that, as former CEO and long-time Chairman, he should have a good idea what's going on within Jayen?

Jon was quick to comment:

Many chairmen don't concern themselves with operating matters or day-to-day nitty-gritty. Among other reasons, it's a way of making sure that the CEO runs the company and can be held accountable.

Ted held his thoughts about the proper role of board chairs. There were more pressing matters for K&P's partners to consider.

What do you think, Jon, about the matter of K&P's prior involvement in these matters? You caught the fact that the author of the letter expressly recommended against using firms who had prior involvement in these deals. Are we even the right firm to do this work?

Jon replied:

It's actually a help that we know something about these transactions. I reviewed all documents and opinions that K&P provided on the Carnival transactions. As a result, I saw all the documentation at closing, including A&B's accounting opinion and Jayen's board resolution authorizing Richard to participate as a principal in Carnival. We know that a lot of the correct steps were taken. This is a case of checking whether anything really new is coming to light. If the partners have any concerns, pick a senior attorney with no Jayen ties to head the team, and put me on it to help him navigate the complexities.

Ted responded:

We'll consider that as one of the options. Here's what I want you to do first. Prepare a detailed brief for the senior partners. Provide background on the underlying transactions, K&P's involvement in them, what you know about Jayen's recent problems, and an analysis of the allegations and the nature of the requested investigation. Have it on my desk by close of business tomorrow. I'll schedule the partners' meeting for Friday morning.

The Partners Meeting

Jon Roper's briefing paper (Attachment 2) was circulated on Thursday morning. Jon had also attached a copy of the American Bar Association's Model Rule of Professional Conduct 1.12, which addresses the client/lawyer relationship and the allocation of authority between the two parties (Attachment 3). Finally, Ted circulated a second summary paper received from Jayen. This one contained excerpts from a second letter sent to Stands by the author of the original letter (Attachment 4).

The partners convened at 8 am Friday morning. Managing Partner Lyle Becker opened the discussion:

We are here today to consider a request from Jayen's CEO, Karl Stands, that K&P conduct an investigation into allegations made by a Jayen executive. The allegations are serious and concern possible accounting improprieties and alleged conflicts of interest by CFO Richard Landsdowne. I'm sure I don't need to remind this group that Jayen is K&P's biggest client in terms of annual billings. On the other hand, K&P did some work on the transactions now being questioned. This may imply a conflict of interest that would disqualify K&P from undertaking the investigation. Details on all this are provided in Jon Roper's briefing paper. The four questions before the partners are these:

1. Should K&P consent to undertake the investigation or decline because our prior involvement compromises independence?
2. If we agree to conduct the investigation, what manner of inquiry should be conducted?
    a. How should the issue(s) be defined?
    b. How broad an investigation should be conducted over what period of time?
    c. Who should be interviewed?
3. Which K&P attorneys and staff should conduct the investigation, under whose lead?
4. If we decline, what explanation should be communicated to Karl Stands in order to minimize the fallout for our relationship?

Who would like to begin the discussion?

Attachment 1

Summarized Content of Anonymous Letter

The following is a summary of key content extracted from an anonymous letter received in the past week from an employee. This summary covers all the allegations and concerns expressed by the employee. The full letter will be made available to K&P upon indicating that it intends to conduct the investigation requested by Jayen Corporation. In the letter, the author states or implies that:

•Jayen Corporation has become a risky place to work, especially for employees who lack seniority, vested benefits, and major incentive pay. The corporation has crossed the line from aggressive accounting to practices that are misleading to investors and possibly illegal. This can only mean that even more difficult days lie ahead, with consequences that can only be guessed at for employees.

- Several of the transactions concluded between Jayen and an array of Special Purpose Entities (SPEs) will not withstand disclosure and scrutiny as presently structured. This is especially the case with the Carnival and OPM deals. These entities have provided hedges for appreciated assets held by Jayen on the basis of arrangements that use Jayen stock to insulate the SPE from any losses. Jayen originally booked these assets' appreciation as fair-value gains. Since then, the underlying assets have deteriorated in value. When Jayen issues stock to the SPEs to offset its losses on the hedges, it will look to outsiders that we sold stock to raise cash but actually booked the transactions as operating cash flow. Outsiders may also conclude that the arrangements were also contrived to hide the losses of value in the underlying assets.

- Carnival and OPM are SPEs in which Jayen's CFO, Richard Landsdowne, also acts as investor and manager of the general partner. When these arrangements were undertaken, several senior Jayen executives complained about these inherent conflicts of interest. As a result, employees are questioning the propriety of our accounting and the adequacy of our controls regarding conflicts of interest.

- This can be fixed. However, doing so will require a thorough investigation of the questionable transactions and may involve taking some unpleasant medicine. The investigation should be undertaken with the help of independent experts who had no past involvement in the transactions in question.

- Taking this course will be the better path: It will allow Jayen to control the repair process and to restore internal and external confidence in our financial statements. The alternative will be to risk increasing external scrutiny, discovery, and the unfolding of a process Jayen will be ill-prepared to manage.

Attachment 2—Historical Recreation (HRC)

MEMORANDUM

To: K&P Senior Partners

From: Jon Roper

SUBJECT:Jayen Request for K&P Investigation: Background

Jayen Corporation CEO Karl Stands has asked K&P to investigate certain allegations made in writing by a Jayen executive. This memo will provide background on matters pertinent to this request. Specific topics covered include the following:

- Substance of the allegations
- Nature of Jayen's request
- Outline of underlying transactions giving rise to allegations
- Summary of Jayen's recent problems
- K&P's prior involvement with subject transactions
- Investigatory requirements and options

Substance of the Allegations

The whistleblowing executive, a woman with accounting expertise, originally submitted an anonymous letter addressed to Karl Stands; subsequently, she came forward and met with the CEO. This woman is making two substantive allegations. One directly concerns Jayen's transactions with certain Special Purpose Entities, and the second indirectly implicates Jayen CFO Richard Landsdowne and others in improper accounting. The accusations in question are that:

1. specific transactions have been accounted for in ways that misrepresent Jayen's financial performance to investors.
2. Landsdowne's relationship with certain 3rd party companies doing business with Jayen constitutes an improper conflict of interest with adverse implications for both Jayen's accounting and its financial controls.

In her letter detailing the accusations, the executive focused attention on Landsdowne's ownership position and management role in these non-Jayen companies. As for accounting improprieties, she alleges that fair-value gains have been booked as income on transactions that were more akin to stock issuance. She indicates that explicit and informal undertakings have been given by Jayen to the third parties for the purpose of insulating these Special

Purpose Entities (SPEs) from losses. She suggests that such arrangements amount to hiding trading losses from Jayen's stockholders and creditors.

Nature of Jayen's Request

Karl Stands recently resumed his position as Jayen's CEO. A series of business reverses and associated unfavorable publicity culminated in the resignation of Ben McKinley, who had succeeded Stands as CEO earlier in the year. Karl Stands served as Jayen's CEO from 1985 to 2001 and has remained chairman through to the present.

The accusatory letter landed on his desk during his first week back. Karl sees his immediate mission to be one of restoring investor and creditor confidence in the company. He is confident that the accusations are wholly without merit. He recalls the board being fully advised regarding the Landsdowne conflict-of-interest issue and its voting to grant a specific waiver. The accounting questions were all reviewed and approved by Jayen's auditor, Aaron & Barkley (A&B). However, Karl wants to ensure that no unfavorable publicity arises from these accusations. An investigation by an independent third party will subject the accusations to appropriate scrutiny and ultimately provide interested parties with confidence that the matter has been dealt with properly.

Karl has turned to K&P to conduct this investigation for several reasons. First, he trusts K&P because of our long-standing and extensive relationship with his company. He knows that K&P would conduct the investigation with due regard to the present condition of Jayen, the need for confidentiality, and the need to protect daily business from disruption. Second, he has a high regard for K&P's credentials and reputation. Karl knows that if something really material has been missed, K&P will bring it to his attention in an appropriate manner. He also knows that a K&P finding of "not substantive" as regards the accusations will carry weight, especially if a need develops to disclose the matter to the capital markets. Finally, he knows that K&P has background on the underlying transactions (see below). This will enable K&P to better understand their nature and to arrive at conclusions more quickly than a less knowledgeable firm.

A subsequent discussion with Jayen's chief legal counsel Harry Rimmer elaborated on this point. Rimmer expressed his view that there should be no "discovery-style investigation" and no second guessing of A&B's accounting judgments. The purpose of the investigation should be "fact finding," i.e. determining whether anything material was missed when the transactions were put in place.

Karl has spoken to no other third parties about this matter. He has approached K&P on the basis of its special relationship with Jayen. Clearly, we are Karl's first choice for the job. Karl made clear, however, that if K&P were to decline the assignment, he would view this as a very negative message from K&P to Jayen and would have to reappraise the relationship accordingly.

Outline of Underlying Transactions Giving Rise to Allegations

Various divisions of Jayen Corporation have purchased minority stockhold-ings in start-up technology ventures. Some of these investments appreciated dramatically. JC determined in several cases that it wished to dispose of its investments but was prevented from doing so by lockup provisions governing its original acquisition of stock. Jayen would thus be exposed to deterioration in the value of these holdings for the duration of the lockup.

To hedge this possibility, Jayen entered into derivative transactions with independent third parties, which took the form of SPEs named Carnival and OPM. These partnerships were formed by investors identified by CFO Landsdowne. According to papers submitted to the JC board, the investors requested that Landsdowne also participate as an investor in the entities and that he manage the General Partner. The rationale given was that the transac-tions were complex and that Landsdowne's participation was judged a good indication that the pricing and terms were fair to the outside investors. From Jayen's point of view, Landsdowne's participation helped ensure timely com-pletion of the project and that the partnership would be responsibly managed going forward. The board, accepting this logic, approved an ethics policy waiv-er for Landsdowne as regards conflict-of-interest.

An example of the transactions in question is as follows. External investors and Landsdowne contributed cash to a partnership, such that they owned at least a 3 percent interest. JC contributed its stock and a note payable; these contributions made up the bulk of the partnership's capitalization. The partnership, acting through a subsidiary, then wrote JC a "put" option, which allows Jayen to "put" the stock of its technology venture to the subsidiary at a strike price that would protect against a major decline in the venture's stock price. Jayen continues to hold the underlying technology stock. However, if and when the stock declines in value, Jayen's losses on the stock would be off-set by gains on its "put" options. The net effect is to preserve the income origi-nally booked by Jayen when its stock holdings originally appreciated. Under mark-to-market accounting, declines in the stock values would have to be rec-ognized as operating losses in the absence of such hedges.

The anonymous writer is alleging that, for several reasons, the hedges are not legitimate. First, she argues that the use of substantial amounts of Jayen stock to capitalize the SPEs should invalidate the accounting hedge. Second, she argues that the SPEs are not independent of Jayen, because the capital of the independent investors is not truly at risk. She furthermore feels that such "non-independence" flaw is rooted in the conflict-of-interest inherent in permitting CFO Landsdowne to develop the transaction for Jayen's benefit but then participate alongside the external Carnival and OPM investors.

Summary of Jayen's Recent Problems

After years of rapid growth and successful financial performance, Jayen has encountered serious difficulties during the past eighteen months.

Several startup ventures and diversifications that were expected to turn profitable during this period have instead generated losses. These losses have grown to the point that they would have reduced Jayen's reported profits by 50 percent if they had not been hedged. It is possible that Jayen will have to sell or shut down several of these ventures. The stock market has evidenced increasing concern about the "quality" of Jayen's earnings, and Jayen stock has fallen from $80/share in February to $45/share today.

Finally, the resignation of Ben McKinley came as a shock to investors and creditors. Ben cited personal reasons for leaving but was not specific in spelling out what that meant. Coming against the backdrop of Jayen's other problems, the overall effect was to reinforce investor concern about Jayen's business strategies and financial solidity.

The cumulative effect of these events has been serious. As noted, Jayen's stock price has declined almost 50 percent from its peak. There have also been increasing difficulties rolling over the company's commercial paper. Attitudes within the investor community have grown skeptical and in some quarters even hostile.

Karl Stands was recalled by Jayen's board to stabilize this situation. As chief architect of Jayen's rise and a respected figure in the investment community, he is well suited to restore confidence in the company.

K&P's Prior Involvement with Subject Transactions

K&P has been Jayen's lead outside counsel for more than ten years. Total billings exceeded $25 million last year, the highest revenue generated by any single client of the firm.

In the course of this relationship, K&P attorneys have worked in some capacity on almost every major acquisition, divestment, and joint-venture transaction entered into by JC. In many instances, K&P has been responsible for drafting all major sale or joint-venture documents and for giving necessary independent opinions on true sale or fairness of value.

Over the last five years, Jayen entered into a growing number of transactions with SPEs. Some of these transactions involved sales of Jayen assets accompanied by complex repurchase agreements. Others involved derivative contracts, such as the transaction described above. K&P reviewed parts or all of several SPE transactions and provided Fair Value, True Sale and True Issuance opinions as warranted by the specific transaction in question. On the derivative contracts at issue here, K&P drafted detailed language based upon a term sheet agreed to among the parties. K&P also reviewed the board paper and supporting documentation associated with CFO Landsdowne's request for a waiver of the Jayen Ethics Policy. The board granted Landsdowne this waiver, which allowed him to participate as an investor and general partner manager in the Carnival and OPM transactions.

Because of this background, individual members of K&P are familiar with the original documents and detailed terms of the transactions to be investigated. They also know the principals at JC who worked on the deals and the A&B accountants who rendered opinions on how to book the transactions. These attorneys will be able to identify material information or agreements not formerly disclosed or such other new information as may cast light on the validity of the accusations now at issue.

It should be noted that the author of the letter to Stands has expressly recommended against using K&P for this investigation, citing conflict of interest given its prior work on the transaction. Please also be aware of the fact that Jayen's Human Resources Department contacted one of our attorneys for advice on the potential issues and ramifications associated with demoting or terminating the author of the letter. Our attorney's advice to Jayen on this matter recommended against taking such action owing to the potential for a subsequent lawsuit and discovery process.

Investigatory Requirements and Options

As the newly returning CEO, Karl Stands needs to assure himself and the Jayen board that nothing material has been missed regarding the transactions questioned by the anonymous letter writer. The focus of the investigation should therefore center on whether new information is forthcoming.

Karl feels that he needs an independent third party to interview the principal individuals involved in structuring the transactions questioned by the author of the anonymous letter. The list of these individuals should include those who may have questioned the transactions at the time or subsequently raised doubts about specific aspects. A partial list of these was subsequently provided by the anonymous letter writer. The investigators can talk to these individuals, talk to the letter writer herself, and determine whether others should be interviewed. The operative question should be: Are you aware of any material facts or circumstances about these transactions that were not then known and/or that were not properly disclosed to the appropriate level of management at the time? A follow-up question should be: Are you aware of necessary levels of review or approval that were not consulted and obtained prior to the closing of the subject transactions?

Any "shades of gray" issues that emerge from this interview process should be noted in any report back to Karl; this same report should make recommendations for any adjustments or actions required to address any doubts hanging over the subject transactions.

Concerns could be raised that K&P should recuse itself from undertaking this investigation, due to its prior work on the underlying transactions. An alternative would be to establish an investigative team headed by an attorney having no connection with the Jayen account and to embed into the team one or more attorneys who do have strong familiarity with the transactions in question. This approach would assure both independence and balance.

Given the importance of this relationship to K&P, the need expressed by Jayen, and the ability of our people to ascertain the facts quickly, it is recommended that we undertake the requested investigation and use the approach described in the immediately preceding paragraph.

Attachment 3

American Bar Association
Model Rules of Professional Conduct

Client-Lawyer Relationship

Rule 1.2: Scope Of Representation And Allocation Of Authority Between Client And Lawyer

(a) Subject to paragraphs (c) and (d), a lawyer shall abide by a client's decisions concerning the objectives of representation and, as required by Rule 1.4, shall consult with the client as to the means by which they are to be pursued. A lawyer may take such action on behalf of the client as is impliedly authorized to carry out the representation. A lawyer shall abide by a client's decision whether to settle a matter. In a criminal case, the lawyer shall abide by the client's decision, after consultation with the lawyer, as to a plea to be entered, whether to waive jury trial and whether the client will testify.

(b) A lawyer's representation of a client, including representation by appointment, does not constitute an endorsement of the client's political, economic, social or moral views or activities.

(c) A lawyer may limit the scope of the representation if the limitation is reasonable under the circumstances and the client gives informed consent.

(d) A lawyer shall not counsel a client to engage, or assist a client, in conduct that the lawyer knows is criminal or fraudulent, but a lawyer may discuss the legal consequences of any proposed course of conduct with a client and may counsel or assist a client to make a good faith effort to determine the validity, scope, meaning or application of the law.

Attachment 4

Excerpts of Follow-up Letter to Karl Stands

After summarizing what she characterized as "accounting irregularities," the author made the following comments:

> I realize that we have had a lot of smart people looking at this and a lot of accountants including A&B have blessed the accounting treatment. None of that will protect Jayen if these transactions are ever disclosed in the bright light of day (Please review the late 90's problems of General Sanitation—where A&B paid $7 million [sued for $130+ M] in litigation re: questionable accounting practices).

> One of the overriding basic principles of accounting is that if you explain the "accounting treatment" to the man on the street, would you influence his investment decision? Would he sell or buy the stock based on a thorough understanding of the facts? If so, you best present it correctly and/or change the accounting.

> My concern is that the footnotes don't adequately explain the transactions. If adequately explained, the investor would know that the "Entities" described in our related party footnote are thinly capitalized, the equity holders have no skin in the game, and all the value in the entities comes from the underlying value of the derivatives (unfortunately in this case, a big loss) AND Jayen stock…

> I firmly believe that executive management of the company must have a clear and precise knowledge of these transactions and they must have the transactions reviewed by objective experts in the fields of securities law and accounting. I believe Karl Stands deserves the right to judge for himself what he believes the probabilities of discovery to be and the estimated damages to the company from those discoveries and decide one of two course of action:

> 1. The probability of discovery is low enough and the estimated damage too great; therefore we find a way to quietly and quickly reverse, unwind, write down these positions/transactions.
> 2. The probability of discovery is too great, the estimated damage to the company too great; therefore, we must quantify, develop damage containment plans, and disclose.

> I firmly believe that the probability of discovery significantly increased with Ben McKinsey's departure. Too many people are looking for a smoking gun…

After providing more details on what she described as "Carnival oddities," the author presented a list of recommended actions:

> 1. Postpone decision on filling the office of the chairman, if the current decision includes the CFO or Chief Accounting Officer (CAO).
> 2. Involve Harry Rimmer to hire a law firm to investigate the Carnival and

OPM transactions to give Jayen attorney client privilege on the work product (Can't use K&P due to conflict—they provided some true sale opinions on some of the deals.)

3. Law firm to hire one of the big 6, but not A&B due to their conflicts of interest.
4. Investigate the transactions, our accounting treatment and our future commitments to these vehicles in the form of stock.
5. Develop clean up plan:
    a. Best case: Clean up quietly if possible.
    b. Worst case: Quantify, develop PR and IR campaigns, customer assurance plans, legal actions, severance actions, disclosure.
6. Personnel to quiz confidentially to determine if I'm all wet:
    a. John McConnell, Jayen Treasurer.
    b. Kurt Fuller, Investor Relations.
    c. Richard Sellers, Chief Risk Officer.
    d. Gene Dauphin, Head of Wholesale Trading.

Author's Note

The purpose of the case is to explore a number of dilemmas that can confront a law firm asked to undertake a delicate investigation for a major client. The first of these involves being asked to conduct the investigation into transactions for which the firm prepared documents or issued opinions. The details cited in Attachment 2 describe the work done on Carnival/OPM by K&P, the case's law firm.

The second dilemma involves attorney responsibility to be guided by the client's requests and its definition of the scope of work. Again, Attachment 2 describes certain guidelines that Jayen is attempting to establish governing the scope of the investigation K&P is being asked to conduct. For reference, Attachment 3 provides the American Bar Association's Model Rule concerning the scope of representation and allocation of authority between client and lawyer.

This case is loosely based on the facts of an investigation commissioned by Ken Lay after he received the anonymous letter penned by Sherron Watkins. Approximately one week after receiving Watkins's letter, Lay and his chief counsel did ask one of Enron's outside law firms to conduct an investigation. This law firm had done work on the Enron-SPE deals in question.

However, this case then departs from the historical record to lay out a set of hypothetical deliberations within the law firm. The purpose of these hypothetical deliberations is to present students with the dilemmas just cited.

Extensive portions of this case have thus been created without having a basis in published accounts. These portions include the attorneys' conversation with Karl Stands, the subsequent dialogue between the two attorneys, the discussions at the senior partners' meeting, and the detailed memo circulated to the senior partners in advance of the meeting (Attachment 2). Because such a large portion of the case is not grounded in the historical record, it has been explicitly fictionalized. None of the names used are those of individuals or organizations involved in the Enron investigation. There is no intent to imply that this case is representative of the facts of that historical episode.

Case readers are expressly advised not to attribute any of the dialogue or conduct depicted in this case to either the individuals or the law firm that conducted the Enron investigation.

Attachment 1 broadly follows the content of Sherron Watkins's first, anonymous letter to Ken Lay. Attachment 4 quotes from her second letter to Lay but uses fictional names. The text of this letter

and thus the quotes in Attachment 4 can be found in Appendix B of
Power Failure (pp. 371-376). Consistent with the fictionalized nature
of this case, the list of names at the end of the attachment has also
been fictionalized.

The allegations attributed to the whistleblower in this case
have been expanded to include the CFO's conflict of interest.
Watkins's letters/memos did not make an explicit issue of this,
focusing instead on just the accounting issues. However, the CFO's
conflicted condition had led to large compensation from the SPEs a
fact that he and others would not want to surface in any investigation. Since students need to determine the appropriate scope of
any investigation, the case provides information on the CFO's conflicts so that they may be considered along with the accounting
issues.

Conclusion:
Ethics Lessons
from the Enron File

THIS BOOK OF CASE STUDIES has tried to do three things with the Enron story:

1. Depict critical moments that determined the ethical environment of the firm
2. Put readers in the shoes of individuals confronting those decisions, thereby exposing them to the business and personal pressures that influenced those individuals
3. Show how the ethical challenges changed over the course of Enron's history

Now, at the end of seventeen case studies, it is possible to shift focus to harvest some lessons. This might seem an easy task. Enron's story certainly has been popularized as a great morality tale. Crimes, outrageous acts of fraud and deception, were committed; more than a few bad guys have been sent to prison. A few heroes stood against the tide and reaped public recognition. More than a few books and articles have massaged this tale to extract the "lessons of Enron."

Saying something meaningful at this point thus involves overcoming two hurdles. The first is that Enron's story is that of only one company. Those who would draw forth lessons must deal with the pitfalls of generalizing from one story. For every Enron that implodes, many companies occupy that 'gray zone' between ethical behavior and fraud and do not implode. Likely overdrawn are lessons suggesting that if one does X like Enron did, it will follow Enron's footsteps into the ditch.

The second hurdle is the need to avoid repetition. Enron's story has been extensively analyzed. At this point, any author demanding readers' attention for more Enron material carries a burden to address questions that have not already been answered.

239

S.V. Arbogast, *Resisting Corporate Corruption* (pp. 239–257)
© 2008 by M & M Scrivener Press

Considering the second issue first, the cases provided herein can serve as a composite case study of corporate ethical deterioration. Virtually all the Enron works to date have concentrated on telling the whole story of why the company failed. This book takes strategic slices to see why Enron decomposed ethically. Having looked at critical threshold moments, the plight of individuals who faced ethical decisions, and how these evolved over time, it is possible to identify more specific questions related to Enron's ethical decomposition:

- What were the critical thresholds that Enron crossed? When, in a sense, "was the battle lost?"
- Could individuals have made a difference? Could they have stopped this organizational decay?
- Were individuals "overmatched" by the corporate culture? Is it unreasonable to expect that they could have behaved differently, and if so, is it reasonable to expect employees in future ethics situations to do much better? And finally:
- What characteristics would allow new employees to spot a severe risk of ethical decomposition from a more normal firm that operates stably in that 'gray zone'?

The Enron story is so dense, so packed with incidents and oversized personalities that none of the chronological accounts makes it easy to answer these questions. Having extracted strategic slices, ones expressly focused on key ethics decisions, it becomes possible to answer the questions more systematically.

As for the fact that Enron is but one story, there is a need to be cautious. Enron's account cannot be used to predict similar fates in other corporate settings. Other stories will be different in so many ways that prediction is hazardous.

What can be said is that Enron serves as a cautionary tale. It shows how bad things can get if major ethics thresholds are crossed and the tide is not reversed. Second, because it is one of the most extensively reported stories of corporate implosion, it provides case material for all stages of ethics decomposition. Students can contrast the early plights of a David Woytek or Ken Rice with those of Mintz, Kaminski, and Watkins. Perhaps most usefully, this book can also serve as a study of "ethical resistance possibilities." By acknowledging Enron to be an extreme case, if it can be shown that employees had effective resistance options, maybe more than they even realized, their stories provide a basis for believing that successful resistance should be possible elsewhere.

With these qualifications, we can now turn to the four questions just cited and see whether the Enron file offers up useful lessons.

Critical Ethics Thresholds: When Did Enron Cross the Line?

One conclusion to be drawn from these cases is that Enron's battle for sound financial control was lost early.

The Valhalla oil-trading cases, circa 1987, give ample evidence that Enron's senior management was prepared to elevate short-term financial results over the maintenance of good controls. Cardinal control sins—not reporting bank accounts, putting company funds into private bank accounts, tampering with bank records, and submitting false evidence to audit/senior management—were excused or treated with the utmost leniency. Even when the trading unit rewarded this leniency with a breathtaking breach of trading limits, Enron senior management drew only a narrow lesson. Henceforth, controls on trading limits would be strict. Controls elsewhere were allowed to become lax.

Far from recognizing and rewarding Internal Audit for spotting the problems at Valhalla, Enron management "outsourced" its audit function to Arthur Anderson (AA) early in the 1990s. This coincided with a period where Enron was imposing its preferred accounting methods on AA and encouraging increasing crossover of AA accountants into Enron's financial functions. The stated reason for the outsourcing was cost efficiency. Since this occurred while Rich Kinder was still COO, that might have been one motive. However, the outsourcing also ensured that Enron would not retain the internal capabilities essential to sustaining sound controls.

Thus, the outsourcing of Internal Audit figures as the first major line that Enron crossed. Why is this conclusion warranted? Because it was the step that solidified for all of Enron the weak-controls mentality revealed in the Valhalla episode. Collectively, the outsourcing to AA sent many signals to the Enron organization:

- **Enron management was comfortable with less-frequent and less-thorough auditing.** If nothing else, it signaled that controls were prioritized below costs. Of course, the principal means for controlling audit costs are to reduce the frequency and duration of audits. The next most effective means is to reduce the number of auditors assigned to audits. Making audit a cost initiative with AA ensured that these means would be used to contain the costs of future Enron audits. Less-frequent and less-intrusive audits would be a not incidental byproduct.
- **Enron favored a more malleable audit activity.** Internal audit is typically insulated from pressures that arise from a service provider's need to please its client. Farming this function out to AA assured Enron that its auditors could be influenced via the auditor/client commercial relationship.

- **Enron was not especially concerned about providing employees with a reliable means to report controls violations.** Properly independent, internal audit is the channel to which internal whistleblowers most often have recourse. Its independence provides the necessary assurance of confidentiality and protection from retaliation. An external auditor with commercial conflicts of interest cannot provide these bulletproof assurances to those considering whether to risk a potentially career-threatening move.

Interestingly, forensic auditing largely disappears from the Enron chronicle once this threshold was crossed. Arthur Anderson continues to figure prominently in its role as certifier of Enron's financial accounts. There are several accounts of AA's Professional Standards Group contesting aggressive accounting approaches and resisting deal structures they felt lacked substance. There is no comparable record of AA auditors questioning asset valuations, expense practices or abuses of company policies. Possibly, AA was an effective auditor, but the Enron chroniclers felt that these matters were now incidental. More likely, AA's audits didn't turn up much. They were happy to provide this reassuring news to Enron's leaders, who were just as happy to receive it uncritically.

A second key threshold concerned the introduction of mark-to-market accounting into multiple Enron business units. The MtM cases (Case Studies 4-6) reveal a story with two major implications: (1) aggressive accounting would not be balanced by compensating controls and (2) MtM could thereafter be used proactively to fix inconvenient profitability issues. This was a major step in the direction of accounting optics taking precedence over business reality; as such, it was a major step away from any culture of accountability.

The account of Jeff Skilling's battle to persuade the SEC that MtM was right for Enron Finance is dramatic but only the opening act of this story. More important but less noted are two other facts:

1. The SEC gave its consent to MtM with conditions. It does not appear that Enron accepted or implemented these conditions. Far from looking to balance an aggressive interpretation with some sense of the potential for abuse, Enron wanted the maximum possible maneuver room.
2. The SEC's MtM decision was specific to Enron Finance. Skilling successfully argued that this business, unlike the rest of Enron, resembled a Wall Street trading house. Yet as the Enron Clean Fuels case (Case Study 6) makes clear, Skilling was willing to encourage adoption of this method by other businesses that: (1) bore little resemblance to a trading house; (2) had profitability problems; and (3) had some contracts where the application of MtM would produce immediate accounting profits.

Revealingly, the Enron controller who promotes this approach to ECF did so with an assurance that the barest factual fig leaf will suffice to get the treatment through AA.

ECF is thus a key threshold. Here, Enron leaves behind the gray zone of seeking aggressive accounting with some grounding in fundamentals and crosses over into manufacturing a picture of restored profitability where no fundamental improvement had taken place.

From here, it would become open season on accounting policies throughout Enron. Shortly thereafter, mark-to-model began to permeate the trading operations. As illustrated by Case Studies 7 and 8, traders discovered that accounting profits and losses could be manufactured out of pure assumptions about the future. Meanwhile, in Enron International, project developers would manufacture assumptions needed to get deals approved and reap their bonuses. A progressive deterioration of both the quality of Enron's financial reports and the economics of its investments was firmly launched.

One sees the final product of this trend in Case Study 16, where the need for the Raptor vehicles is discussed. There, Sherron Watkins finds merchant assets whose fair values are way below what resides on Enron's books. By initially classifying Avici and Hanover Compressor as merchant assets, Enron convinced itself (and AA) that these were marketable assets with readily ascertainable values–and hence eligible for MtM treatment; gains based on aggressive valuation assumptions were then booked Later, facing gross deterioration in those values and reluctant to reverse gains it never should have booked, Enron resorted to related-party transactions whose only purpose was to perpetuate its existing, dubious accounting.

It is important to draw a lesson from these early battles: The importance of controls and accounting in combination is often underestimated. With Valhalla followed by MtM, a weak controls/aggressive accounting virus was released. By dismantling the audit function, Enron management signaled its low regard for financial controls to employees. With the control function impaired, the accountants became the focus of pressures that turned many into willing agents of overly aggressive approaches. With only a few exceptions, it is difficult to find evidence of Enron's auditors or accountants fighting to ensure that MtM was narrowly applied or administered with rigor. This handed business unit managers a free pass; the accountants were largely on board with earnings manipulation. Why not be as creative as possible and deliver wins to management?

Thus, by the early 1990s Enron had crossed two critical thresholds. Outside of the trading arena, it had abandoned the effort to sustain strong financial controls, and it had decoupled its financial accounting from accurate representation of business results.

Henceforth, individuals troubled by specific Enron transactions would not have recourse to a trustworthy, independent audit function. Henceforth,

Enron's management would have an ever-increasing stake in maintaining the appearance of being a profit machine, even as its knowledge of what was actually happening in the firm progressively deteriorated.

In these senses, the financial-control battle at Enron was already lost. Turning things around would have required another battle, one to reverse the dangerous momentum already in motion. Was this still possible?

Could Individuals Have Arrested Enron's Descent?

Pretty clearly, Ken Lay as CEO could have arrested Enron's descent. In the Valhalla incident, Lay had the opportunity to:

- Discipline the oil-trading management while preserving its activities.
- Investigate thoroughly with an eye to reinforcing controls around Valhalla.
- Use the subsequent trading scandal to reestablish Enron's controls environment.

Ken Lay did none of these things. As a result, he missed the chance to use the Valhalla affair to direct Enron onto a sounder ethical path.

The CEO sets the tone on financial control. He determines whether the message to the organization is lip service to traditional pieties or accountability for delivering ethical conduct and financial control. The CEO also determines the resources allocated to and the authority given the financial-control organization. As we have just seen, these were not priorities for Ken Lay.

Lay's business persona has been described as one of not being involved in the details; thus, he is often portrayed as somewhat distant from the scandals that brought Enron down. What surfaces in the Valhalla account is quite a bit different. Lay is involved in the details. He hears this story of misappropriated funds, unauthorized bank accounts, tampered bank records, and the excuses given by the perpetrators. He gives guidance, sets corrective wheels in motion, and then disappears from the public record of the account. His subordinates make the decision to bring audit back to Houston and later to outsource Internal Audit to AA. Lay's involvement in these decisions is not reported.

Having given such direct instructions to David Woytek and his team, it is hard to imagine subordinates countermanding the CEO without at least checking to make sure that this was acceptable. Lay seems to have had a talent for quietly letting his wishes be known and for carefully distancing his person from the decisions and events that followed. None of this is consistent with how a CEO truly concerned about the firm's ethical environment would have handled such matters.

Other individuals who could have arrested Enron's descent were its chief financial officers. With the exception of Andy Fastow, Enron's CFOs appear as shadowy figures in the published chronicles. Especially during the early years, their names pop up in various episodes but are never associated with major initiatives. That is exactly the point. Enron's CFOs never embraced the role of guardian of financial control. The public record contains no cases where an Enron CFO is resisting some questionable practice or abuse. To some extent, this record must be traced back to Enron's operating management, which picked the CFOs. Apparently, Lay and Skilling used the CFO position as a rotational assignment, as a chief accounting officer position, or as a reward for clever deal making. They never intended the CFO to be a financial-control guardian.

This absence of a CFO with ownership of financial control had far-reaching consequences. Most Enron chronicles don't emphasize this point. However, the controls void at CFO meant many things:

- There was no senior officer to protect audit from business-line executives looking to impede an investigation.
- There was no one to resist the outsourcing of Internal Audit.
- There was no one in Enron management to whom AA could go in an attempt to maintain some balance between sound accounting principles and the wishes of Enron's business line managers.
- There was no one to set boundaries or implement controls to compensate for risks Enron was taking on as it moved to mark-to-market accounting.

Effective leadership and resistance by an adroit CFO could have made a difference in all these areas. The cases show that on many occasions Enron management was happy to accept "half a loaf." Jeff Skilling celebrated when the SEC endorsed MtM with limits and controls. A strong CFO could have made sure that those limits/controls materialized. With this, Enron might have stayed on the right side of the aggressive/abusive line during its formative years. Case Studies 7 and 8 especially illustrate the difference a strong CFO could have made.

The absence of strong ethics and controls leadership at the top placed midlevel Enron executives in difficult circumstances. When ethics questions arose, there was no controls organization with integrity to which one could turn. Even worse, gatekeepers, such as AA, were already compromised. This meant that individuals upset by questionable practices were isolated. They would have to fly on their own and go out of channels to try to reverse questionable dealings. Proponents, on the other hand, could confidently cite support from AA or from attorneys for whatever they were promoting.

Did this mean that all individuals at Enron were destined to be ineffectual resisters? Not so. One of the lessons from these cases is that even under very difficult circumstances, individuals could still be effective resisters. However, they would have to be both determined and tactically adroit to have any success. One key was to undertake resistance as a campaign, adopting tactics appropriate to an extended struggle. Both Vince Kaminski and Jordan Mintz did this. Mintz waged a six-month battle to force Fastow's LJM compensation out in the open. Ultimately, enough questions and heat began to envelop Fastow's role that Skilling forced him to give up his LJM position.

Kaminski conceived of his "Probability of Ruin" study as a non-accusatory framework with which to expose questionable practices that could produce an unintended avalanche of liabilities. Approaching the matter this way allowed him to ask in non-inflammatory fashion: What are we doing here? Kaminski invested more than a year in the work; he then took the findings to multiple audiences: Buy, Glisan, and Whalley. In the end, Kaminski was convinced that this effort failed. On closer inspection, he at least got his message in front of senior management. At the August 2001 board meeting, Rick Buy presented enterprise risk scenarios that resembled the findings in Kaminski's study. Apparently, he must have been listening to Kaminski's team. (However Skilling, eager to resign without the impression of "fleeing the scene," dismissed the risks as remote.)

Thus, it can be concluded that individuals prepared to battle tactically could achieve some small-scale success. This was possible right down to the end of Enron's run. Indeed, more tactical possibilities opened up as Enron's plight became more severe and outside demands for full disclosure mounted.

It is considerably less clear that Mintz, Kaminski, or Watkins could have achieved more than such local successes. For one thing, there is legitimate debate over whether Enron was still salvageable at the time their cases were coming to a head. Some studies have argued that by 1999, Enron was already insolvent; as Kaminski's study demonstrated, the company didn't really know its own liability position. For another, Enron's senior management denied any need for reform almost to the bitter end. As demonstrated in Case Study 15 (Lay Back...), management seemed to have believed that in its core business "things were never better." This belief and a shaky grasp on the magnitude of Enron's problems undercut any sense of urgency to consider a basic change of course.

Given gridlock at the top, it is difficult to imagine even the most adroit resisters turning the ship around. In their own ways, Kaminski and Watkins tried. The former was politely told by Glisan and Whalley to go away. Watkins's accusations became the object of a carefully circumscribed investigation wherein her express recommendations on the conduct of the investigation were ignored.

However, the Enron file also reveals the efficacy of the external options. Persons named and unnamed began to provide the SEC and the financial press with information targeting Enron's dark shadows. During the period March to September 2001, the financial market's mood toward Enron turned dramatically. Superlatives and benefits of the doubt gave way to skepticism

and relentless digging for the facts. Thrown on the defensive, Enron's managers responded clumsily, piling negative surprise on top of bombshell until
nothing remained of the company's credibility.

There is a tantalizing "what if" question: What if Skilling's resignation
had triggered a deeper introspection at Enron, one resulting in a more res-
olute conviction that medicine needed to be taken? Even as late as Case
Study 15 (Lay Back…), it is still possible to conceive of a path by which Enron
might have escaped as a going concern. It would have involved draconian
measures to generate/conserve cash–measures that would have punctured
immediate profit reports and acknowledged past errors; quite possibly, managers such as Ken Lay wouldn't have survived the fallout. But for a leader
who had truly measured the depth of Enron's hole and who had resolved to
pay the price of recovery, it may have been possible to salvage Enron as a
going concern.

This possibility also implies that the resistance of Kaminski, Mintz, and
Watkins actually had some shot at triggering a broader turnaround. In retrospect, it looks like a long shot. Still, it could have happened in as simple
a fashion as Ken Lay's refusing to replace Skilling as CEO. Things could
have turned out very differently if Lay had told the Enron board something
like: "I'm too old and too out of touch. I've been phasing out for more than
a year. I'll stay six months as Chairman but then you have to find someone
else."   Quite possibly, attracting a new CEO would have involved the
board's doing thorough due diligence as preparation for identifying and
interviewing candidates. Such a process would have taken shape against
the backdrop of growing market scrutiny. Serious candidates would be
focused on understanding what they were getting into. This truly could
have been a new deal.

Effective resistance, even at the local level, thus contains a kernel
from which broader reform can suddenly spring. Outside events can
evolve, suddenly providing a context favorable to housecleaning. Thus,
even if the efforts of Kaminski, Mintz, and others ultimately proved in
vain at Enron, they were not inevitably doomed to that result. With some
changes in facts along the way, the result could have been different.
Similar resistance efforts in other contexts might indeed achieve better
results.

Even if successful resistance was possible all the way to Enron's ending,
the question of whether most individuals can be expected to step up to that
kind of ethics challenge is still open. As the cases make clear, the pressures
on Enron resisters were daunting. Only highly exceptional people can be
expected to face down such pressures. If so, is it even possible to draw lessons from these cases for the average employees? It is to this issue that we
now turn.

Were Enron's Employees Overmatched' by the Decayed Ethical Culture?

It is easy to argue that Enron's internal culture presented daunting obstacles to its more ethically inclined employees. Senior management demonstrated time and again that it would embrace expedient practices to fix immediate problems. Moreover, the instruments of intimidation were well honed. Employees who crossed powerful individuals could find themselves ranked near the bottom by the Performance Review Committee (PRC); from there, the next step was being transitioned out of the company, bearing the stigma "couldn't make it at Enron." Recourse to the traditional gatekeepers soon ceased to be an option. The culture in general took on a tone of lionizing those who got results by whatever means; meanwhile, those who pushed back on questionable deals were regarded as mediocrities that "didn't get it." Even one as unarguably bright as Vince Kaminski felt the sting of this culture, as recounted in Case Study 14. Skilling personally removed his group from reviewing enterprise-wide transactions. Skilling's explanation was: "We don't need cops, Vince."

And then, the unapologetically corrupt Fastow rose to CFO, the position normally reserved for the firm's controls and ethics watchdog.

So, it must be acknowledged that a new employee waking up inside Enron would have found the environment hostile to scruples and intimidating to resisters. No doubt many employees at Enron simply fell into line. They came, learned to survive, played the game and when necessary, looked the other way. Some absorbed one stinging lesson before "wisdom" set in. A small group of others decided that Enron was an unhealthy place and got out. They look prescient in retrospect. In sum, Enron did present formidable obstacles to average employees otherwise disposed to behave ethically.

But when looked at within a broader selection of major corporate workers, were Enron's employees "average?" Certainly, the vast majority of them didn't think so. Whether they were indeed the "smartest guys in the room" can be debated, but most Enron employees considered themselves an exceptional lot. Brian Cruver, who joined the company late in the game (March 2001) and then went on to write a book about his nine months there (*Anatomy of Greed*) described his mood going to work on his first day:

> I was built to work at Enron. Like anyone from Houston and anyone who went to business school in Texas, I had always known that Enron was the ultimate launching pad for a business career. Highly respected, bitterly admired—if you were craving the fast track, you dreamed of working at Enron. Everyone knew it, and everybody talked about it: the people of Enron were simply "the best and the brightest"... and now, I was finally one of them. On that first day... I remember trying to project the image of brilliance, sophistication, and self control. But inside, Enron's newest manager was a kid, and he was ready to scream, "This place is bad-ass!"[1]

This hopped-up rhetoric was not exceptional. All the Enron chronicles contain similar statements and classic phrases, such as "Guys with Spikes." So, perhaps it is more accurate to consider the Enron workforce as a self-selected group who came in seeking the big score. Clearly, this label is not valid for everyone and risks being unfair in particular cases. Still, before exonerating Enron's workforce on the grounds that they woke up in a tough situation, it is fair to consider the alternative hypothesis—that this was a group not especially concerned with ethics or financial control and not pre-disposed to risk much when confronted with ethics issues

They also were largely unprepared in terms of what their business school training had provided. Prior to Enron's demise, most U.S. business schools either provided a low-priority business ethics course or no training at all. Steve Salbu, Associate Dean of the McCombs School of Business, University of Texas-Austin, wrote the Foreword to Cruver's book. In it, he captures the state of business school ethics training ante-Enron:

> "Business schools must accept some of the responsibility. Recent sur-
> vey data suggest that M.B.A. students graduate with less concern about
> social and ethical issues than they had when they entered business school.
> Sad, yes, and how can it be? Few top M.B.A. programs require students to
> take a class in ethics. B-school assurances that ethics are examined through-
> out the curriculum sound hollow, if not downright laughable, to most stu-
> dents and recent M.B.A. graduates...
>
> Students and alumni—from my own school and others—routinely
> recount stories of being rebuffed, or even ridiculed, for so much as raising
> ethical questions in some finance, marketing, and accounting classes.
> Elective work in ethics, when available, is singularly ill-equipped to address
> the managerial gap. Why? Because those students most in need of the elec-
> tive courses offered by most high-quality M.B.A. programs routinely self-
> select out of the classes. Like it or not, business school faculty—myself
> included—must accept some of the responsibility for the managers we
> train...Too many of the business leaders we graduate are hitting the ground
> running, but we have forgotten to help them to build their moral muscles." [2]

Were Enron's employees 'overmatched' by the decayed ethical culture? The answer to the question emerges as annoyingly circular. Yes, the Enron business culture was daunting, enough so that reasonable people could be overwhelmed. But that culture was created by an employee group that went there for the sizzle and wasn't on the whole overly particular about how it was being produced. This employee group, in turn, was part of a larger group that was left unprepared by its education to spot, let alone handle, ethics issues.

Where does this circle get broken? It is impossible to say whether sus-tained and serious ethics training at U.S. business schools might have pre-vented Enron's ethical decomposition. Possibly it might have embedded more and more able resisters there who could have supported one another and made a difference. Possibly, they would have had no more effect on Ken

Lay and Jeff Skilling than those Enron resisters who did rise up. Or, possibly, it would have simply produced more good employees who spotted the signs and stayed clear of Enron or left quickly after experiencing its culture. Guessing among these alternatives would be pure conjecture.

What can be said with more certainty is that solid ethics training at business school would have reduced the hype that surrounded Enron. The company was understood to be over the line in many areas. In a business community better grounded in morality and decency, this would have put Enron into a rogue category much sooner. Rating agencies, analysts, and banks would have been more careful. More than a few would have decided not to do business with Enron, regardless of the compensation lost. More analysts would have challenged Enron's opaque accounting. The market would have imposed discipline sooner.

That could have made all the difference.

And that brings us to the last question: presuming that a future generation of business school graduates has acquired more interest in the subject, what signs and signals would help them to spot another Enron in the making?

Signals to Distinguish Ethical Decay from the "Normal Gray Zone"

Signs abound when a corporation poses more than a normal ethical risk. However, potential employees must first want to look for them. Second, they must know where to look.

Company policies, surprisingly, can be an informative source. Consider, for example, the two ethics policies attached to the end of Essay 2. On first look, both seem to contain suitably stern words about the need to be honest and trustworthy. Look closer, however, this time searching for differences. The ExxonMobil Ethics Policy is shorter, yet it contains three items missing from the Enron policy:

1. Strict instructions to accurately record all transactions on company books of account.
2. A preoccupation with the corrupting effects of unethical behavior: signals sent to the rest of the organization, demoralization of those who would act ethically, and so on.
3. Explicit instructions to support those who would act ethically even when there is a cost to the business.

In contrast, the Enron policy is a bit of a grab bag. There is good language about observance of all laws and regulations, both U.S. and foreign. There is explicit instruction to honor both legal and moral obligations. On the other hand, much of the policy is concerned with protecting the company from its employees: Employees cannot publish sensitive materials after leaving the company, must review all contracts with legal counsel, cannot hire outside counsel except through the corporate law office, and so on. There is no language about the course of highest integrity to address conflicts among various laws. There is no awareness of and concern over the debilitating effects of internal corruption.

Most tellingly, there is not a word in Enron's ethics policy about accurate and honest accounting.

Comparisons of ethics policies can thus be a rewarding source of information about company ethics standards. Graduating business students and those considering job changes should review prospective employer policies before going to job interviews. Most major publicly traded companies now post their ethics policies on their Websites. Usually, these policies are found under Investor Relations, Governance, or Citizenship categories. Pick out a couple of major companies with good reputations. Study their ethics policies. Then examine others with dodgy backgrounds. Compare both with the policies posted by your prospective employer. Look for major areas of commonality and difference.

Company ethics policies come in varieties, several of which will interest perspective employees:

- Firms with a strong tradition of sound practices and controls
- Firms with a checkered history that includes recent problems or lawsuits
- Firms about which one hears rumors but have not yet experienced a major scandal

Firms in the first category back up their commitment to be law-abiding with an understanding that accurate accounting is a prerequisite to following the law. Individuals who would break the law will have to cover their tracks in the company's books of accounts. A strong financial function with integrity will deter many illegal transactions and detect most others. Consequently, companies in the first category will give accurate reporting a prominent place among their ethics policies. It is not uncommon also to see a strong interest in employee and community safety. Seasoned firms recognize that the early signals of trouble often arise in matters of accounting and safety compliance.

Another characteristic of the first group is a practical focus on incident prevention and legal compliance. These firms have taken on board the idea that ethical conduct involves enculturation and constant reinforcement. Their policies evidence concern with the consequences of unethical behavior; consequently, they are replete with questions or examples that signal a focus on real dilemmas. Such questions as "Can we pay for the Disney World visit of a visiting minister's family?" are posed and discussed. Employees are encouraged to raise questions and are promised anonymity if need be. Finally, these firms go the extra mile to signal protection for those who would report questionable behavior. Employees can report possible violations through multiple channels. If employees are uncomfortable with their immediate supervisors, they are offered options that vary from compliance officers/auditors and counsel to a company ethics official or ombudsman. Throughout, the company is signaling that it knows that employees are always skeptical about whether ethics policies mean what they say; this they will counter with tangible signals of substance behind the words.

Firms with a problematic history will often post ethics policies that are quite comprehensive and often have a recent enactment/revision date. Some of the policy rhetoric will be reminiscent of or copied from policies of firms in the first category. Closer inspection, however, reveals key differences. One of the first differences will be in the order and intensity of the individual ethics policies. Most companies have a general code of conduct complemented by individual policies on specific issues: Foreign Corrupt Practices Act, conflict of interest, protection of company assets, and so on. Firms that have had recent problems usually end up with ethics policies that "fight the last war." Their most recent problem areas will figure early and large in their policy book. More fundamental areas, such as accounting and safety, are treated nearer the back and more perfunctorily or don't appear at all.

Another tell-tale difference for the "recent problem" firm is its approach to lobbying in the political arena. Very often, the language will be carefully crafted to acknowledge the existence of legal constraints while leaving maximum maneuver room for the company's ongoing lobbying efforts. Instead of emphasizing what is legally and expressly forbidden, these firms tend to state that lobbying activities will be carried out "only to the extent permitted by law." From there, concern often focuses on preventing political activities that are not properly coordinated with senior management.

The other interesting characteristic of such problem firms is their approach to compliance. Having been burned, they will be interested in catching future problems before they go public. So, there will be words encouraging employees to identify issues. However, firms that have not truly embraced sound controls will temporize on protecting their issue identifiers. There won't be an independent go-to contact insulated from managerial pressure. Instead, there might be a committee of internal lawyers, whose preoccupation will be with preventing the company from being sued. Long standing employees know what this means: identify problems at the risk of becoming secondary to the firm's legal risk.

Some firms with recent problems will undertake more thorough reforms. Their policies may still signal a focus on wherever their recent problems arose. However, these firms will demonstrate seriousness by importing the enculturation and employee-protection features of the first group. The general content of a serious approach to business ethics is now well established. Firms wishing to adopt such an approach don't need to reinvent it.

Firms in the last category will be long on strong rhetoric but show an almost total lack of interest in the practical problems of compliance. Their policies "say all the right things" while communicating an implicit belief that they will never be caught.

Contrasting ethics policies is only a beginning for personal due diligence. Beyond the ethics policy, other accessible information to examine includes: (a) published financial statements and accounting policies, and (b) recent prospectuses and information memoranda for financings, mergers, or other capital market transactions

Again, a simple process of comparing the approach of competitors with good reputations to that of the target employer will illuminate the subject. Particular areas of interest include discussions of recent litigation, tax disputes, government consent decrees, and the general intelligibility or opaqueness of the financial reports.

This information will usually provide a suggestion of whether there are deeper issues about a firm's ethics climate. Its primary utility is to help prepare for the interview process itself.

Scoping the Ethical Climate During Job Interviews

Scoping a potential employer's ethics climate is usually not at the top of the objectives list for someone going on an interview. Making a good impression, learning about the business opportunity, pay and benefits: These dominate the first-interview agenda. Serious job searches, however, typically involve an extended interviewing process. Along the way, there will be opportunities to ask questions that can reveal whether the firm has a problematic culture. Here is how to use these opportunities to best advantage.

The general approach is to ready several questions that probe a firm's attitudes toward business ethics without revealing your own. This involves phrasing the questions in a sufficiently neutral way that no signal is given of the answer being sought. This forces interviewers to speak out of their own firms' context. Generally speaking, they will assume that you are "their kind of person" and will tell you something that they think you want to hear about the firm. In this way, they will say something revealing about the firm.

When doing this, it is important to pick a topic that doesn't set off obvious alarm bells. Financial control is a good subject for these purposes. Attitudes toward financial control can be very revealing of a firm's ethics climate. Yet when such questions are properly phrased, few interviewers can find fault with a question exploring a firm's approach to controlling its assets/employees.

Let us consider potential employees as divided into two groups: those seeking jobs in the financial functions and those interviewing for general management/operations. Financial professionals can be more explicit in their questions. In concept, promoting good financial control will be part of their responsibilities; consequently, it could form part of the career of an aspiring finance person. For these candidates, an illustrative sequence of four questions might unfold as follows:

1. In what way does financial control form part of the responsibilities of the firm's finance functions? Can or should I expect to work in financial control during my career at the firm?
2. How is this organized? Is there an internal audit function and to whom does it report? Is this function primarily responsible for controls practices, or are those assigned to line managers?
3. Why do types of control issues typically arise? Are they identified by people in the business units or usually discovered during audits?
4. Can I expect to receive controls training early in my career? What sort of controls training, if any, is routinely provided to the workforce?

Note that the questions don't reveal much about the asker. They are studiously ambiguous about whether the asker's motive is to probe the ethics climate or to clarify the possible roles he or she may play during a finance career at this firm.

These four questions won't reveal everything but they can tell you a lot. They will reveal whether (1) the finance organization is involved in financial control, (2) the firm views the finance function as "the police" or whether it expects managers to instill and monitor controls, (3) the organization at large participates in identifying controls issues or leaves it to "the audit police," and (4) the firm invests in having sound controls by training all employees.

These insights will not reveal the presence of serious corruption but can indicate whether controls are weak, poorly conceived, or robust. If the firm in question has a reputation for questionable activity and has not addressed this by putting a robust controls environment in place, caution is warranted.

General management types can get at some of this same information by probing the issue from the opposite direction. The firm's interviewer will not expect a long series of financial-control questions and might be put on guard by an interviewee's overconcentration here. Thus, the questions must be more limited and crafted for maximum effect. A possible two question sequence might go as follows:

1. What part will financial control play in my managerial responsibilities? Will I be involved in self-assessments and controls training, or will that be handled by specialists?
2. Who conducts audits and how frequently? What issues come up most often? Do people generally feel that the firm is over- or undercontrolled?

Again, the intent is to be ambiguous about one's purpose, i.e. exploring the controls environment or clarifying what constitutes the manager's job in this firm.

These questions should reveal some of the same answers sought by the financial questions: Who is primarily responsible for controls, and how does the finance/line management relationship function? Mentioning self-assessments is a good way to probe whether managers really have continuous responsibility for controls. Testing the over/undercontrolled relationship can bring out whether controls are poorly structured and burdensome, whether managers/employees have not bought in and what sort of work-in-progress is going on.

Depending on the number of interviews involved, prospective employees can work these questions in over the course of several conversations; it may make sense to seed one question per interview. Depending on the number of interviews, one may also be able to ask them multiple times to test earlier responses and deepen the composite picture.

The ultimate point here is that discussing financial control is the best proxy for asking about the ethics climate. Controls are an accepted part of management science. Asking about them is consistent with showcasing oneself as a good manager. Leavening one's questions with content drawn from an understanding of what it takes to achieve good control can help determine whether a prospective employer is on the same ethics page.

The Enron Story: A Final Word

Tucked deep inside *Conspiracy of Fools* is an event that took place on June 20, 2000. This episode did not involve Enron directly. However, the subject of the meeting in question forms part of Enron's unfinished legacy.

The meeting took place at the Manhattan offices of Deloitte & Touche. Arthur Levitt, then SEC chairman, had invited Deloitte, Arthur Anderson, and KPMG Peat Marwick to meet and discuss the relationship between public auditing and consulting. Levitt's theme? Consulting is incompatible with auditing when the same client is involved. He wanted an orderly and negotiated transition to phase out the practice. The three firms unambiguously turned him down.[3]

Seven years, Enron's demise, and Sarbanes-Oxley's (SOX) passage later, much has changed. SOX has dramatically altered the auditor/client relationship in the following four ways:

1. Public firms must place the hiring, compensation, and firing of the audit firm in the hands of an audit committee of independent directors.
2. Auditors may not also provide a host of "prohibited services" including bookkeeping, valuation, fairness opinions, and internal audit outsourcing services.
3. Lead audit partners must be rotated off engagements every five years.
4. Various restrictions are placed on the ability of firms to hire personnel from their audit clients.

Although these provisions go far to address the abuses at Enron and other scandal-ridden firms, some gaps remain. Public accounting firms can still provide certain non-audit services, including tax planning and compliance. Thus, their potential conflicts of interest are reduced but not eliminated. Management still gets to make recommendations to its audit committee on auditor hiring, compensation, and retention. Most significantly, there is no forced rotation of audit firms off their clients' accounts. Clients that have gotten comfortable with their auditors don't have to fear what a new firm would discover. Auditors must still balance accounting judgment on tough calls versus their financial incentive to retain a client indefinitely.

Arguably, these gaps represent a reasonable compromise between the demands for reform and the corporate world's aversion to regulatory cost and disruption. So far, the voices complaining most loudly about SOX don't seem to be focusing on loosening the rules surrounding auditor/client relations. With success weakening other provisions and more time, this could change.

In retrospect, the Enron story and the reforms that followed in its wake seem eerily reminiscent of a previous scandal-filled era. While reading about Enron, one will come across references to Ivan Boesky, Mike Milliken, and Drexel Burnham Lambert. It then hits home that Wall Street's scandal unfolded only slightly more than a decade before Enron's surfaced. One feels surprised that a regulatory environment so recently challenged by insider trading and market manipulation could take so long to pick up on the issues brewing at Enron, WorldCom, Adelphia, and the rest.

The truth is that memories fade quickly in the business world. Corporations have to focus relentlessly on the present and the future. Where the memories involved are embarrassing, managers are even happier to consign them to the archives. For this reason, the corporate mood on ethics seems ever-cyclical, waxing into penitent reform only to slide quietly and then with accelerating momentum back toward the giddy sense that anything goes.

Today, a counterattack on SOX is visible. Establishment heavyweights, such as Treasury Secretary Paulson, have joined with crusading reformer turned Governor Eliot Spitzer to call for legislative revisions. New York's future as the financial markets' center of gravity is reputed to be at stake.

In all likelihood, there may be some aspects of SOX that could stand some pruning. That, however, is not the main point to be grasped. America's financial markets absorbed two of their worst scandals within a period of only fifteen years. Existing law and regulatory oversight failed to preempt either. This history should sober anyone tempted to think that business has learned the lessons of Enron.

Although some businesses learn to value ethical cultures and good controls, others will always find the pressures or temptations to cheat irresistible. What has allowed our financial markets to develop and deepen has not been some self-governing improvement throughout the corporate world but rather the development of strong law and regulation backed by effective enforcement. My own corporation, Exxon, probably learned some lessons from its Cazzaniga affair. Most employees today don't know who Cazzaniga was. They do, however, pay close attention to the strong controls that Exxon put in place in response to the subsequent SEC consent decree.

The core reforms enacted in Enron's wake must thus be protected and preserved. They address real problems that will emerge again if the law is weakened or enforcement slackens. And, should the ever-inventive business world find new routes around these latest boundaries, further steps to ensure the independence of corporate gatekeepers and the accuracy of the reports they bless will be warranted.

Only by preserving this legacy will the destruction wrought at Enron be partially redeemed by an enduring improvement in the ethical climates of our corporations and our capital markets.

Notes

1. *Anatomy of Greed: The Unshredded Truth from an Enron Insider,* pp. 1-2.
2. Salbu, Steve; Ibid., p. xiii.
3. *Conspiracy of Fools,* pp. 350-352.

A Note on Sources

Since this is not a work of company history, its focus has not been a comprehensive investigation of all aspects of Enron's rise and fall. That story has been compiled and told several times already. Rather, the focus was to identify critical moments in Enron's ethics path and to develop the factual basis to construct representative case studies. Sources were thus selected and used for this purpose.

Three comprehensive accounts of the Enron story provided most of the material from which these cases were constructed:

1. Mimi Swartz with Sherron Watkins, *Power Failure, The Inside Story* of the Collapse of Enron, New York: Doubleday, 2003.
2. Bethany McLean and Peter Elkind, *The Smartest Guys in the Room, The Amazing Rise and Scandalous Fall of Enron*, New York: Penguin, 2003.
3. Kurt Eichenwald, *Conspiracy of Fools, A True Story*, New York: Random House, 2005.

The last two of these works built upon the one(s) before, telling essentially the same story but with progressively more detail and data. With relatively minor exceptions, they agree on the stories told in these case studies. The Author's Notes provide comments clarifying where one or another provided unique information or elaborative detail. *Conspiracy of Fools*, coming last and with the benefit of extensive interviews with the major protagonists, provides most of the insider-account material.

Other, earlier accounts were less useful but contributed in spots: Robert Bryce, *Pipe Dreams: Greed, Ego, and the Death of Enron*, New York: Perseus, 2002, Loren Fox, *Enron, the Rise and Fall*, Hoboken, N.J.: Wiley, 2003, and Peter C. Fusaro and Ross M. Miller, *What Went Wrong at Enron*, Hoboken N.J.: Wiley, 2002

The *Report of the Special Investigation Committee of the Board of Directors of Enron Corporation* (the Powers Committee Report), issued on February 1, 2002, is an indispensable guide to the details of Enron's most complex and ethically questionable transactions. The Powers Committee had unique access to Enron's internal information, to its then-current and now-former executives, and to independent accounting and legal advice (Deloitte & Touche LLP and Wilmer, Cutler, respectively). The starkness and clarity of the report's conclusions, such as the importance it attributed to Enron's

Chewco-related accounting restatements (October 2001) helped identify which events were critical to Enron's ethical decomposition. Many of the Enron's SPE details and structural diagrams presented in the cases were also taken from or confirmed by the Powers Committee Report.

The Final Report of Neal Batson, Court-Appointed Examiner re: Enron Corp., et al., Debtors, Appendix C, provides extensive information and analysis of the role of attorneys in various Enron episodes. Batson was appointed by the U.S. Bankruptcy Court, Southern District of New York. This appendix covers the conduct of both in-house and outside counsels in many of Enron's questionable transactions, including Condor, Chewco, the LJM deals, and the Raptors. Vinson and Elkins' conduct of the Sherron Watkins investigation is also covered. The report is extensively documented, draws upon depositions of key figures, and provides considerable legal analysis regarding proper and questionable conduct by the various attorneys.

Enron, Corporate Fiascos and Their Implications, ed. Nancy B. Rapoport and Bala G. Dharan, New York: Foundation Press, 2004 is a valuable anthology of analytical pieces on Enron's demise. Portions of the book deal directly with ethics issues. Some articles provide informative technical material on Enron's accounting methods. Bala G. Dharan's article and congressional testimony were particularly useful in this regard. Leslie Griffin's article, "Whistleblowing in the Business World," provided legal background and insights helpful to understanding Sherron Watkins's situation. Griffin's article also throws light on the dilemma of in-house legal counsels, such as Jordan Mintz, as they consider whether to work ethics issues inside the company or to take their issues to external regulators.

Brian Cruver's Anatomy of Greed: the Unshredded Truth from an Enron Insider, (New York: Carroll & Graf, 2002) provides a personal memoir of an Enron new hire who joined the company early in 2001. Much of the book is anecdotal, but it does capture some sense of Enron's culture. Cruver's description of the motivational signs posted as one drove up Enron's parking garage is telling for both what is emphasized and what is left out. Cruver's account also includes reproductions of some companywide e-mails, including the e-mail announcement of Jeff Skilling's resignation, which is incorporated into Case Study 15 as an attachment.

Sherron S. Watkins's "Ethical Conflicts at Enron: Moral Responsibility in Corporate Capitalism," California Management Review, Summer 2003: is a helpful look back at Enron's demise by perhaps its most famous resister. The article also provides insights into Watkins's thinking at the time and includes her reflection that in retrospect she should have taken her complaint to the Audit Committee of the Enron board.

Several case studies on Enron and ethics were published in the wake of the company's demise. Two of the better ones were The Enron Collapse by Professor Stewart Hamilton (IMD, Lausanne Switzerland, 2003) and Broken Trust by Professor Ashish Nanda (Harvard Business School #903-084,

February 28, 2003). The former provides a condensed story of the events that caused the collapse. The latter details the role played by various professional gatekeepers and watchdogs, including the Accountants, analysts, investment bankers, lawyers, consultants, and credit raters. Broken Trust highlights the conflict-of-interest issues faced by all these groups when confronting an aggressive client and as such, serves as a useful counterpoint to earlier Harvard Business School cases extolling Enron's culture of creativity (see, for example: *Enron's Transformation: From Gas Pipelines to New Economy Powerhouse* by Christopher Bartlett and Meg Glinska, HBS # 301-064, March 16, 2001, and *Enron: Entrepreneurial Energy* by Pankaj Ghemawat and David Lane, HBS # 700-079, February 17, 2000) .

Numerous newspaper and magazine articles are worth reading to capture the 'perception at the time' as the Enron story unfolded. Of special note are "Is Enron Overpriced?" by Bethany McLean (*Fortune*, March 5, 2001, pp. 123-126), "Enron Posts Surprise 3rd Quarter Loss after Investment, Asset Write-downs" by John Emshwiller and Rebecca Smith (*Wall Street Journal*, October 17, 2001) and "Enron's CFO's Partnership Had Millions in Profit" by the same authors (October 19, 2001). These and similar articles bracket the changing mood in the press toward Enron and the increasingly aggressive investigative climate that confronted Ken Lay when he returned as CEO in August 2001.

Enron's financial data and notes are taken from the company's 10-Q and 10-K filings with the U.S. Securities and Exchange Commission. Numerous brokerage reports reveal the financial market's understanding or lack thereof of Enron's financials. An interesting example of both is *The New, New Valuation Metrics: Is Enron Really Worth $126 per share?* published by John S. Herold, Inc., on February 21, 2001. The report analyzes not Enron's stock price but Jeff Skilling's assertion that the stock should rise to $126/share. Although the report does latch on to Enron's eroding profit margins, it ignores cash flow and arrives at the conclusion that $111/share was a more reasonable price (Enron's stock never broke $90/share). This and many similar pieces testify to the longevity of Enron's success in masking its financial issues from financial market analysts and thus the mountain of establishment thinking facing resisters who favored more honest disclosure.

Enron's Code of Ethics, July 2000 was taken off www.TheSmokingGun.com. ExxonMobil's Ethics Policy is taken from the company's Standards of Business Conduct that is provided to all executives, available to all employees and posted on the company's Web site (www.exxonmobil.com).

Finally, various former Enron employees were willing to be interviewed and to read draft cases of which they had some personal knowledge. In particular, Jordan Mintz, Vince Kaminski, David Woytek, and Sherron Watkins reviewed the cases that involved them, providing factual corrections and enhancements.

Index

Conflicts and Trends™ in Business Ethics

Series Editor: Nicholas Capaldi

Business and Religion: A Clash of Civilizations?
Edited by Nicholas Capladi
2005, vi + 442pp. ISBN 978-0-9764041-0-1

Renewing American Culture: The Pursuit of Happiness
Theodore Roosevelt Malloch and Scott T. Massey
2006, xviii + 203pp. ISBN 978-0-9764041-1-8

The Two Faces of Liberalism: How the Hoover-Roosevelt Debate Shapes the 21st Century
Original Material Selected and Edited by Gordon Lloyd
2007, x + 420pp. ISBN 978-0-9764041-2-5

Resisting Corporate Corruption: Lessons in Practical Ethics from the Enron Wreckage
Stephen V. Arbogast
2008, xvi + 264pp. ISBN 978-0-9764041-4-9